Glorious Vegetables

IN THE

MICROWAVE

PATRICIA TENNISON

CONTEMPORARY
BOOKS, INC.
CHICAGO • NEW YORK

Library of Congress Cataloging-in-Publication Data

Tennison, Patricia.
   Glorious vegetables in the microwave.

   Bibliography: p. 274
   Includes index.
   1. Cookery (Vegetables)   2. Microwave cookery.
I. Title.
TX801.T46   1987   641.6′5   87-6807
ISBN 0-8092-4773-9

On cover: Shrimp-Stuffed Chayote, Carrot-Dill Salad, and Cheddar Beans

Published by Contemporary Books, Inc.
180 North Michigan Avenue, Chicago, Illinois 60601
Manufactured in the United States of America
Library of Congress Catalog Card Number: 87-6807
International Standard Book Number: 0-8092-4773-9

Published simultaneously in Canada by Beaverbooks, Ltd.
195 Allstate Parkway, Valleywood Business Park
Markham, Ontario L3R 4T8 Canada

CONTENTS

ACKNOWLEDGMENTS

This book could not have been written without the inspiration and expertise of many colleagues and friends, chefs, writers, produce buyers, library researchers, language teachers, and young neighborhood "sous chefs" who gave up their sunny Saturdays to help me chop vegetables.

Editor Nancy Crossman wisely guided the original concept of this book; Georgene Sainati fashioned the artwork with particular style; Richard Phillips kept my words and grammar pure; colleague JeanMarie Brownson generously advised me and creatively did the food styling for the cover and inside photographs; and photographer Bill Hogan made sure, as usual, that his work is nothing less than spectacular.

Gisela Riess served as my soul mate throughout this venture, conscientiously checked every recipe, and contributed many recipes of her own, including Gila's Extra-Creamy Vichyssoise; Curried Tomato Halves; Hot German Potato Salad; Gila's Asparagus, Mushrooms, and Crabmeat Casserole; Asparagus with Hollandaise Sauce; Nutty Carrot Cupcakes; Zucchini Bread; and Red Snapper with Fennel and Tomatoes.

Information and advice are sincerely appreciated from chef Paul Prudhomme of New Orleans; Frieda Caplan and Judi Greening of Frieda's Finest Produce Specialties Inc., Los Angeles; and Princess Marie-Blanche de Broglie of Normandy, France.

Also, the International Microwave Power Institute, Clifton, Virginia; Don Winslow, buyer, Treasure Island stores, Chicago; Nancy Tucker, staff vice president, Produce Marketing Association; Mary Mardiguian, librarian for United Fresh Fruit and Vegetable Association; Bill O'Neill, editor, *The Packer*; Herbs Now of Highland Park, Illinois; El Zocalo Foods, Chicago; Gary Massel, vice president, engineering, Packaging Corporation of America; and Ronald R. Miller, chief of economic analysis and program review branch, and Ruth H. Matthews, nutritionist, United States Department of Agriculture, Washington, DC.

Of the many people who helped, I would like to thank Bonnie Ballinger, Barbara Banghart, Margaret Duncan, Carol Haddix, Elizabeth Laubhan, Phyllis Magida, Virginia Partain, Barbara Sullivan, Janie Tennison, Catherine Vary, Monica Weinles, Julie Williams, and Jane Wolf.

For inspiration a thanks to my mother, Sophie, who many years ago trusted me to water rows of fresh garden peas, then graciously turned her back as I ate them all.

And a special thanks to my family, Tom, Jeff, and Ashley, for patiently putting up with dinners of "parsnips—five ways."

INTRODUCTION

Glorious Vegetables in the Microwave is the first volume to enlist old favorites and new exotic vegetables in one special cookbook for microwave cooking.

Jicama from Mexico, chayote from South America, fiddlehead ferns from the woods of Maine, and plantain from Jamaica. Add these to traditionals like fresh corn now available virtually year-round or mounds of zucchini from the garden, and our choice of bountiful produce bursts its baskets.

At the same time, the microwave oven enters our lives, and the two couldn't be a better match. Vegetables are low in fat and cholesterol but high in vitamins—and the microwave can retain those nutrients better than conventional cooking methods. We want to eat healthful vegetables, but we want them ready fast: the microwave is at our service. Fresh carrots are marvelous, but we want to try a lovely spaghetti squash or present guests with a taste of the breadfruit that caused the mutiny on the *Bounty*. The microwave makes it easy.

Presented here are 250 recipes for 50 vegetables, from tasty blue cheese–stuffed mushrooms to aromatic asparagus in parchment, from a light green bean side dish to hearty eggplant parmesan, from crunchy jicama-cranberry sauce to creamy chestnut- and wild mushroom–studded soup served in individual baby pumpkins.

Many of the recipes are inspired by avant-garde restaurant dishes sampled in my 12 years as a Chicago restaurant reviewer. Others are simpler fare enjoyed in my own home. There are old classic European dishes adapted for the microwave, as well as new classics like corn on the cob cooked in its own husk, a technique made possible by the microwave.

1

Some of the recipes are side dishes, a smart way to approach a new vegetable. Others are substantial enough to serve as the main course.

Each of the alphabetical chapters in Part II starts with information on how to purchase and store the fresh vegetable. But don't snub your nose at frozen vegetables. Frozen vegetables can be just as tasty and often nutritionally superior to fresh produce, especially when prepared in the microwave.

When fresh vegetables are at their peak, and especially when home gardeners are harvesting their labor, these recipes will be your gold mine of ideas. Pick a new vegetable to try or serve an old favorite with new inspiration.

HOW TO USE THIS BOOK

Glorious Vegetables in the Microwave is the missing link when you have a mound of zucchini in one arm, a microwave on the counter, and dinner around the corner.

If you have been using your microwave primarily to defrost or reheat foods, vegetables are the next step. Vegetables not only cook faster in the microwave, but, because you need less water and fat than in conventional cooking, they can be more nutritious.

Start with some of your favorite vegetables, perhaps corn, potatoes, or broccoli. Then branch out into exciting produce that is becoming more and more common in our groceries: tomatillos, yellow or black sweet peppers, Jerusalem artichokes, even baby or mini vegetables.

Even those familiar with microwave ovens will want to thumb through the first chapter in Part I, which explains the microwave. The type of cover used in cooking can make the difference between mush and crunch. And a few extra utensils will earn back their price in convenience.

In addition to accolades for frozen and canned vegetables as well as garden-fresh, the second chapter, "Vegetables," offers a nutrition chart, an availability chart, and addresses to help you order the more unusual vegetables and seeds.

In the third chapter, you'll find sample menus that give ideas on how to combine dishes for color and texture.

Part II brings you recipes for 50 vegetables from artichokes to zucchini, plus information on how to select the best fresh vegetables, how to store them, and how to cook them in the microwave. To make it easier to select a recipe, each lists preparation time, microwaving time, and the number of servings the recipe yields.

A special chapter on baby vegetables gets these tiny delights dressed for dinner. A handy chapter on "Five-Minute Vegetables" gets you out of a jam and down at the dinner table with grace and taste.

Before you start a recipe, glance through the whole chapter for that vegetable, reading the tips. Much of the advice in these tips can be applied to other recipes as well.

The first recipe in each vegetable chapter offers food as honest food, a simple presentation using basic microwave oven technique. Herbs, spices, and sauces are minimal so that the vegetable itself stars. You'll find you use this first recipe frequently.

Subsequent recipes in each chapter dress the vegetable with more creative sauces or other vegetables, fish, or meat. The final recipes anchoring each chapter may require more time or unusual or expensive ingredients. Flip right to these recipes for entertaining ideas.

The index will help you find other recipes in this cookbook where your favorite vegetable appears as a major ingredient. The "Recipes List" before the index categorizes the recipes by appetizer, salad, soup, side dish, entree, and dessert.

Ingredients may be listed by both amount and weight to make it easier for you to estimate how much to buy. *Butter* means *unsalted* butter; eggs are Grade A large.

In creating these recipes, I reached for ingredients that I love most: mushrooms, pine nuts, basil, pepper, lemon, sesame oil, onions, and garlic. You'll find no raisins, cocktail onions, or creme de menthe.

Let's start with the basics, because understanding your microwave will open your culinary world.

Patricia Tennison

PART I
THE BASICS

THE MICROWAVE

HOW A MICROWAVE WORKS

Microwaves are short radio waves. The waves themselves are not hot; that is, they do not give off heat like charcoal on a grill or like an electric coil that heats air in a conventional oven.

Instead, microwaves pass through many materials, such as glass, ceramic, paper, and most plastic, without causing heat. That is why you can cook food in a glass bowl in a microwave and still find the bowl cool enough to handle.

However, microwaves are absorbed by water, sugar, starches, and fats. Microwaves excite water molecules, and when the molecules move, the friction causes heat, just as rubbing your hands together causes heat.

The magnetron tube in a microwave oven works like a broadcasting station, sending out the waves. The waves travel in a straight line, bouncing off metal walls and any fans designed to move the waves within a microwave oven. It is important that you never operate your microwave oven when it is empty, or the microwaves could damage the magnetron tube.

Microwaves penetrate about $\frac{1}{3}$ inch to $1\frac{1}{2}$ inches into foods, depending on the density of the food. This outer inch of food heats up, and the heat tranfers to cook the rest of the food.

Some foods, like a whole head of cauliflower, cook perfectly in the microwave with little fuss. Others need to be stirred or rearranged so that the microwaves can reach uncooked portions.

COOKING TIMES

Recipes in this book were tested in countertop microwave ovens that operate on 600 to 700 watts. Cooking times are approximate because microwave ovens vary by manufacturer. Small or early models generally have lower wattage and require longer cooking time; check your machine's manual.

Common power settings are not yet standardized. As a guide, however, *high* means 100 percent power or full power, *medium-high* is 70 percent power, *medium* is 50 percent or half power, *defrost* is 30 percent, and *warm* is 10 percent power.

EQUIPMENT

Microwave cookware gets more practical and beautiful each year. But your cupboards probably already contain enough equipment to get you started.

Do not use metal pans, gold or silver-rimmed plates, or utensils with screws or metal handles. Microwaves will be reflected off the metals and may damage the oven. Delicate glassware and china are not recommended.

Glass, ceramic, and plastic bowls and dishes are best. Microwaves pass through these materials. To test to see if a favorite plate or bowl is microwave-proof, put it in the microwave oven next to a glass measure filled with a cup of cool water. Microwave on high power for one minute. If the water is warm but the plate you are testing feels cool to the touch, the plate is fine for the microwave. If it feels slightly warm, you could use it to reheat foods but not for long cooking. If the dish feels hot, do not use it in the microwave.

Even if dishes are suitable for the microwave, heat may transfer from the cooked food and make the container too hot to handle. Use oven mitts when removing dishes from the microwave.

Just as with conventional cooking, recipes work best if you use cooking equipment of the recommended size. If a bowl is too large, the food will spread out and may cook unevenly. If a bowl is too small, certain foods such as sauces may overflow. In general, foods cook best in the microwave in bowls that are just large enough to hold them; that is, in bowls that are not too large.

Most of the dishes in this book can be made if you have one-quart and two-quart covered casseroles, a three-quart bowl, two-cup and four-cup measures, and plastic or wooden spoons. A ring mold is useful for breads and puddings.

COVERING TECHNIQUES

Covering holds in heat and moisture, helping foods to cook faster and more evenly in the microwave. When a recipe says "cover," use a tight-fitting lid or plastic wrap. When using plastic wrap, fold back a corner to create a vent; this helps prevent the wrap from splitting and also makes it possible to stir food without removing the wrap.

Some recipes call for other coverings. Waxed paper is used when you want to prevent splattering and promote even cooking but don't want to trap in moisture. Paper towels are used for a similar purpose, and they also absorb moisture.

Take care when removing covers. Open casseroles and remove plastic wrap by lifting the far corner. This allows hot steam to escape and helps you avoid burns.

COOKING WITH A MICROWAVE

A microwave oven saves you time, allows you to cook with less water and fat than conventional methods for more nutritious results, creates easier cleanup, and doesn't heat the house in summer.

But you can't just push buttons and walk away.

Feel the food as it cooks; use your fingers or a fork to test for doneness and stir or rearrange as necesary. Ingredients straight from the refrigerator will need more time to cook than those at room temperature. Chopped vegetables need less time than whole ones. Very fresh vegetables with a high water content cook faster than three-day-old produce. Recipe times can serve only as a guide.

And taste as you cook. The intensity of herbs and spices varies, and you may need to adjust the seasoning. If you are using canned ingredients such as chicken or beef broth, taste before adding salt.

WHAT A MICROWAVE CAN'T DO

While a microwave oven is ideal for many dishes, it doesn't replace all conventional cooking methods.

Large amounts of water take longer to boil in a microwave, so use your stove to cook a pot of pasta. A cup of uncooked rice is a toss-up; it takes about the same amount of time, so use whichever appliance is more convenient at the time.

Deep frying takes too long in the microwave. Ditto for a large turkey. Soft- or hard-boiled eggs are best left to the stove, too; steam builds up inside the shells and causes the eggs to explode into a sticky mess in the microwave.

MICROWAVE TIPS

Be sure to read your oven's manual for specific instructions and read each recipe through once before you start cooking. But here are some general tips:

- Do not overcook vegetables. They are brighter, crisper, and more nutritious when cooked briefly. If a recipe gives a range of cooking time, test after the shortest suggested time.
- Remember to allow for standing time. Dense vegetables and larger dishes will continue to cook for several minutes after you remove them from the microwave. Take this time into account when you judge for doneness.
- Many wooden spoons may be left right in the bowl when you are cooking in a microwave and remain cool to the touch. However, I find that old wooden spoons that have darkened from age and oil do get quite hot. Experiment carefully.
- Many vegetables need no additional water if you wash them just before using and do not dry them.
- Salt most vegetables after cooking. Salt attracts microwaves and can cause

uneven cooking if sprinkled directly on vegetables before cooking. It doesn't matter as much if the salt is dissolved in enough cooking liquid. Check each recipe carefully.

• A larger mass of food takes longer to cook in the microwave. If you double a recipe, add one-half more time and check for doneness.

• Thicker shapes take longer to cook than thin ones. Position thicker parts, like broccoli stems, toward the outside of the dish, where they will receive more microwave energy.

• Arrange larger vegetables on the outside of the dish for more even cooking.

• Turn over large vegetables such as squashes for more even cooking.

• Stir cooked, outside portions to the inside.

• If dishes can't be stirred, rotate a quarter or a half turn midway through cooking for more even results.

• Use small pieces of aluminum foil to shield areas that you don't want to cook. This is a good technique if you want to defrost only a few slices of bacon.

• To make squashes easier to pierce, cook first for one minute on high power.

• Microwave vegetables until slightly limp and easy to pierce before putting on a skewer.

• Weigh vegetables to get a more precise cooking time.

• Reheat at medium-high or medium temperature.

VEGETABLES

COOKING VEGETABLES IN A MICROWAVE

The most nutritious and tasty vegetable dishes start with the best produce. Check each vegetable chapter in Part II of this book for tips on how to select and store each vegetable, then demand the best from your grocer.

Very fresh vegetables from the garden are ideal, but frozen and canned produce is more than convenient. These commercially prepared vegetables can be more nutritious than fresh produce that has been stored too long at the grocery or in your refrigerator. Buy the freshest produce you can at least once a week and supplement with frozen or canned vegetables.

You get the most nutrients from vegetables if you eat them raw. So although we like to cook vegetables for variety and to make them more palatable, simplicity is the rule.

In general, cooking vegetables in the microwave oven requires less water and fat than conventional methods, so microwave cooking gives us a good head start toward healthier eating. In addition, keep trimming of leaves and stalks to a minimum and peel only thin layers so nutrients are not wasted.

Vegetables generally are cooked on high power. But when they are cooked with eggs or meat, the recipe may call for medium power so that the protein does not toughen.

Most vegetables cooked in the microwave are covered to hold in moisture and to help them cook evenly. Whole potatoes and squashes serve as their own containers but need to be pierced to allow steam to escape and to prevent exploding. A baked potato isn't dangerous if it explodes in a closed microwave oven—but it is messy.

Vegetables cook more evenly if they are the same size. Select whole vegetables that are similarly sized and give the larger ones a head start in the microwave, if necessary. Cut vegetables into uniform sizes. Vary the shapes for interest.

Julienne strips (carrots)

Slices (mushrooms)

Dices (onions)

Diagonal slices (celery)

Flowers (carrots)

Half moons (turnips)

WHERE TO ORDER SEEDS

The following seed companies may be helpful, particularly if you seek some of the more unusual vegetables and mini vegetables. The price noted is for a catalogue.

W. Atlee Burpee Company
300 Park Ave.
Warminster, PA 18991
(215) 674-4900

Farmer Seed and Nursery Co.
Faribault, MN 55021
(507) 334-1623

Gurney Seed & Nursery Co., Inc.
Yankton, SD 57079
(605) 665-4451

Johnny's Selected Seeds
Albion, ME 04910
(207) 437-9294

George W. Park Seed Company, Inc.
101 Cokesbury Rd.
P.O. Box 31
Greenwood, SC 29646
(800) 845-3369

Shepherd's Garden Seeds
7389 W. Zayante Rd.
Felton, CA 95018
($1)
(408) 335-5400

Stokes Seeds, Inc.
28 Water St.
Fredonia, NY 14063
(716) 672-8844

NUTRITION

Vegetable (Edible portion of common measure of food; cooked, boiled, drained, unless noted)	Calories	Protein (g)	Fat (g)	Carbohydrate (g)	Calcium (mg)	Phosphorus (mg)	Iron (mg)	Sodium (mg)	Potassium (mg)	Vitamin A (IU)	Ascorbic acid (Vitamin C) (mg)
Artichokes, 1 medium	53	2.7	.2	12.3	47	72	1.6	79	316	172	8.9
Asparagus, ½ cup	22	2.3	.2	3.9	22	54	.5	4	279	746	18.2
Beans (snap green), ½ cup	22	1.1	.1	4.8	29	24	.7	2	185	413	6.0
Beets, ½ cup slices	26	.9	.04	5.6	9	26	.5	42	266	11	4.7
Belgian Endive, ½ cup raw	28	.4	.05	1.4	—	9	.2	3	82	0	4.5
Bok Choy, ½ cup shredded	10	1.3	.14	1.5	79	25	.8	29	315	2,183	22.1
Breadfruit, ¼ small fruit	99	1.0	.22	26.0	17	29	.5	2	470	38	27.8
Broccoli, ½ cup chopped	23	2.3	.22	4.3	89	37	.8	8	127	1,099	49
Brussels Sprouts, ½ cup	30	1.9	.40	6.7	28	44	.9	17	247	561	48.4
Cabbage, ½ cup shredded	16	.7	.18	3.5	25	18	.2	14	154	64	18.2
Carrots, ½ cup slices	35	.8	.14	8.1	24	24	.4	52	177	19,152	1.8
Cauliflower, ½ cup	15	1.1	.11	2.8	17	22	.2	4	200	9	34.3
Celeriac, ⅔ cup	25	.9	.19	5.9	26	66	.4	61	173	0	3.6
Celery, ½ cup diced	11	.3	.08	2.6	27	18	.1	48	266	81	3.5
Chard, ½ cup chopped	18	1.6	.07	3.6	51	29	1.9	158	483	2,762	15.8
Chayote, ½ cup	19	.4	.38	4.0	10	23	.1	1	138	37	6.4
Corn, ½ cup	89	2.7	1.05	20.5	2	84	.5	14	204	178	5.1
Cucumber, ½ cup raw slices	7	.2	.07	1.5	7	9	.1	1	78	23	2.4
Eggplant, ½ cup	13	.4	.11	3.1	3	11	.1	2	119	31	.6
Fennel, 100g raw	28	2.8	.4	5.1	100	51	2.7	—	397	3,500	31
Garlic, 1 clove, raw	4	.1	.02	.9	5	5	.05	1.	12	0	.9
Greens (mustard), ½ cup chopped	11	1.5	.17	1.4	52	29	.4	11	141	2,122	17.7
Jerusalem Artichokes, ½ cup raw slices	57	1.5	.01	13.0	10	58	2.5	—	—	15	3.0
Jicama, about 8 ⅛-inch thick slices	23	.5	.03	5.2	8	12	.1	3	90	0	7.8

Vegetable (Edible portion of common measure of food; cooked, boiled, drained, unless noted)	Calories	Protein (g)	Fat (g)	Carbohydrate (g)	Calcium (mg)	Phosphorus (mg)	Iron (mg)	Sodium (mg)	Potassium (mg)	Vitamin A (IU)	Ascorbic acid (Vitamin C) (mg)
Kohlrabi, 1/2 cup slices	24	1.4	.09	5.4	20	37	.3	17	279	29	44.3
Leeks, 1/4 cup chopped	8	.2	.05	1.9	8	4	.2	3	23	12	1.1
Mushrooms, 1/2 cup pieces	21	1.6	.37	4.0	4	68	1.3	2	277	0	3.1
Okra, 1/2 cup slices	25	1.4	.14	5.7	50	45	.3	4	257	460	13.1
Onions (dry), 1/2 cup chopped	29	.9	.17	6.5	29	24	.2	8	159	0	6
Parsnips, 1/2 cup slices	63	1.0	.23	15.2	29	54	.4	8	287	0	10.1
Peas (green), 1/2 cup	67	4.2	.17	12.5	22	94	1.2	2	217	478	11.4
Peppers (sweet, green), 1/2 cup chopped	12	.4	.22	2.6	3	10	.6	1	88	264	75.8
Plantain, 100g raw	119	1.1	.4	31.2	7	30	.7	5	385	approx. 1,000	14.0
Potatoes, 1 microwaved, skin and flesh	212	4.9	.20	48.7	22	212	2.5	16	903	—	30.5
Pumpkin, 1/2 cup mashed	24	.8	.09	5.9	18	37	.7	2	281	1,320	5.7
Radishes, 1/2 cup raw slices	10	.3	.31	2.0	12	10	.1	14	134	4	13.2
Rutabagas, 1/2 cup cubes	29	.9	.16	6.5	36	42	.4	15	244	0	18.6
Salsify, 1/2 cup slices	46	1.8	.11	10.4	32	38	.3	11	192	0	3.1
Snow Peas, 1/2 cup	34	2.6	.18	5.6	33	44	1.5	3	192	104	38.3
Spinach, 1/2 cup	21	2.6	.23	3.3	122	50	3.2	63	419	7,371	8.9
Squash (summer), 1/2 cup	18	.8	.28	3.8	24	35	.3	1	173	259	5.0
Squash (winter), 1/2 cup cubes	39	.9	.64	8.9	14	20	.3	1	445	3,628	9.8
Sweet Potatoes, 1/2 cup mashed (baked in skin)	103	1.7	.11	24.2	28	55	.4	10	348	21,822	24.6
Tomatoes, 1/2 cup cooked, boiled	30	1.3	.32	6.7	10	35	.7	13	312	1,623	25.1
Turnips, 1/2 cup cubes	14	.5	.06	3.8	18	15	.1	39	106	0	9.0
Watercress, 1/2 cup raw chopped	2	.3	.02	.2	20	10	.03	7	56	799	7.3
Zucchini, 1/2 cup slices	14	.5	.05	3.5	12	36	.3	2	228	216	4.2

Source: U.S. Department of Agriculture, Agriculture Handbook No. 8–11 and No. 8.

AVAILABILITY

Vegetable	Jan.	Feb.	Mar.	Apr.	May	June	July	Aug.	Sept.	Oct.	Nov.	Dec.
Artichokes												
Asparagus												
Beans												
Beets												
Belgian Endive												
Bok Choy												
Breadfruit												
Broccoli												
Brussels Sprouts												
Cabbage												
Carrots												
Cauliflower												
Celeriac												
Celery												
Chard												
Chayote												
Corn												
Cucumbers												
Eggplant												
Fennel												
Fiddlehead Ferns												
Garlic												
Greens												
Jerusalem Artichokes												
Jicama												

Vegetable	Jan.	Feb.	Mar.	Apr.	May	June	July	Aug.	Sept.	Oct.	Nov.	Dec.
Kohlrabi												
Leeks												
Mushrooms												
Okra	Generally available	Generally available	Generally available								Generally available	Generally available
Onions												
Parsnips						Generally available	Generally available	Generally available	Generally available			
Peas									Generally available	Generally available	Low availability	Generally available
Peppers		Generally available										
Plantain												
Potatoes												
Pumpkins	Generally available	Generally available	Generally available	Generally available	Generally available		Low availability	Low availability	Generally available		Generally available	Generally available
Radicchio												
Radishes						Generally available	Generally available	Generally available	Generally available	Generally available		
Rutabagas					Generally available	Generally available	Generally available	Generally available	Generally available			
Salsify												
Snow Peas												
Spinach												
Squash, Summer												
Squash, Winter												
Sweet Potatoes					Generally available	Generally available	Generally available	Generally available	Generally available			
Tomatillos	Generally available	Generally available	Generally available	Generally available	Generally available	Generally available	Generally available	Generally available	Generally available	Generally available	Generally available	Generally available
Tomatoes												
Turnips					Generally available	Generally available	Generally available	Generally available	Generally available			
Watercress	Generally available	Generally available	Generally available	Generally available	Generally available	Generally available	Generally available	Generally available	Generally available	Generally available	Generally available	Generally available
Zucchini												

Source: United Fresh Fruit and Vegetable Association

■ Very available   ■ Generally available   □ Low availability

SAMPLE MENUS

Vegetables can find their way into your meal from appetizers through dessert.
Here are some suggested menus to get you started.
Starred (*) dishes are recipes in this book.

Apricot Turkey Breast on a Bed of Turnips*
Sesame Spinach*
Carrot-Dill Salad*
Yogurt

Broccoli and Ham Kabobs*
Sweet Onion–Tomatoes*
Brown Rice
Whiskey Corn Pudding*

Baked Apples with Leeks and Sausage*
Fresh Brussels Sprouts with Caraway Seeds*
Fresh Tomato Slices
Crusty Rye Bread
Spice Cake

Gila's Extra-Creamy Vichyssoise*
Chicken Breasts Stuffed with Watercress*
Yellow Squash with Rosemary*
Rice
Red and Green Grapes

Duxelles-Stuffed Cabbage*
New Potatoes with Butter and Lemon*
Carrot-Dill Salad*
Zucchini Bread*

Garlic-Studded Whole Artichokes*
Spinach Lasagna*
Marinated Mushrooms*
Spumoni

18

Carrot Soup*
Broiled Chicken with Lemon
Dirty Potatoes*
Peppers in Olive Oil*
Cheddar Cheese and Apples

Roast Lamb
Peas with Figs and Apple Butter*
Fresh Onion Rings with Basil*
Yogurt-and-Dill-Stuffed Potatoes*
Fresh Strawberries

Classic Onion Soup*
Niçoise Salad*
Crusty French Bread
Fresh Pears

Jicama and Shrimp Rumaki*
Spicy Cucumber Soup*
Thin Wheat Toast
Pineapple-Plantain Pie*

Chicken Gumbo*
Jalapeño Cornbread*
Tossed Salad
Strawberry Ice Cream

Baked Catfish
Sweet Potatoes and Apples*
Skid-Free Okra Salad*
Fresh Oranges

Mushroom Soup*
Meat Loaf
Cabbage Wedges Vinaigrette*
Beets with Tops*
Nutty Carrot Cupcakes*

Cucumber-Chicken Salad*
Tomatoes with Mozzarella and Basil*
Sourdough Bread
Fresh Peaches

Veal Cutlets
Hot Waldorf Salad*
Salsify with Cream*
Broccoli with Hot Peppers and Garlic*
Fresh Pears

Carrot Wontons*
Snow Peas with Shrimp and Cashews*
Sesame Bok Choy*
Rice
Tea, Cookies

Pork Chops
Rutabaga with Thyme*
Tart Apple–Onion Sauce*
Peas with Mint*
Fresh Apricots

Eggs with Jerusalem Artichokes and Mushrooms*
Asparagus with Hollandaise Sauce*
Whole Wheat Toast
Fresh Strawberries

Blue Cheese–Stuffed Mushrooms*
Cabbage and Pork Paprika*
Buttered Noodles
Green Beans with Dill*
Fresh Apples

Baked Trout
Fennel and Tomatoes Au Gratin*
Greens with Vinegar and Mint*
Sweet Potato Pudding Grand Marnier*

Garlic Soup*
Green Beans with Beef and Cashews*
Curried Tomato Halves*
Brown Rice
Fresh Oranges

Roast Chicken
Jicama-Cranberry Sauce*
Turnip and Potato Puree*
Wilted Spinach Salad*
Apples

Sautéed Scallops
Jerusalem Artichokes Provençale*
Almond Zucchini*
Crusty French Bread
Cheese and Pears

PART II
THE RECIPES

ARTICHOKES

"When a man is tired of artichokes, he is tired of life."

I am sure this is what 18th-century wit Samuel Johnson actually had in mind when he penned a similar line about his beloved London. But paying homage to a thistle just wasn't in vogue.

Thankfully, it is now. Once a rare treat, California artichokes abound in supermarkets. Yet these large, unopened flower buds of the thistle family never fail to draw appreciation from diners. Artichoke (and shrimp) appetizers are among the first to disappear. Fresh, whole artichokes are constant scene stealers. And our repertory is widened with canned and frozen artichoke hearts, two handy time savers.

It is hard to believe that anything as fun to eat as a fresh artichoke can be good for us. But, like a baked potato, the sins in an artichoke dish exist in the butter and sauces. An average whole artichoke touts a mere 58 calories, while being a good source of potassium.

The drawback to artichokes for dinner has been the time involved, almost an hour by conventional cooking methods. With the microwave, however, fresh, whole artichokes can be ready in 15 minutes.

Select heavy, compact globes with tightly clinging, leaflike scales. To test for freshness, rub two artichokes together. Fresh ones will be so crisp they squeak. Look for a fresh green color, especially in the peak months of April and May. Between November and March, however, artichokes may show a harmless brown tinge or "winter kiss" from the frost. Avoid those with dark spots or with wide, spreading scales.

Store loosely wrapped in a plastic bag in the refrigerator for up to a week.

GARLIC-STUDDED WHOLE ARTICHOKES

"Candy." That's what my young son used to call the plentiful, mild garlic chunks he'd find in this family favorite. The small amount of oil seeps through the artichoke leaves, eliminating the need for a calorie-laden dipping sauce.

Preparation time: 10 minutes
Microwave time: 16 minutes
Servings: 4

4 fresh, whole artichokes, bottoms trimmed to sit flat, leaf tips snipped
⅓ cup pea-sized chunks fresh garlic
1 teaspoon salt
½ teaspoon freshly ground pepper
½ cup minced fresh parsley
4 tablespoons vegetable oil
¼ cup water

1. Place artichokes upright on plate or in flat-bottomed casserole, leaving an inch between artichokes. Use fingers to gently open leaves. Drop garlic cubes within leaves, scattering them evenly. Sprinkle with salt, pepper, and half (¼ cup) the parsley. Drizzle with oil. Add the water to bottom of plate. Cover.
2. MICROWAVE (high) 14–16 minutes, rotating quarter turn every 4 minutes. Artichokes are done when a middle leaf pulls out easily or the bottom can be pierced easily with a knife. Sprinkle with remaining parsley. Serve.

TIP: *To eat, pull off outer petals one at a time. Pull through teeth to remove soft, pulpy portion of petal. Eat garlic chunks right on the petals. Continue until all petals have been removed.*

Spoon out fuzzy center at base. Discard. The bottom, or heart, is the best part. Cut into small pieces and eat.

ARTICHOKES IN LEMON SAUCE

The microwave makes this tangy lemon sauce foolproof. Serve over rice or warm, sliced lamb.

Preparation time: 10 minutes
Microwave time: 9 minutes
Servings: 3–4

3 tablespoons butter
3 tablespoons flour
1 cup chicken broth
3 tablespoons fresh lemon juice
1 10-ounce package frozen artichoke hearts, defrosted and drained

1. Put butter in 2-quart casserole. MICROWAVE (high), uncovered, 45 seconds to 1 minute until butter melts. Blend in flour until smooth. Gradually stir in chicken broth and lemon juice until well blended.
2. MICROWAVE (high) uncovered 2–3 minutes until thickened, stirring every minute.
3. Stir in artichokes. MICROWAVE (high) 3–5 minutes until tender.

ARTICHOKE KABOBS IN MUSTARD-CHEESE SAUCE

Serve this like a fondu with crusty French bread cubes. Your artichoke slipped off the toothpick and into the sauce? The same fondu rule applies: you buy the wine.

Preparation time: 10 minutes
Microwave time: 10 minutes
Servings: 4

1 can (6–8 count) artichoke bottoms, rinsed, drained
6 tablespoons butter
⅓ cup flour
1½ cups milk
3 tablespoons Dijon mustard
1 tablespoon fresh lemon juice
¼ teaspoon salt
¼ teaspoon freshly ground black pepper
1 cup grated cheddar cheese

1. Cut artichokes into quarters. Stick an uncolored toothpick through each. Set aside.
2. Put butter in 1-quart casserole. MICROWAVE (high) 1 minute to melt. Blend in flour. Stir in milk. MICROWAVE (high), uncovered, 4–5 minutes to thicken, stirring twice.
3. Stir in mustard, lemon juice, salt, pepper, and cheese. MICROWAVE (high) 1–2 minutes to melt cheese.
4. Add artichoke quarters to casserole so that toothpicks stick out for easy retrieval. MICROWAVE (high) 2–3 minutes to warm artichokes. Serve.

TIP: *This recipe is designed to work right in a microwave-proof serving dish. The sauce and artichokes get nice and hot, but because microwaves don't heat wood, the toothpicks stay cool.*

SAUSAGE-STUFFED ARTICHOKES

These are wonderful to make ahead for parties because the flavors blend yet the artichokes stay firm during a wait in the refrigerator.

Preparation time: 15 minutes
Microwave time: 5 minutes
Servings: 4–6

⅓ cup pork sausage
1 teaspoon minced garlic
2 green onions, whites and first 2 inches of green, chopped
1 tablespoon olive oil
2 tablespoons fine bread crumbs
4 tablespoons minced fresh parsley
½ teaspoon dried sage
¼ teaspoon freshly ground pepper
2 14-ounce cans (6–8 count) whole artichoke hearts, drained

1. Crumble sausage in 1-quart casserole. Add garlic and onions. Cover loosely with waxed paper. MICROWAVE (high) 2–3 minutes, breaking up and stirring once, until no pink remains. Drain. When cool enough to handle, crumble well between fingers.
2. Mix oil, bread crumbs, parsley, sage, and pepper into sausage.
3. Gently open artichoke hearts and stuff about a teaspoon of mixture into each. Place on flat, microwave-proof serving dish. (Artichokes can be made ahead to this point, covered, and stored in refrigerator.)
4. Cover. MICROWAVE (high) 1–2 minutes, rotating twice, until heated through.

TIP: For safety reasons, don't let this or other meat-enhanced party dishes sit around for hours on the kitchen counter. Keep in the refrigerator, then reheat in the microwave.

ARTICHOKE AND OYSTER SOUP

Cuddled together in a smooth, creamy broth, this combo makes a lovely light supper, accompanied by crusty French bread.

Preparation time: 10 minutes
Microwave time: 17 minutes
Servings: 4

  1 **5-ounce can oysters with juices**
1⅓ **cups chicken broth**
  1 **tablespoon butter**
  1 **tablespoon flour**
  ¼ **teaspoon dried thyme**
  ½ **teaspoon salt**
  ⅛ **teaspoon freshly ground pepper**
  1 **10-ounce package frozen artichoke hearts, defrosted and drained**
  2 **cups half-and-half**
  1 **green onion, white part and first 2 inches of green, sliced**

1. Drain oyster juice into 2-cup measure. Add enough chicken broth to make 1½ cups liquid. Reserve liquid and oysters.
2. Put butter in 2-quart casserole. MICROWAVE (high) 15–30 seconds, until melted. Blend in flour until smooth. Stir in thyme, salt, and pepper. Gradually stir in oyster-chicken liquid.
3. Cover. MICROWAVE (high) 4–5 minutes until it boils, stirring twice. Stir in artichokes. Cover. MICROWAVE (high) 4–5 minutes.
4. Stir in half-and-half and oysters. Cover. MICROWAVE (medium-high) 4–6 minutes to heat thoroughly. Serve, sprinkled with green onions.

TIP: Store leftovers in a microwave-proof bowl, covered with plastic wrap. To reheat, MICROWAVE (high) 2 minutes, then (medium-high) 2–3 minutes.

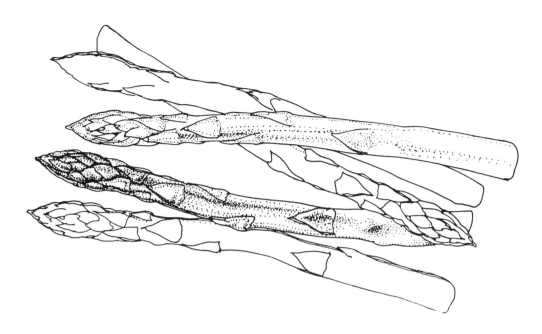

A S P A R A G U S

It is rare to find someone dispassionate about asparagus. Those unfortunates who actually dislike asparagus ignore this harbinger of spring, while the rest of us gorge ourselves as if time were limited—which indeed it is.

Part of the appeal of asparagus, no doubt, is its short season. Unless money is absolutely no factor, March, April, May, and June are the reasonable times to purchase asparagus. So we do, by the pound, week after week, until spring slips into summer and astronomical prices mark the end of fresh asparagus for that year.

Those who have tried to grow asparagus can appreciate the price tag it bears. An asparagus bed takes a good three years to develop, and then, as I can attest, one joyful puppy can wipe it out in an afternoon. Most of the asparagus in our groceries comes from southern California, supplemented by imports in off-season.

Europeans grow white asparagus by mulching the spears to prevent them from getting sunshine. I haven't yet seen domestic white asparagus on the market, but with the current strong interest in vegetables, I wouldn't be surprised to find them soon.

Asparagus deserves extra care in preparation. Very tough, white ends need to be cut off. But most of the rest of the stem can be salvaged by peeling lightly. The old method of snapping asparagus until it breaks wastes a lot of good stem.

Less-than-pristine asparagus can be refreshed by setting them in water, like a bunch of flowers. Indeed, a good grocer will store them this way. Use them as soon as possible.

Stalks take slightly longer to cook than tender tips, so position them to the outside of dishes in the microwave. If you have the discipline to wait, cut and cook the tips for one meal, then store the stems for a follow-up dish. Or, stir in the tips a minute after the stems. For whole asparagus, give larger, thicker asparagus a head start in the microwave and add others a minute later. Asparagus are best when cooked only until crisp; avoid overcooking.

Select rich-green-colored spears with close, compact tips and firm, crisp stalks. Pick stalks of similar thickness for even cooking. Avoid asparagus with wet tips, a sign of decay.

Store with stalk ends wrapped in wet towels in a plastic bag in the refrigerator for two or three days.

ASPARAGUS WITH HOLLANDAISE SAUCE

Since these are so good, we're a little generous with the asparagus. A little half-and-half thins the hollandaise so that it pours well. Be sure to stir the sauce well and frequently to keep it smooth.

Preparation time: 20 minutes
Microwave time: 11 minutes
Servings: 4

1½ **pounds fresh asparagus,**
    stems lightly peeled
¼ **cup water**
⅓ **cup (5⅓ tablespoons) butter**
2 **tablespoons fresh lemon juice**
¼ **cup half-and-half**
2 **egg yolks, well beaten**
¼ **teaspoon salt**
⅛ **teaspoon ground nutmeg**

1. Arrange asparagus in 2-quart rectangular casserole, alternating tips and ends. Add water. Cover. MICROWAVE (high) 6–8 minutes, until just tender, rearranging stalks after 4 minutes. Drain. Arrange on serving dish.

2. To make sauce, put butter in 4-cup measure. MICROWAVE (high) 1 minute to melt. Stir in lemon juice and half-and-half. Gradually whisk in egg yolks.

3. MICROWAVE (high) 1½–2 minutes, whisking every 20 seconds, until mixture has thickened. Stir in salt and nutmeg. Pour over asparagus or serve separately in sauceboat.

SESAME ASPARAGUS

When sliced, fresh asparagus need just five minutes in the microwave. Sesame oil is quite strong-tasting, so it is diluted here with vegetable oil for a smooth-tasting dish. There is no salt; add ½ teaspoon of soy sauce at the end if you wish.

Preparation time: 10 minutes
Microwave time: 6 minutes
Servings: 4

1 **pound asparagus, stems lightly peeled, cut into 2-inch diagonal slices**
½ **teaspoon vegetable oil**
¼ **teaspoon sesame oil**

Put asparagus, vegetable oil, and sesame oil in 1-quart casserole. Cover. MICROWAVE (high) 4–6 minutes, until just tender.

TIP: For perfect texture, stir in tips one minute after stem pieces; tips take slightly less time to cook.

ASPARAGUS AND ARTICHOKE SALAD

Two wonderful treats in one salad. Asparagus are cooked until just crisp. Tarragon vinegar and a little mustard add zip to the dressing.

Preparation time: 15 minutes
Microwave time: 5 minutes
Servings: 4

1 **pound asparagus, stems peeled**
¼ **cup water**
1 **14-ounce can (6–8 count) artichoke hearts, rinsed well and drained**
2 **tablespoons tarragon vinegar**
⅛ **teaspoon salt**
⅛ **teaspoon freshly ground white pepper**
2 **teaspoons vegetable oil**
1 **teaspoon prepared mustard**
1 **tablespoon water**

1. Arrange asparagus in 2-quart rectangular casserole, alternating tips and ends. Add water. Cover. MICROWAVE (high) 4–5 minutes, until just tender but still crisp, rearranging stalks once. Drain. Arrange on plate with artichokes.
2. In 4-cup measure, mix vinegar, salt, and pepper. Whisk in oil, then mustard and water. Pour over vegetables and toss gently. Serve immediately or refrigerate, covered, then drain before serving.

GILA'S ASPARAGUS, MUSHROOMS, AND CRABMEAT CASSEROLE

When fresh asparagus are out of season, this makes a nice straight-from-the-larder luncheon dish for drop-in guests or a quick dinner for two.

Preparation time: 15 minutes
Microwave time: 23 minutes
Servings: 2–4

1 10-ounce package frozen crabmeat
1 10-ounce package frozen asparagus
2 tablespoons water
3 tablespoons butter
3 tablespoons flour
1½ cups milk
1 teaspoon salt
1 tablespoon soy sauce
3 tablespoons sherry
1 4-ounce can sliced mushrooms, drained
¼ cup grated Parmesan cheese

1. Defrost crabmeat in microwave oven according to package directions.
2. Put asparagus in 1-quart casserole icy side up and add water. Cover. MICROWAVE (high) 7–8 minutes, rearranging stalks after 4 minutes. Drain.
3. Put butter in 4-cup measure. MICROWAVE (high) 30–45 seconds, until melted. Stir in flour. Gradually add milk, stirring constantly until blended. MICROWAVE (high) 2–3 minutes or until thickened, stirring three or four times. Stir in salt, soy sauce, and sherry.
4. Place crabmeat in 2½-quart casserole. Sprinkle with mushrooms. Arrange asparagus on top, alternating tips and ends. Pour sauce over asparagus. Cover. MICROWAVE (high) 5–7 minutes. Sprinkle with grated cheese. Do not cover. MICROWAVE (high) 2–4 minutes.

AROMATIC ASPARAGUS IN PARCHMENT

Sliced asparagus are mixed with sesame oil and fresh ginger, then wrapped and cooked in individual parchment packages. Take a moment to enjoy the fine aroma before you plunge in.

Preparation time: 20 minutes
Microwave time: 6 minutes
Marinating time: 10 minutes
Servings: 4

2 tablespoons soy sauce
¼ teaspoon sesame oil
½ teaspoon minced fresh ginger
1 pound asparagus, lightly peeled, cut into 2-inch diagonal slices

1. In 1-quart bowl, mix soy sauce, sesame oil, and ginger. Stir in asparagus and let marinate on counter 10 minutes.
2. Cut parchment or waxed paper into four 12-inch pieces. Divide asparagus mixture into fourths and place in center of each paper. Fold long sides toward center, creasing paper well, then fold and tuck under ends to form neat packages. Place packets smooth side up on plate.
3. MICROWAVE (high) 4–6 minutes, until asparagus are tender. Let stand 2 minutes. Use knife to slit open each packet just before eating. Discard the parchment or other wrapping.

TIP: *Parchment paper, sometimes called* greaseproof *or* kitchen paper, *is porous like waxed paper but does not contain wax. It may be difficult to find; look for it in specialty food and equipment and houseware stores.*

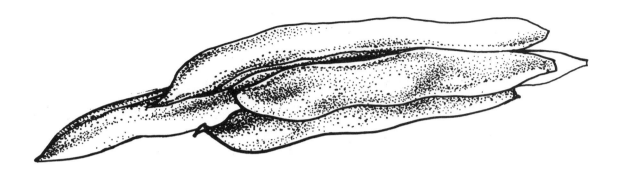

BEANS

Green beans, or snap beans, are so plentiful and easily accepted by even the most finicky eaters that the vegetable has become a cliché. Banquet diners typically face a choice of beef or chicken—plus plain green beans. Cafeterias historically steam, then team them with soggy spaghetti. And the home cook is faced with presenting the overused vegetable in an appealing way.

In midsummer, this presents no problem. Green beans straight from the garden or vegetable market—so fresh that you can feel a slight velvety fur on the outside—need nothing more than a brief cooking and a pat of butter. Their absolute freshness sets them well apart from institutional fare. Indeed, very fresh green beans rank right up with asparagus as some of my favorite vegetables.

During the rest of the year, when green beans are still plentiful but not pristinely fresh, the solution is to get creative. Add fresh dill, marjoram, or basil. If you usually serve green beans whole, cut them into French-style strips or on an angle, or chop them. Make a green bean puree and use it to stuff other vegetables. Or top them with a favorite cheddar cheese sauce.

Green beans and yellow wax beans are the most common fresh snap beans available and can be used in any of these recipes. Larger markets may carry Chinese long beans, which are green beans up to two feet long. They can be cooked whole, then braided for an unusual presentation. Very slender green snap beans from France are a find; cook them very briefly and check often for doneness.

Microwave time for green beans varies according to the freshness of the beans, how you cut them, and the desired crispness. Very fresh beans with a higher moisture content will take slightly less time to cook. Sliced or diced beans need less time than whole beans.

Prosciutto-wrapped green beans call for shorter cooking time to keep beans crisp; the puree requires longer cooking so the dish will be smooth.

Select firm, crisp beans with a bright, fresh-looking green color (or yellow for yellow wax beans). The very freshest will have a slight fur on the outside of the pods and snap easily when broken. Avoid wilted, flabby beans with thick, tough pods or large, overmature seeds.

Store dry and loosely wrapped in refrigerator. Wash just before using.

GREEN BEANS WITH DILL

Fresh green beans get a healthy dose of yogurt sparked with dill.

Preparation time: 10 minutes
Microwave time: 11 minutes
Servings: 4

1 **pound fresh green beans, ends trimmed, cut into 2-inch pieces**
½ **cup water**
⅓ **cup plain yogurt**
1 **tablespoon minced fresh dill** *or* ½ **teaspoon dried**

1. Put beans and water in 1½-quart casserole. Cover. MICROWAVE (high) 6–11 minutes, until tender, stirring twice. Let stand 2 minutes. Drain.
2. Blend yogurt and dill. Spoon over beans. Serve.

GREEN BEAN PUREE

A touch of rosemary elevates this puree from baby food to adult fare.

Preparation time: 15 minutes
Microwave time: 14 minutes
Servings: 4

1 pound green beans, ends trimmed
½ cup water
2 tablespoons butter
¼ cup cream
½ teaspoon dried rosemary, crushed

1. Put green beans and water in 2-quart casserole. Cover. MICROWAVE (high) 12–14 minutes, until quite tender, stirring twice. Let stand 3 minutes. Drain.
2. Puree in blender or processor. Add butter, cream, and rosemary. Puree again.

TIP: Reduce cream to 2 tablespoons to make a thick puree ideal for stuffing other vegetables or for piping onto an assorted vegetable platter. Gradually increase cream or milk to make the puree thinner.

CHEDDAR BEANS

Fresh green beans and cheddar cheese are a very likable combination that appeals especially to children.

Preparation time: 10 minutes
Microwave time: 16 minutes
Servings: 4

1 pound fresh, whole green beans, ends trimmed
½ cup water
2 tablespoons butter
2 tablespoons flour
1 cup milk
½ cup grated sharp cheddar cheese
¼ teaspoon salt
⅛ teaspoon freshly ground pepper

1. Put green beans and water in 2-quart casserole. Cover. MICROWAVE (high) 5–8 minutes, stirring twice. Let stand, covered, 2 minutes. Drain.
2. Put butter in 4-cup measure. MICROWAVE (high) 40–50 seconds to melt. Blend in flour until smooth. Slowly whisk in milk. MICROWAVE (high) 1–3 minutes to thicken, stirring every minute. Stir in cheese, salt, and pepper. MICROWAVE (high) 3–4 minutes, until thick, stirring every minute. Pour cheese sauce over beans and serve.

GREEN BEANS IN PROSCIUTTO

Green beans, cooked al dente *and wrapped in paper-thin slices of this Italian ham, make wonderful finger-food appetizers. Select thin beans and try to wrap beans of the same thickness and length together.*

Preparation time: 20 minutes
Microwave time: 9 minutes
Marinating time: 15 minutes
Servings: about 20

1 pound fresh green beans, ends trimmed, cut into 3-inch pieces	1. Put beans and water in 2-quart casserole. Cover. MICROWAVE (high) 5–8 minutes, until just tender but not soft, stirring twice. Let stand, covered, 2 minutes. Drain.
½ cup water	
2 teaspoons chopped shallots	
1 tablespoon olive oil	2. Put shallots and oil in 4-cup measure. MICROWAVE (high) 1 minute. Whisk in vinegar and salt. Mix in beans. Let marinate on counter 15 minutes. Drain.
1 tablespoon wine vinegar	
¼ teaspoon salt	
½ pound prosciutto, sliced very thin	3. Cut prosciutto slices in half across the width, creating 2- to 3-inch-long semicircles. Use 1 strip of prosciutto to wrap 2–3 green beans around the middle, leaving the beans a little exposed at both ends. Serve immediately or store covered in refrigerator and remove 15 minutes before serving.

GREEN BEANS WITH BEEF AND CASHEWS

The directions may look long, but this stir-fry is very easy to make, especially after you've done it once and gotten a feel for timing the beef. Cashews may be replaced by peanuts, and the oyster sauce by a prepared teriyaki sauce.

Preparation time: 20 minutes
Microwave time: 13 minutes
Servings: 4

½ **pound boneless sirloin steak**
4 **tablespoons oyster sauce**
1 **pound green beans, ends trimmed, cut into 3-inch pieces**
½ **cup water**
1 **cup cashews**

1. Trim fat from steak. Cut across grain into ¼- by ½- by 3-inch strips. (Partially frozen meat is easier to cut.) Mix steak and half (2 tablespoons) oyster sauce. Let marinate for 10 minutes on counter while you prepare beans.
2. Put green beans and water in 2-quart casserole. Cover. MICROWAVE (high) 5–8 minutes, stirring twice. Let stand, covered, 2 minutes. Drain. Add remaining 2 tablespoons oyster sauce. Set beans aside.
3. Put beef in 2-quart rectangular casserole. Do not cover. MICROWAVE (high) 2–3 minutes, until exterior of beef just loses redness, stirring once. (The beef will cook more later and turn from rare to medium rare. For a medium finished product, cook here another minute until interior of meat turns from red to pink.)
4. Stir in cashews to coat. Stir in beans. Do not cover. MICROWAVE (high) 2 minutes, until vegetables are warm and meat is done as desired. Serve with rice.

TIP: *Do not cover the meat, or moisture will be trapped and the texture will be more like a stew than a stir-fry.*

TIP: *Oyster sauce can be purchased in specialty Oriental food stores or some major supermarkets.*

CHOPPED BEANS WITH SHRIMP

There is very little shrimp in this dish—it just looks like a lot because they are chopped up. It reheats well and makes an unusual contribution to a potluck dinner.

Preparation time: 15 minutes
Microwave time: 15 minutes
Servings: 6–8

½ **pound ground pork**
1 **pound green beans, chopped into ¼-inch pieces**
½ **cup apple juice**
1 **teaspoon grated fresh ginger**
2 **tablespoons soy sauce**
1 **teaspoon sesame oil**
¼ **teaspoon salt**
1 **tablespoon cornstarch, dissolved in 1 tablespoon water**
1 **cup chopped raw fresh or frozen shrimp**

1. Put pork in 2-quart casserole. Cover. MICROWAVE (high) 2 minutes, until fat starts to come out. Stir in beans. Cover. MICROWAVE (high) 5–7 minutes, until pork turns from pink to grey and beans are almost tender. Let stand, covered, 2 minutes. Drain.

2. Add apple juice, ginger, soy sauce, sesame oil, salt, and cornstarch mixture to beans. MICROWAVE (high) 3–4 minutes, until sauce boils and thickens, stirring twice. Stir in shrimp. MICROWAVE (high) 1–2 minutes, until shrimp turn pink. Take care not to overcook shrimp, or they will be tough.

TIP: Since the shrimp will be chopped, there is no need to purchase large, expensive shrimp. The smallest shrimp or shrimp pieces will do.

BEETS

Fresh beets are a vegetable I seem to rediscover every summer. The sweet taste of cooked yet still crisp beets is unlike that of beets in jars, useful though canned beets may be. And there is a special pleasure to peeling back its mundane skin to reveal the vibrant red beet.

Indeed the tendency of beets to bleed their red color when cooked too long in water may make some cooks wary of this fine vegetable. The microwave can help.

Beets cook best in the microwave with just a little water, far less than is needed to cover them. Because of the small amount of water, the flavor is superior and less color is lost, especially if beets are cooked whole.

Select similarly sized beets, if possible, to assure more even cooking. Look for beets that are small to medium-sized, firm, smooth, and deep red. If beets are bunched, you can judge freshness by the condition of the tops. The freshest beets will have full, crisp tops with little wilting. However, the beet root may still be satisfactory after the tops wilt. Check for firmness. Wash beets carefully before using, but take care not to tear the skin, or the color will bleed.

Store uncovered in the refrigerator for up to a week. Use green tops as soon as possible.

BEETS WITH TOPS

Don't waste the tops when cooking fresh beets. They cook down into a pretty bed for the sliced red vegetable.

Preparation time: 15 minutes
Microwave time: 26 minutes
Servings: 4

1 pound 2-inch-diameter unpeeled whole beets with 1-inch stems, washed
½ cup water
1½ pounds beet tops (see Tip), washed, stems removed, chopped
2 tablespoons malt vinegar
¼ teaspoon freshly ground pepper

1. Put beets and water in 1½-quart casserole. Cover. MICROWAVE (high) 14–18 minutes, until just tender, rearranging once. Let stand, covered, 3 minutes. Drain. Cool slightly. Slip off skins. Leave whole.
2. Meanwhile, put tops in 3-quart casserole. Cover. MICROWAVE (high) 6–8 minutes, until tender, stirring after 3 minutes. Drain.
3. Put tops in serving dish. Toss with half (1 tablespoon) vinegar. Top with beets. Sprinkle with remaining vinegar and the pepper. Serve.

TIP: Leave beet skin intact and stems attached to help prevent beets from bleeding their vibrant red color.

TIP: A pound of fresh whole beets provides enough of the root vegetable for 4 people, but enough tops for only 1 serving. Buy extra tops, or use what you have, chop well, and sprinkle over cooked roots for color.

BEETS AND CAPERS SALAD

Use this pretty light red salad to add color to a green vegetable plate.

Preparation time: 15 minutes
Microwave time: 18 minutes
Servings: 4

1 pound 2-inch-diameter
unpeeled whole beets with
1-inch stems, washed
½ cup vinegar
⅛ teaspoon ground cloves
⅛ teaspoon ground cinnamon
½ teaspoon sugar
2 tablespoons mayonnaise
1 tablespoon capers
1 hard-boiled egg, diced (see
Tip)

1. Put beets and vinegar in 1½-quart casserole. Cover. MICROWAVE (high) 14–18 minutes, until just tender, rearranging once. Let stand, covered, 3 minutes. Strain and reserve liquid. Cool beets slightly. Slip off and discard skins. Dice beets.
2. Combine diced beets and reserved liquid, cloves, cinnamon, and sugar. Stir in mayonnaise, capers, and egg. Serve immediately or refrigerate, covered, for an hour.

TIP: *Don't use the microwave to hard-cook eggs in the shell. The built-up heat will cause the shell to explode. To hard-cook an egg, break 1 large egg into a greased custard cup. Pierce yolk with a fork. Cover with plastic wrap. MICROWAVE (medium) 1¼ minutes, until yolk is set. Let stand, covered, 1 minute.*

BEET AND CABBAGE SOUP

This classic Russian soup needs only some beer and a loaf of black bread.

Preparation time: 20 minutes
Microwave time: 28 minutes
Servings: 4–6

2 tablespoons butter
½ cup chopped onion
2 cups finely shredded cabbage
(half a small head)
1 pound beets, peeled and cut
into ¼-inch cubes
2 cups beef broth or stock
1 tablespoon vinegar

1. Put butter, onions, and cabbage in 3-quart casserole. Cover. MICROWAVE (high) 6 minutes, stirring once. Add beets. Cover. MICROWAVE (high) 12–15 minutes, until vegetables are tender, stirring twice.
2. Add broth and vinegar. Cover. MICROWAVE (high) 6–7 minutes, until boiling. Serve.

BEETS AND MANDARIN ORANGES

Naturally sweet beets team well with citrus fruits.

Preparation time: 15 minutes
Microwave time: 24 minutes
Servings: 4

1 pound 2-inch-diameter unpeeled whole beets with 1-inch stems, washed
½ cup water
1 11-ounce can mandarin oranges in light syrup
2 teaspoons cornstarch
1 tablespoon butter
¼ teaspoon ground cinnamon
½ teaspoon sugar

1. Put beets and water in 1½-quart casserole. Cover. MICROWAVE (high) 14–18 minutes, until just tender, rearranging once. Let stand, covered, 3 minutes. Drain. Cool slightly. Slip off skins. Cut into ¼-inch slices.
2. Drain about ½ cup of syrup from mandarin orange can into 2-cup measure. Stir in cornstarch until dissolved. MICROWAVE (high), uncovered, 2–3 minutes, until thickened, stirring after 2 minutes. Stir in butter, cinnamon, and sugar. MICROWAVE (high) 1 minute, until blended.
3. Arrange beets and oranges on serving platter. Cover with waxed paper. MICROWAVE (high) 1–2 minutes to heat through. Pour sauce over beets and oranges.

TIP: Canned plain—not pickled—beets may be substituted.

TIP: Four larger, 3-inch-diameter beets take 20–25 minutes to cook in the microwave.

TIP: Whole beets will sizzle a little but don't need to be punctured like potatoes.

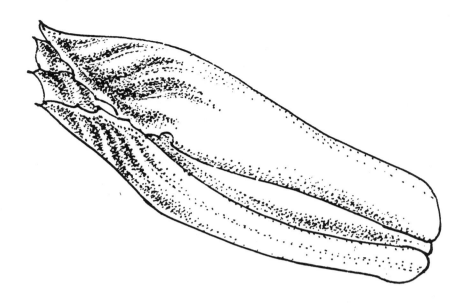

BELGIAN ENDIVE

Pale, cone-shaped Belgian endive, or witloof chicory, is actually the sprouts from chicory roots and was discovered by a Belgian farmer. He stored the roots covered in his barn to use as fodder for his animals. But when he uncovered the roots, he saw that the chicory had sprouted white, crisp, sweet leaves.

The sprouts became known as Belgian endive, and most of the commercial supply is still grown in Belgium and France. The process is laborious. Chicory must be planted in the ground as usual, then its roots are dug up and stored covered with sand until the delicate sprouts grow.

Hand labor and air transporation costs add up to a high price at the grocery. But fortunately a little Belgian endive goes a long way.

Belgian endive has a crisp texture and pleasantly bitter taste. When cooked in the microwave, its bitterness is accentuated and may be unacceptable to some people. In general, cook Belgian endive briefly, as in the following recipe for goat cheese on Belgian endive spears, or serve it raw with a topping such as the warm anchovy sauce.

Select crisp, pale yellow or white leaves that are firm and plump. If the tips have been exposed to light too long and turned green, it will be more bitter.

Store wrapped in plastic in refrigerator for two to three days.

BELGIAN ENDIVE BRAISED IN WINE

The slightly bitter taste of endive is realized in this simple braised dish.

Preparation time: 5 minutes
Microwave time: 7 minutes
Servings: 4

4 Belgian endive hearts
¼ cup dry white wine
Freshly ground black pepper

Rinse endive, discarding any wilted leaves, leaving hearts whole. Arrange in 2-quart rectangular casserole, with stem portions to outside. Pour wine over. Cover. MICROWAVE (high) 5–7 minutes, until tender. Drain. Sprinkle with pepper and serve.

BELGIAN ENDIVE SALAD WITH WARM ANCHOVY SAUCE

This is one of the most delightful ways to enjoy Belgian endive: in a raw salad with crisp apples and oranges, topped with an anchovy and bacon dressing. It also stretches one expensive endive to serve four people.

Preparation time: 20 minutes
Microwave time: 4 minutes
Servings: 4

1 Belgian endive heart, washed, leaves separated
2 medium Granny Smith apples, cored and sliced thin, unpeeled
1 orange, peeled and sectioned
6 tablespoons fresh lemon juice (about 1½ whole lemons)
3 strips bacon
3 anchovy fillets, cut up
1 teaspoon minced garlic
2 tablespoons wine vinegar
¼ teaspoon salt
⅛ teaspoon freshly ground pepper
4 tablespoons vegetable oil

1. Arrange endive, apples, and oranges attractively on a plate. Sprinkle with 2 tablespoons of the lemon juice to keep apples from turning brown. Keep chilled until ready to use.
2. Put bacon between two layers of paper towels on plate. MICROWAVE (high) 2–3 minutes, until crisp. Let cool. Crumble bacon. Reserve.
3. In a large bowl, mash anchovies and garlic. Stir in remaining 4 tablespoons of lemon juice, vinegar, salt, and pepper. MICROWAVE (high) 1 minute. Beat in oil. Pour over salad. Sprinkle with bacon.

TIP: *Crisscross any leftover anchovies on top of the salad.*

GOAT CHEESE ON BELGIAN ENDIVE SPEARS

A brief stint in the microwave brings out the flavors of both the goat cheese and the endive. These can be prepared ahead and kept covered in the refrigerator until ready to heat.

Preparation time: 15 minutes
Microwave time: 2 minutes
Servings: appetizers for 6

2 ounces soft goat cheese (Montrachet)
½ pound Belgian endive, pulled apart into spears and washed
¼ cup pine nuts

Spread cheese inside individual spears. Arrange in spoke fashion on two or three serving plates, with thicker stem portion of spears facing out. Sprinkle with nuts. Put one plate in the microwave. MICROWAVE (high) 30 seconds until cheese warms. Repeat with other plates. Serve warm.

BELGIAN ENDIVE HEARTS WITH ROQUEFORT DRESSING

This recipe is designed for the small inner core of Belgian endive hearts, the tight, compact leaves that are too small to use in many recipes. Here they are microwaved briefly, then covered with a light Roquefort dressing.

Preparation time: 10 minutes
Microwave time: 3 minutes
Servings: 4

10–15 Belgian endive inner cores, stems trimmed to ¼ inch
2 tablespoons fresh lemon juice
4 tablespoons olive oil
2 tablespoons Roquefort or blue cheese, crumbled

1. Put endive hearts in 1-quart casserole with stems facing outside. Sprinkle with 1 tablespoon of the lemon juice. Cover. MICROWAVE (high) 2–3 minutes, until just tender. Drain.
2. Whisk olive oil and remaining 1 tablespoon lemon juice. Beat in cheese. Pour over tips of endive hearts. Serve.

TIP: *Use the same microwave technique and dressing for 4 whole endive hearts. Increase microwave time to 5–7 minutes and double the dressing recipe.*

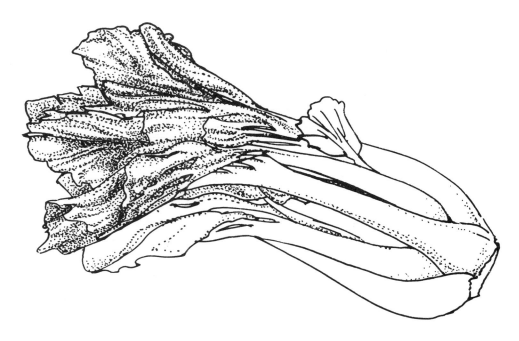

BOK CHOY

It wasn't long ago that bok choy was an oddity on supermarket shelves. The rather clumsy-looking plant, resembling a marriage between a celery stalk and a head of cabbage, hardly looked familiar. Yet were it marketed already cut into diagonal slices, it would be recognized as the background vegetable in popular Cantonese dishes.

Indeed, the stir-fry craze pushed bok choy from the back of Chinese restaurant kitchens into our own homes. It is indispensable in stir-fry dishes and serves as a fine stand-in for either celery or cabbage in other dishes.

Because it contains a large amount of water, little extra water is needed to cook bok choy in the microwave. Cut it into uniform pieces to assure even cooking and try it straightforward with a little sesame seed or stir-fried with pork. To retain crispness, be sure not to overcook bok choy.

Select firm, smooth stalks with fresh-looking leaves.

Store loosely wrapped in the refrigerator for several days.

SESAME BOK CHOY

The sesame touch is Oriental, but this side dish easily accompanies entrees such as simple broiled fish or roast chicken.

Preparation time: 10 minutes
Microwave time: 6 minutes
Servings: 4

1½ **pounds bok choy, greens trimmed, white portion julienned**
¼ **cup chicken broth**
¼ **teaspoon sesame oil**
2 **teaspoons sesame seeds**

1. Put bok choy and broth in 1-quart casserole. Cover. MICROWAVE (high) 4–6 minutes, until tender, stirring twice. Let stand 3 minutes. Drain. (Reserve cooking broth for a soup.)
2. Stir in sesame oil and seeds. Serve.

WARM BOK CHOY SALAD WITH PEANUTS

With a little imagination and a warm buttermilk dressing, bok choy can be as upscale as more expensive vegetables.

Preparation time: 10 minutes
Microwave time: 6 minutes
Servings: 4

1½ **pounds bok choy, white portion only, cut into ¼-inch diagonal slices**
¼ **cup water**
½ **cup buttermilk**
¼ **cup sour cream**
2 **tablespoons chopped roasted peanuts**

1. Put bok choy and water in 2-quart casserole. Cover. MICROWAVE (high) 4–6 minutes, until just tender, stirring twice. Let stand 3 minutes. Drain.
2. In 2-cup measure, mix buttermilk and sour cream. MICROWAVE (high) 20–30 seconds to warm, taking care not to let cream boil. Pour over bok choy. Sprinkle with peanuts. Serve.

JAPANESE NOODLE SOUP

One of my favorite quick lunches, this soup starts with a package of ramen noodles, plus fresh bok choy and a little shrimp. I leave out the too-salty seasoning packet and substitute chicken broth or stock.

Preparation time: 15 minutes
Microwave time: 16 minutes
Servings: 4

1 pound bok choy, white portion cut into 2-inch julienned strips, green tops cut into ¼-inch strips
4 cups chicken stock or broth
1 3-ounce package ramen noodles
½ cup (about 3 ounces) small frozen shrimp
2 green onions, white portion and first 2 inches of green, sliced

1. Put white portion of bok choy and the broth in 2-quart casserole. Cover. MICROWAVE (high) 10–12 minutes, until broth boils, stirring once.
2. Drop in noodles. (Noodles first may be broken in half for easier eating.) Cover. MICROWAVE (high) 2 minutes, stirring once to break up noodles.
3. Add shrimp and bok choy green tops. MICROWAVE (high) 1–2 minutes, until shrimp are just pink and greens wilt. Serve sprinkled with green onions.

TIP: Note the order in which ingredients are added to make soup in the microwave. Start with long-cooking root or stalk vegetables, then a quick-cooking noodle, and finally delicate shrimp and thinly sliced greens.

STIR-FRY WITH PORK

Bok choy is practically essential in a stir-fry. Its white portion adds crunch, and its leafy top donates contrasting greenery.

Preparation time: 20 minutes
Microwave time: 20 minutes
Servings: 6

¾ **pound boneless pork, sliced into ¼-inch by 2-inch strips**
3 **tablespoons soy sauce**
2 **tablespoons vegetable oil**
½ **teaspoon minced garlic**
¼ **teaspoon red pepper flakes**
½ **pound fresh mushrooms, sliced**
1 **pound bok choy, white portion cut into ¼-inch diagonal slices, green tops cut into ¼-inch strips**
2 **green onions, white portion and first 2 inches of green, sliced**

1. Mix pork, soy sauce, oil, garlic, and pepper flakes in 2½-quart casserole. Let stand 5 minutes to marinate. Cover. MICROWAVE (medium) 8–10 minutes, until pork is no longer pink inside, stirring every 2 minutes.
2. Stir in mushrooms, then white portion of bok choy. Cover. MICROWAVE (medium) 6 minutes. Add bok choy green tops. MICROWAVE (medium) 4 minutes, until vegetables are tender and green tops just wilt. Sprinkle with green onions. Serve with white rice.

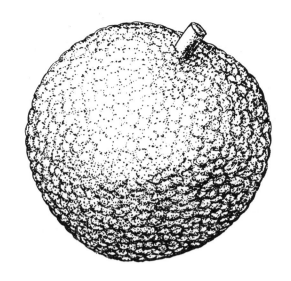

BREADFRUIT

Mild, slightly chestnut-flavored, and heavy, almost sticky in texture, the white meat of tropical breadfruit can be touted as lackluster. Yet there is romance to the fruit that hangs like green volleyballs from lush-leaved trees in the Caribbean, Pacific islands, and parts of South America.

This is the staple food that Capt. William Bligh envisioned for the Caribbean and thus set out to transport from Tahiti to Jamaica on the H.M.S. *Bounty* in the 1780s. The precious little water on board was used for the thousand seedlings first, not for the crew—a disenchanted group that made mutiny, not breadfruit, the top priority.

The first time I had breadfruit was in Jamaica, where they love to simply bake it and serve it sliced with meals. Before leaving for home, I purchased a beautiful specimen in the market and asked the chef at The Plantation Inn to bake and wrap it for me. It survived customs and the spot under my seat on the airplane, arriving still slightly warm to share with friends in Chicago.

Technically breadfruit is available all year, and it is not impossible to purchase breadfruit here. But supplies are unpredictable. Your dinner party will be at the mercy of "the shipment"; and then, if your local merchant is as proud as mine, he still won't sell the breadfruit if the quality is poor.

Expect to pay $5 to $6 for a 3- to 4-pound breadfruit, which will serve 12 generously or give a taste to 24 people.

The exterior of the breadfruit is slightly sticky, and this tackiness increases when cooked. However, the stickiness easily washes off hands and knives.

Select breadfruit that is firm and heavy for its size, with clear, evenly sized scales.

Store green-colored breadfruit at room temperature until it ripens to a mottled brown. Refrigerate ripe fruit for only one or two days.

BAKED BREADFRUIT

Baked or broiled breadfruit is a common staple in the Caribbean, served sliced and buttered with meals. A 3- to 4-pound breadfruit generously serves 12 or gives a taste to 24 people. I've written this recipe so that you cook the whole breadfruit but use only half to serve six; fill another casserole and double the butter mixture to serve 12 or use the remaining half to make salad or dessert recipes, also in this chapter. Don't let the length of the recipe fool you; baking a breadfruit in the microwave is as easy as baking a winter squash.

Preparation time: 10 minutes
Microwave time: 23 minutes
Servings: 6

1 3- to 4-pound green breadfruit
3 tablespoons butter
¼ teaspoon salt
⅛ teaspoon freshly ground white pepper
¼ teaspoon ground nutmeg

1. Pierce breadfruit several times with fork to allow steam to escape while cooking. Place on plate. Do not cover. MICROWAVE (high) 20–22 minutes, until knife pierces through easily (the center core still will be slightly resistant), turning breadfruit over and rotating dish once. Let stand 5 minutes.
2. Cut breadfruit in half lengthwise. Use small knife and spoon to remove core. Save half the breadfruit for another use or double the butter sauce.
3. Cut breadfruit again lengthwise into quarters. Peel. Cut lengthwise into 1-inch wedges. Arrange overlapping slices in 2-quart rectangular casserole. (Recipe can be made ahead to this point. Cover and refrigerate for 24 hours. To reheat, cover, MICROWAVE [high] 4–5 minutes. Let stand, covered, 2 minutes.)
4. Put butter in 2-cup measure. MICROWAVE (high) 45 seconds to 1 minute to melt. Stir in salt, pepper, and nutmeg. Pour over breadfruit. Spoon over extra butter sauce as you serve.

TIP: For breakfast breadfruit, pour on warmed maple syrup. It's not a Caribbean specialty, but it's good.

HAWAIIAN BREADFRUIT SALAD

Bland breadfruit teams with pineapple and a sesame-honey dressing for this make-ahead salad. The dish marinates for a day to let the breadfruit absorb the oil and liquid. If the salad seems too dry after marinating, refresh it with reserved pineapple juice. The recipe calls for using only half the cooked breadfruit; double the dressing if you use both halves.

Preparation time: 20 minutes
Microwave time: 26 minutes
Marinating time: 24 hours
Servings: 8–10

1 3- to 4-pound green breadfruit
2 tablespoons sesame seeds
2 tablespoons white wine
    vinegar
3 tablespoons vegetable oil
2 tablespoons honey
¼ teaspoon salt
2 cups fresh pineapple chunks
    plus ¼ cup juice *or* 1 15-ounce
    can pineapple chunks,
    drained, ¼ cup juice reserved

1. Pierce breadfruit several times with fork to allow steam to escape while cooking. Place on plate. Do not cover. MICROWAVE (high) 20–22 minutes, until knife pierces through easily (the center core still will be slightly resistant), turning breadfruit over and rotating dish once. Let stand 5 minutes.
2. Cut breadfruit in half lengthwise. Use small knife and spoon to remove core. Save half the breadfruit for another use or double the sesame-honey dressing.
3. Cut breadfruit again lengthwise into quarters. Peel. Cut into long wedges, then thin, bite-sized pieces.
4. Put sesame seeds in 2-cup measure. Do not cover. MICROWAVE (high) 3–4 minutes to toast. Mix in vinegar. Whisk in oil, then honey and salt. In serving bowl, pour dressing over breadfruit and mix well. Marinate, covered, in refrigerator overnight.
5. Before serving, gently mix in pineapple and, if desired, ¼ cup of pineapple juice.

COCONUT BREADFRUIT DESSERT

This is a favorite recipe: easy and good. Half of a cooked breadfruit is mixed with half a can of cream of coconut. Serve this very sweet dessert slightly warm or after chilling in the refrigerator.

Preparation time: 15 minutes
Microwave time: 22 minutes
Servings: 6–8

1 green breadfruit
1 cup cream of coconut
¼ cup chopped macadamia nuts
¼ cup grated dry coconut

1. Pierce breadfruit several times with fork to allow steam to escape while cooking. Place on plate. Do not cover. MICROWAVE (high) 20–22 minutes, until knife pierces through easily (the center core still will be slightly resistant), turning breadfruit over and rotating dish once. Let stand 5 minutes.
2. Cut breadfruit in half lengthwise. Use small knife and spoon to remove core. Save half the breadfruit for another use or double the coconut dressing and nuts.
3. Cut breadfruit again lengthwise into quarters. Peel. Cut into long wedges, then thin, bite-sized pieces. In serving bowl, mix breadfruit and cream of coconut. Top with macadamia nuts and coconut.

TIP: Thick, creamy, sweetened cream of coconut (used to make piña coladas) can be purchased in 15-ounce cans. Mix well before using.

TIP: For a prettier presentation, leave some of the macadamia nuts whole.

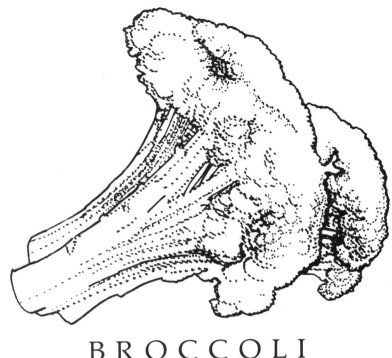

BROCCOLI

Broccoli is the wonder vegetable of modern times. It is plentiful and cheap. It stores well and dresses up or down for meals. Kids love it. And it is remarkably healthful.

Historians note that Thomas Jefferson grew Italian-bred broccoli in his garden, but commercial development in this country started only in the 1920s in California.

Broccoli is a good source of iron and vitamins C and A, as well as calcium and potassium. It is low in sodium, low in fat, and has but 40 calories per cup. Also, scientific evidence indicates that eating broccoli, cauliflower, cabbage, and brussels sprouts reduces cancer in humans.

To keep as many nutrients as possible, cook broccoli only briefly and with the least possible amount of water.

The floweret and stalk sections should be treated separately for best results in the microwave. Peel the stalks and give them a head start before you add the flowerets or save the stalks for special recipes such as the following stuffed tortillas or kabobs.

Select broccoli with good green color, tight buds, and firm stalks. Avoid open bud clusters, yellowed buds or leaves, and thick, woody stems.

Store loosely wrapped in the refrigerator for several days.

BROCCOLI WITH LEMON JUICE

Broccoli has a more even texture if you microwave either flowerets or stems separately. However, long spears may be prepared if you arrange the thicker stem portions facing the outside. Soaking in water also helps the broccoli cook more evenly. For this basic recipe, no butter, cream, or salt is needed. Lemon juice alone suffices.

Preparation time: 10 minutes
Microwave time: 8 minutes
Servings: 4

4 large broccoli spears (about 1 pound)
4 tablespoons fresh lemon juice

1. Trim ends of stems and peel lightly to remove tough skin. Soak in cold water for 5 minutes. Drain but do not dry.
2. Arrange spears in spokelike fashion on serving plate or in 2-quart rectangular casserole. Sprinkle with lemon juice. Cover with plastic wrap. MICROWAVE (high) 6–8 minutes, until tender enough to pierce with fork, rotating dish once. Let stand, covered, 2 minutes. Drain.

BROCCOLI WITH OYSTER SAUCE

This dish is wonderful—and embarrassingly simple. Oyster sauce, a thick, brown, salty sauce made with oysters and seasonings and used largely in Oriental cooking, is readily available in major supermarkets. If you've just opened the bottle, there is no need to heat it. Just spread it on and gather the compliments.

Preparation time: 10 minutes
Microwave time: 8 minutes
Servings: 4

1 pound broccoli, flowerets only
¼ cup water
⅓ cup prepared oyster sauce

1. Soak broccoli flowerets in water for 5 minutes. Drain.
2. Put broccoli and water in 2-quart casserole. Cover. MICROWAVE (high) 5–8 minutes, until tender enough to pierce with fork, stirring twice. Let stand, covered, 2 minutes. Drain. Spread with oyster sauce. Serve.

BROCCOLI WITH HOT PEPPERS AND GARLIC

The first two steps of this recipe are a good basic way to cook broccoli flowerets. A chili-hot vinaigrette enlivens the dish.

Preparation time: 10 minutes
Microwave time: 10 minutes
Servings: 4

1 pound broccoli, flowerets only
¼ **cup water**
1 tablespoon minced, seeded chili pepper
2 teaspoons minced garlic
2 tablespoons white wine vinegar
¼ **teaspoon salt**
4 tablespoons olive oil

1. Soak broccoli flowerets in water for 5 minutes. Drain.
2. Put broccoli and water in 2-quart casserole. Cover. MICROWAVE (high) 5–8 minutes, until tender enough to pierce with fork, stirring twice. Let stand, covered, 2 minutes. Drain.
3. Whisk chili pepper, garlic, vinegar, salt, and olive oil in 4-cup measure. MICROWAVE (high) 2 minutes. Whisk again. Pour over broccoli and toss gently. Serve.

TIP: *It is best to cook broccoli in small batches to achieve even cooking. However, up to 4 cups of flowerets can be microwaved at one time in a 4-quart casserole. Add ½ cup water. Cover. MICROWAVE (high) 10–12 minutes, stirring twice. Let stand 2 minutes. Drain.*

BROCCOLI WITH MACADAMIA NUTS

Butter-soaked macadamia nuts are a classy addition to broccoli.

Preparation time: 10 minutes
Microwave time: 10 minutes
Servings: 4

1 pound broccoli, flowerets only
¼ **cup water**
3 tablespoons butter
¼ **cup chopped macadamia nuts**

1. Soak broccoli flowerets in water for 5 minutes. Drain.
2. Put broccoli and water in 2-quart casserole. Cover. MICROWAVE (high) 5–8 minutes, until tender enough to pierce with fork, stirring twice. Let stand, covered, 2 minutes. Drain.
3. Put butter and nuts in 2-cup measure. MICROWAVE (high) 2 minutes, until softened, stirring once. Pour over broccoli.

BROCCOLI AND CHICKEN TORTILLAS

Don't discard the stems when you clean fresh broccoli. Save them for a healthy crunch in these colorful tortillas.

Preparation time: 20 minutes
Microwave time: 9 minutes
Servings: 8 tortillas

1 tablespoon fresh lemon juice
1 tablespoon oil
⅛ teaspoon cayenne
½ pound boneless, skinned chicken breast
1 cup (from one bunch) broccoli stems, lightly peeled and julienned
½ teaspoon salt
¼ cup water
8 8-inch flour tortillas
1 cup chopped tomatoes
1 green onion, chopped
¾ cup prepared salsa
¼ cup roughly chopped cilantro

1. Mix lemon juice, oil, and cayenne in small bowl. Turn chicken several times in lemon marinade and let sit in bowl 5 minutes while you peel and chop vegetables.
2. Put broccoli, salt, and water in 1-quart casserole. Cover. MICROWAVE (high) 2 minutes, until just tender. Drain.
3. Put chicken on roasting rack. Cover with waxed paper. MICROWAVE (high) 5–6 minutes, until no longer pink, turning after half the time. Cut into thin strips.
4. Put tortillas between damp paper towels. MICROWAVE (high) 30 seconds to 1 minute, until warm. Fill center of each tortilla evenly with chicken, broccoli, tomatoes, onions, and salsa. Sprinkle with cilantro. Fold over bottom of tortilla, then sides.

TIP: *If tortillas are sold in a plastic bag, MICROWAVE (high) 1–2 minutes right in the unopened bag.*

TIP: *People love or hate cilantro. If it hits home, team it again with tomatoes or avocados.*

BROCCOLI AND HAM KABOBS

Here is another use for broccoli stems, designed to serve a crowd. Broccoli and ham are marinated in a sweet bean sauce (readily found in Oriental food sections of major supermarkets), then threaded with pineapple chunks on bamboo skewers. Use a good-quality canned ham and ask your grocer to cube it. The microwave is ideal for reheating the kabobs because the bamboo handles don't get hot.

Preparation time: 1 hour
Microwave time: 11 minutes
Marinating time: 10 minutes
Servings: 25–30 skewers (2 per person for dinner)

4 cups broccoli stems (from about 4 bunches)
¼ cup water
2 pounds boneless, cooked ham, cut into 1-inch cubes
½ cup prepared bean sauce
2 20-ounce cans pineapple chunks, drained
1 10-ounce jar maraschino cherries

1. Peel broccoli stems and cut into 1-inch cubes to match the ham. Put broccoli and water in 2-quart casserole. Cover. MICROWAVE (high) 6–8 minutes, until just tender, stirring twice. Let stand, covered, 2 minutes. Drain.
2. In a large bowl, mix cooked broccoli, ham, and bean sauce until well coated. Let stand 10 minutes to cool and marinate. (Don't let mixture stand long at room temperature or the sauce will become too thin.)
3. Thread three rows of ham, broccoli, and pineapple on each 12-inch bamboo skewer, making sure each piece is secure. Leave three inches at one end clean for a handle; leave room at the very tip for a last-minute cherry. Use immediately or cover and refrigerate. Skewers can be made 24 hours ahead to this point.
4. Just before serving, add cherry to end of skewer. (If you add the cherry before you refrigerate the skewers, the cherries tend to dry out and the cherry juice runs.) To reheat, arrange skewers in single- or double-layer batches on serving plate. Do not cover. MICROWAVE (high) 3 minutes, until warm.

BRUSSELS SPROUTS

Bless the English for Devonshire cream, plum pudding, and "Masterpiece Theatre," but don't let them touch the brussels sprouts. Nothing ruins the gems quicker than a long sojourn in boiling water, a British tradition adopted in this country and perfected in our school cafeterias.

Fresh, properly prepared brussels sprouts are wonderful. They are green, not grey; crisp, not soggy. Carve a little X on each cute bottom, and they cook up perfectly in the microwave.

As a concession to convenience, I have included one recipe for doctoring up frozen brussels sprouts. Don't let me regret this.

Try, by all means, Quick Dilled Brussels Sprouts made from frozen sprouts, but only if you agree to venture later into Fresh Brussels Sprouts with Caraway Seeds. Even better, offer the two dishes side by side in a friendly taste testing, anywhere outside of England.

Select firm, compact sprouts with tight leaves. Avoid those with yellowed or wilted leaves.

Store loosely wrapped in the refrigerator for up to a week.

FRESH BRUSSELS SPROUTS WITH CARAWAY SEEDS

Very simple, very good. Fresh brussels sprouts need only a touch of butter and herbs to make a fine side dish.

Preparation time: 10 minutes
Microwave time: 7 minutes
Servings: 4–6

1½ **pounds fresh brussels**
   sprouts, trimmed, with an X
   cut into the bottom of each
   stem
¼ **cup water**
1 **tablespoon butter**
2 **teaspoons caraway seeds**
¼ **teaspoon salt**

1. Put brussels sprouts and water in 1½ quart casserole. Cover. MICROWAVE (high) 5–7 minutes, until just tender, stirring once. Let stand, covered, 3 minutes. Drain.
2. Add butter, caraway seeds, and salt. Toss. Serve warm.

TIP: Brussels sprouts are done when the center can be pierced easily with a fork. Don't overcook or they turn to mush.

QUICK DILLED BRUSSELS SPROUTS

Fresh brussels sprouts are superior, but frozen can do in a pinch. Be careful not to overcook frozen brussels sprouts, which already have a softer texture.

Preparation time: 5 minutes
Microwave time: 10 minutes
Servings: 4–6

2 **10-ounce packages frozen**
   brussels sprouts
3 **tablespoons oil**
1 **tablespoon white vinegar**
¼ **teaspoon salt**
⅛ **teaspoon freshly ground**
   pepper
½ **teaspoon dried dill**

1. Remove sprouts from package. Put in 2-quart casserole. Cover. MICROWAVE (high) 8–10 minutes, until tender, stirring once. Drain.
2. In 2-cup measure, whisk oil, vinegar, salt, pepper, and dill. Toss with sprouts, Serve warm.

BRUSSELS SPROUTS WITH APPLES AND ONIONS

Enhanced with sage and thyme, this generous dish teams well with turkey or roast pork. It's healthful, too: no butter and only apple juice for sweetening.

Preparation time: 10 minutes
Microwave time: 15 minutes
Servings: 6–8

1 pound fresh brussels sprouts, cut in half lengthwise
1 medium onion, sliced thin
½ cup apple juice
2 medium Granny Smith apples, peeled, cored, and sliced ½ inch thick
1 teaspoon cornstarch
1 tablespoon water
1 tablespoon fresh thyme *or* ½ teaspoon dried
¼ teaspoon dried sage, crushed

1. Mix brussels sprouts, onions, and apple juice in 2½ quart casserole. Cover. MICROWAVE (high) 6–8 minutes, until sprouts are almost tender, stirring once.
2. Mix in apples. Cover. MICROWAVE (high) 4–5 minutes, until apples are fork-tender.
3. In 2-cup measure, dissolve cornstarch and water. Pour juices (about ½ cup) from brussels sprouts casserole into measure. Blend.
4. MICROWAVE (high) cornstarch mixture 1–2 minutes to thicken, stirring every 30 seconds. Stir in thyme and sage. Pour over brussels sprouts. Mix gently. Serve warm.

BRUSSELS SPROUTS WITH HAM IN MUSTARD SAUCE

Serve over a pile of mashed potatoes for a hearty winter supper.

Preparation time: 15 minutes
Microwave time: 17 minutes
Servings: 4–6

1½ **pounds fresh brussels sprouts, trimmed, with X cut into bottom of each stem**
¼ **cup water**
2 **tablespoons butter**
1 **cup chopped onions**
2 **tablespoons flour**
¾ **cup chicken broth**
2 **tablespoons prepared mustard, preferably Dijon with whole grains**
⅛ **teaspoon freshly ground pepper**
1 **1-pound ham steak, cut into 2- by ¼- by ½-inch strips**

1. Put brussels sprouts and water in 2-quart rectangular casserole. Cover. MICROWAVE (high) 6–8 minutes, stirring once. Let stand, covered, 3 minutes. Drain. Put in dish and cover to keep warm.
2. Put butter and onions in the casserole. MICROWAVE (high) 3 minutes, until onions are tender, stirring once. Blend in flour. Stir in broth, mustard, and pepper.
3. Stir in ham. Cover with waxed paper. MICROWAVE (high) 5–6 minutes, until sauce is thickened and ham heated through, stirring twice. Stir brussels sprouts into casserole. Serve warm.

TIP: *When cooking dishes that include ham, taste before adding salt to the sauce. This one is fine without salt.*

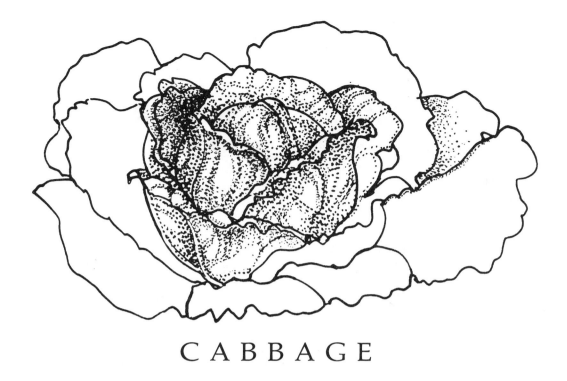

CABBAGE

Cabbage is the most humble member of the cruciferous plant family, which also includes broccoli, brussels sprouts, and cauliflower. These vegetables have gained status lately because of their apparent cancer-fighting ability. Cabbage also is high in vitamin C and low in sodium and calories.

The most common variety of cabbage is green cabbage. However, savoy cabbage, with its curly leaves and softer head, imparts a more delicate touch. And red cabbage is a good choice to add color to dishes. To help maintain its color, cut red cabbage with a stainless steel knife and add lemon juice or vinegar to the cooking water. Because it takes longer to grow, red cabbage can be a little tougher than green cabbage; cook it a little longer.

Cabbage can emit an odor when cooked by conventional methods for long periods of time. The odor isn't as much of a problem with enclosed microwave ovens, which also cook cabbage much more quickly.

Select solid cabbage heads that are heavy for their size. For green cabbage, avoid flabby, yellow leaves. Savoy is naturally pale green to yellow.

Store wrapped in plastic in the refrigerator for one to two weeks. Remove the tougher two or three outer leaves before cooking. Wash just before using.

CABBAGE WEDGES VINAIGRETTE

Topped with a tangy shallot vinaigrette, cabbage seems anything but plain.

Preparation time: 5 minutes
Microwave time: 16 minutes
Servings: 4

1 small to medium cabbage (1–2 pounds), quartered
¼ cup water
2 tablespoons minced shallot
8 tablespoons olive oil
6 tablespoons red wine vinegar
1 tablespoon Dijon mustard

1. Arrange cabbage in 2-quart rectangular casserole. Add water. Cover. MICROWAVE (high) 12–14 minutes, rearranging once. Let stand, covered, 3 minutes.
2. Put shallot and olive oil in 2-cup measure. MICROWAVE (high) 1–2 minutes to soften shallots. Whisk in vinegar and mustard. Pour vinaigrette over cabbage wedges and serve.

CREAMY CABBAGE WITH CARAWAY

Caraway seeds are a traditional accent to cabbage. Note that you first cook the seeds briefly in the microwave to soften them and develop flavor.

Preparation time: 10 minutes
Microwave time: 9 minutes
Servings: 4–6

½ medium (2-pound) cabbage, cored and chopped (about 5 cups)
¼ cup water
1 tablespoon butter
2 teaspoons caraway seeds
1 cup half-and-half
½ teaspoon salt
¼ teaspoon freshly ground pepper

1. Put cabbage and water in 2½-quart casserole. Cover. MICROWAVE (high) 6–7 minutes, until tender. Drain well.
2. Put butter and caraway seeds in 4-cup measure. MICROWAVE (high) 1 minute, stirring once. Stir in half-and-half. MICROWAVE (high) 1 minute to heat. Mix into cabbage. Add salt and pepper and serve.

TIP: Note that cabbage and other vegetables take less time in the microwave if they are cut into small pieces. A cabbage cut into four large quarters needs 14 minutes in the microwave. The same cabbage sliced needs 8 minutes; and chopped, 7 minutes.

CABBAGE POTAGE

Slow cooking—made faster in the microwave—gives depth to this hearty, beef-enhanced soup. Serve with crusty French bread and butter.

Preparation time: 25 minutes
Microwave time: 1 hour, 17 minutes
Servings: 6–8

3 slices bacon, cut into 1-inch pieces
½ pound boneless beef chuck, cut into 1-inch pieces
1 tablespoon brown sugar
2 cups chopped onions
1 cup diced carrots
½ cup diced celery
½ teaspoon dried thyme
½ teaspoon freshly ground black pepper
3 parsley sprigs
1 bay leaf
4 whole cloves
2 13½-ounce cans beef broth
1 28-ounce can tomatoes, with juice
7 cups coarsely chopped cabbage (1 large head)
1 15½-ounce can kidney beans, drained

1. Place bacon in 4-quart casserole. Cover with paper towels. MICROWAVE (high) 2 minutes. Stir. MICROWAVE (high) 3–4 minutes, until crisp. Use slotted spoon to remove bacon, leaving 2 tablespoons fat in casserole. Drain bacon on paper towels. Reserve.
2. Coat beef with sugar. Place in casserole with still-hot bacon grease. Cover with paper towel. MICROWAVE (high) 3 minutes, stirring and turning several times until partially browned.
3. Stir in onions, carrots, celery, thyme, and pepper. Cover. MICROWAVE (medium) 10–14 minutes, stirring several times. Skim fat.
4. Tie parsley, bay leaf, and cloves in cheesecloth. Add tied herbs, beef broth, and tomatoes to casserole. Cover. MICROWAVE (medium-low) 20 minutes. Stir. Discard herb bag.
5. Stir in cabbage. Cover. MICROWAVE (medium-low) 30 minutes. Add beans. Cover. MICROWAVE (medium-low) 4 minutes. Serve sprinkled with bacon.

TIP: Keep bacon in the freezer. To defrost, pull back plastic wrap to expose the number of slices desired. Wrap the rest in aluminum foil. Place in microwave at least one inch away from the walls. Defrost. The part protected by foil will remain frozen. Remove desired slices. Return the rest of the bacon to the freezer.

SLICED CABBAGE WITH PINE NUTS

Pine nuts and a bit of butter elevate humble cabbage to a lovely side dish.

Preparation time: 10 minutes
Microwave time: 10 minutes
Servings: 4–6

½ **medium (2-pound) cabbage, cored and cut into ¼-inch slices (about 5 cups)**
¼ **cup water**
3 **tablespoons butter**
¼ **cup pine nuts**
   Freshly ground pepper

1. Put cabbage and water in 2½-quart casserole. Cover. MICROWAVE (high) 6–8 minutes, until just tender, stirring once. Drain.
2. Put butter and pine nuts in 2-cup measure. MICROWAVE (high) 2 minutes, stirring once. Pour over cabbage wedges. Top with freshly ground pepper as desired. Serve.

CABBAGE AND PORK PAPRIKA

Use good Hungarian paprika in this robust entree. Note that the dish is cooked on medium to keep the pork tender.

Preparation time: 20 minutes
Microwave time: 45 minutes
Servings: 4

1 **pound pork shoulder roast, cut into 1-inch cubes**
½ **cup chopped onion**
1 **teaspoon minced garlic**
½ **medium (2-pound) cabbage, cored and cut into ¼-inch slices (about 5 cups)**
½ **cup apple juice or beer**
½ **teaspoon dried rosemary, crushed**
½ **teaspoon salt**
1 **tablespoon paprika**
1 **tablespoon flour**
1 **cup sour cream**
Hot, cooked noodles

1. Put pork, onion, and garlic in 2-quart casserole. Cover. MICROWAVE (medium) 10–12 minutes, until meat is no longer pink, stirring every 3 minutes.
2. Stir in cabbage. Cover. MICROWAVE (medium) 5 minutes, until cabbage softens. Stir in apple juice or beer, rosemary, salt, paprika, and flour. Cover. MICROWAVE (medium) 24–28 minutes, until pork and cabbage are tender stirring every 5 minutes.
3. Stir in sour cream. Let stand, covered, 3 minutes. Serve over noodles.

TIP: *Sauerkraut may be substituted for the fresh cabbage. Serve with boiled potatoes.*

DUXELLES-STUFFED CABBAGE

No rice. No tomato sauce. No meat. Cabbage rolls go upscale here with a walnut and mushroom filling that has a meatlike texture of its own.

Preparation time: 40 minutes
Microwave time: 43 minutes
Servings: 6

1 medium (2-pound) cabbage
1 pound mushrooms, chopped fine
1 cup minced onions
½ cup finely chopped walnuts
¼ teaspoon freshly ground pepper
½ teaspoon dried thyme
½ teaspoon salt
2 cups beef broth
1 tablespoon cornstarch
1 tablespoon water

1. Cut out cabbage core and discard. Wrap cabbage tightly in plastic wrap. MICROWAVE (high) 6–8 minutes. Plunge into sink or bowl of cold water to loosen leaves. Remove leaves, taking care not to tear them, and reserve about 20 of the largest. Chop the remaining small leaves in the center.
2. Mix the chopped cabbage (about 2–3 cups), mushrooms, onions, walnuts, pepper, thyme, and salt in 2-quart casserole. MICROWAVE (high) 3–5 minutes, until just tender.
3. Carve away a triangle of hard stem from the largest leaves to make them easier to roll. Put a heaping tablespoon of mushroom filling in center of each leaf. Starting at the thicker end, roll, tucking in sides, and fasten with toothpick. Arrange rolls in 3½-quart rectangular casserole, with the largest rolls to the outside. Pour beef broth over rolls. Cover.
4. MICROWAVE (high) 5 minutes, then MICROWAVE (medium) 18–22 minutes. Let stand, covered, 3 minutes.
5. Use large spoon to lift rolls onto serving platter, reserving cooking broth. Mix cornstarch and water in 4-cup measure. Stir cooking broth into measure. MICROWAVE (high) 2–3 minutes, until broth thickens. Pour over cabbage rolls. Serve with rice.

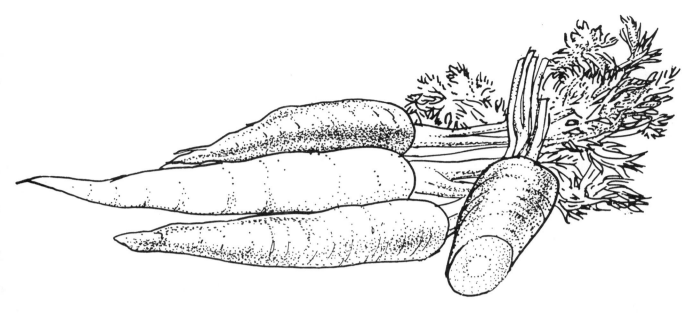

C A R R O T S

Even if they weren't good for you, fresh carrots would be a pleasure to eat. Nothing can quite replace crisp, raw carrots for low-calorie nibbling. And cooking only enhances their fine, sweet flavor.

But carrots, as every child learns early, are indeed good for you. A one-half cup serving of cooked carrots has a whopping 19,152 international units of vitamin A and significant potassium. And it has only 35 calories and a fraction of a gram of fat. You'll save more nutrients if you don't peel carrots.

Carrots belong to the same family as fennel, parsnips, the flower Queen Anne's Lace, and poisonous hemlock. When it comes to taste, the same carrot seed produces a different-quality product, depending on the soil. Carrots grown on the West Coast are considered sweeter.

Because foods cook better in a microwave if they are the same size, I find that julienned, sliced, or diced carrots work better than whole.

If you have very large carrots with tough cores, cut the carrots in half lengthwise, then cut again in the same direction. The core will stick out at the point of a triangle. Slice out and discard the core. Use only the outer portion of the carrot.

Select small or medium, deep orange carrots that are smooth and firm. Avoid those with very thick, then tapered roots as these tend to be bitter and are hard to cut. Avoid limp carrots. If sold with green tops, look for bright, fresh tops with no wilting.

Store in plastic wrap in the refrigerator for a month.

ORANGE CARROTS

Orange marmalade is stirred in at the last moment to sweeten julienned carrots.

Preparation time: 10 minutes
Microwave time: 7 minutes
Servings: 4

1 pound carrots (4–6 medium)
2 tablespoons water
3 tablespoons orange marmalade

Peel and trim carrots. Cut into 2-inch julienne strips. Put carrots and water in 1-quart casserole. Cover. MICROWAVE (high) 5–7 minutes, until just tender, stirring after 3 minutes. Let stand, covered, 2 minutes. Drain. Stir in marmalade.

CARROT SOUP

The natural sweetness of carrots, plus a little honey, makes a surprisingly pleasant soup. Carrots and the potato, which works as a thickener, are cooked in only a small amount of broth until tender. The vegetables would take longer to cook in the microwave if you added all the broth at once.

·Preparation time: 25 minutes
Microwave time: 22 minutes
Servings: 4

2 tablespoons butter
½ cup chopped onion
1 pound carrots (4–6 medium), sliced
1 small potato, peeled and sliced
2 cups chicken stock or broth
1 tablespoon honey
½ teaspoon salt
¼ teaspoon freshly ground pepper

1. Put butter and onion in 3-quart casserole. MICROWAVE (high) 2 minutes to soften. Add carrots, potatoes, and ¼ cup of the chicken broth. Cover. MICROWAVE (high) 12–14 minutes, until quite tender. Puree in blender or processor.
2. Return carrot mixture to casserole. Add remaining chicken broth. Cover. MICROWAVE (high) 4–6 minutes to boiling. Stir in honey, salt, and pepper.

CARROT-DILL SALAD

Brief cooking helps blend flavors of this cold salad which can be quick chilled (see Tip).

Preparation time: 10 minutes
Microwave time: 2 minutes
Chilling time: 1 hour
Servings: 4

10 medium-sized carrots, peeled and julienned or sliced very thin
¼ cup water
¼ teaspoon salt
3 tablespoons fresh dill *or* 1 tablespoon dried
2 medium green onions, white parts and first 2 inches of green, sliced thin
2 tablespoons chopped fresh parsley
½ teaspoon salt
¼ teaspoon freshly ground pepper
¾ cup sour cream
¾ cup mayonnaise

1. Put carrots, water, and ¼ teaspoon salt in 2-quart casserole. Cover. MICROWAVE (high) 1–2 minutes, until just starting to soften. Drain.
2. Toss in dill, green onions, parsley, ½ teaspoon salt, and pepper. Mix in sour cream and mayonnaise. Refrigerate, covered, for at least 1 hour.

TIP: *In a hurry? Work in reverse. Mix sour cream and mayonnaise in a metal mixing bowl. Put in the freezer while you cook carrots and toss with herbs and spices. Add carrots to cream mixture. Return, uncovered, to freezer. And don't forget to take it out. The salad will be cold in 10 minutes—but frozen on the edges in 12.*

ORLANDO CARROT COINS

These addictive, sweet-and-sour, marinated carrot slices are popular in Orlando, Florida, where my sister, Virginia Partain, lives. I kept nibbling at them during a visit, so she sent the recipe up north. Because carrots and canned tomato soup already are sweet, I cut the amount of sugar in half; sweet tooths may want to add it back.

Preparation time: 20 minutes
Microwave time: 18 minutes
Chilling time: 24 hours
Servings: 12–16

2 pounds carrots, cut into ¼-inch slices
4 tablespoons water
1 10-ounce can tomato soup
¾ cup vinegar
½ cup sugar
1 tablespoon dry mustard
1 tablespoon Worcestershire sauce
1 medium onion, sliced
1 green pepper, cored and diced

1. Put half the carrots (1 pound) and half the water (2 tablespoons) in 2½-quart casserole. Cover. MICROWAVE (high) 5–7 minutes, until carrots can be just pierced with a fork but still are firm, stirring twice. Drain. Put carrots in 3-quart casserole. Repeat with remaining carrots and water.
2. Add rest of ingredients to carrots. Stir well. Do not cover. MICROWAVE (high) 3–4 minutes, until onions soften a little but sauce is still thick and carrots are still a little firm. Refrigerate, covered, 24 hours.

CARROT WONTONS

These delightful, bite-sized wontons or dumplings are easy and fun to make, but they do take time to assemble. The filling is prepared in the microwave, then the stuffed wontons are boiled in a pot on the stove. (A large amount of water takes too long to boil in the microwave.) As one batch of wontons is cooking, you have just enough time to stuff the next batch. Serve the wontons as a side dish or in chicken stock for homemade wonton soup. I also have brought them as appetizers to a party. The wonton skins stick together when wet, so arrange the finished dumplings on a plate in a single layer without touching. Cover with plastic wrap to reheat.

Preparation time: 1 hour
Microwave time: 4 minutes
Servings: 60 dumplings

1 **tablespoon butter**
4 **green onions, white and first 2 inches of green, sliced**
1 **teaspoon minced garlic**
1 **tablespoon flour**
3 **medium-sized carrots, grated (2 cups)**
½ **cup pine nuts**
1 **teaspoon minced fresh ginger**
3 **tablespoons soy sauce**
½ **teaspoon salt**
¼ **teaspoon freshly ground pepper**
1 **teaspoon cornstarch**
1 **tablespoon water**
15 **egg roll skins *or* 60 wonton skins**

1. Put butter, green onions, and garlic in 2-quart casserole. MICROWAVE (high) 2 minutes, stirring after 1 minute. Stir in flour, carrots, pine nuts, and ginger. Do not cover. MICROWAVE (high) 2 minutes. Mix in soy sauce, salt, and pepper. Let mixture cool a little.

2. Bring 4 quarts of water to boil in a stockpot on the stove. Mix the cornstarch and water in a cup and set on work counter.

3. Cut three of the egg roll skins into quarters to make 12 little rectangles. Put a scant teaspoon of filling in center of one rectangle. Use your finger to paint the edges with the cornstarch mixture. (This helps the skins to stick together.) Fold the long sides together so that it looks like a long ravioli and press edges firmly to seal. The dumplings may be cooked like this, or you may continue to paint, fold, and press the bottom of the short sides to form little wontons.

4. Drop stuffed dumplings 12 at a time into boiling water. Cook for 5 minutes. Remove with slotted spoon, set in single layer on a plate, and cover with plastic wrap. Repeat with remaining egg roll skins.

TIP: Fresh ginger is essential for the underlying Oriental flavor. Sliced almonds or minced cooked pork may be substituted for pine nuts.

TIP: Egg roll skins can be purchased in Oriental markets and in many supermarkets, wrapped in clear plastic, in the produce or other refrigerated sections.

NUTTY CARROT CUPCAKES

Chopped walnuts give a browned look to these buttery cupcakes. They freeze well. To defrost two cupcakes, MICROWAVE (high) for 30 seconds.

Preparation time: 15 minutes
Microwave time: 12 minutes
Servings: 18 muffins

1½ cups flour
 1 teaspoon baking soda
 ¾ teaspoon salt
 1 teaspoon ground cinnamon
 2 eggs
 6 tablespoons butter or margarine
 1 cup light brown sugar
 ½ cup orange juice concentrate, defrosted
1½ cups finely grated carrots
 ¼ cup finely chopped walnuts

1. In small bowl, sift together flour, baking soda, salt, and cinnamon. Set aside.
2. In 3-quart bowl, beat eggs. Beat in butter and sugar until creamy. Stir in orange juice concentrate, scraping sides well. Gradually beat in flour mixture until smooth. Stir in carrots.
3. Place paper liners in microwave-proof, circular, 6-cup muffin pan. Fill each cup half full with cupcake mixture. Sprinkle each with about ½ teaspoon nuts.
4. Do not cover. MICROWAVE (high) 3–4 minutes, until toothpick inserted in middle comes out dry, rotating pan one-half turn after 2 minutes. Cupcakes may still be moist but will finish cooking while standing. Let stand 1 minute. Remove cupcakes to wire rack to cool. Repeat with remaining batter.

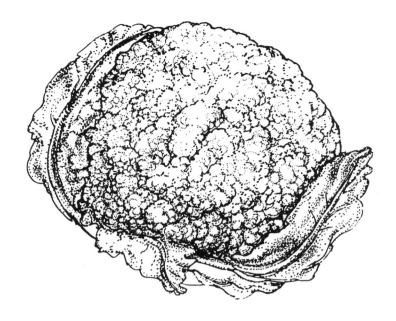

CAULIFLOWER

A head of cauliflower is almost perfectly designed for the microwave oven—and what a wonderful break for healthy diets.

As a proud member of the cruciferous family, cauliflower—like broccoli, brussels sprouts, and cabbage—gets high grades as a possible deterrent to cancer. And if that isn't enough, you can count on it for a good serving of vitamin C and calcium, just 22 calories per 100-gram serving.

Then, to make the deal almost impossible to refuse, cauliflower's round, compact shape makes it ideal to cook in the microwave. Just remove the core, cover the head of cauliflower with plastic wrap, and set the microwave for seven minutes. The result will be outstanding in taste and nutrition. Just take care not to overcook cauliflower, or it becomes unpleasantly mushy.

Although cauliflower may be green-with-purple, the most common variety by far is the familiar white cauliflower, which may have slight purple tones near the flowerets. Cauliflower is available all year, with a peak in October and November.

To freshen a head of cauliflower, use a trick from grocers: soak it head down for an hour in cold water with a teaspoon each of vinegar and salt added.

Select heavy, compact heads with clear white buds. Avoid those with brown spots and spreading, a sign of overmaturity.

Store loosely wrapped in refrigerator up to five days.

CAULIFLOWER WITH LEMON-CRUMB TOPPING

This simple recipe requires no water so that nutrient loss is minimum.

Preparation time: 5 minutes
Microwave time: 8 minutes
Servings: 4–6

1 medium head cauliflower, core removed
¼ cup butter
3 tablespoons finely ground bread crumbs
1 tablespoon fresh lemon juice

1. Wrap washed, whole cauliflower in plastic wrap. MICROWAVE (high) 6–8 minutes, until just tender, rotating one-quarter turn every 2 minutes. Let stand, covered, 3 minutes.
2. Put butter in 1-cup measure. MICROWAVE (high) 30–45 seconds to melt. Stir in crumbs and lemon juice. Pour over cauliflower. Serve.

CAULIFLOWER CUSTARD RING

This dish holds its shape well for dinner presentation. Fill the center with tiny flowers or parsley sprigs. If the edges look uneven, add more parsley there, too.

Preparation time: 15 minutes
Microwave time: 20 minutes
Servings: 6–8

1 medium head cauliflower, chopped (about 4 cups)
¼ cup water
¼ teaspoon salt
2 cups shredded sharp cheddar cheese
2 green onions, white and first 2 inches green, sliced
¼ cup minced fresh parsley
¼ cup biscuit mix
¼ teaspoon salt
⅛ teaspoon freshly ground white pepper
¼ teaspoon ground nutmeg
4 eggs, well beaten
Butter

1. Place cauliflower, water, and ¼ teaspoon salt in 1½-quart casserole. Cover. MICROWAVE (high) 9–11 minutes, stirring once. Drain.
2. In 3-quart bowl, combine cauliflower, cheese, onions, parsley, biscuit mix, ¼ teaspoon salt, pepper, and nutmeg. Stir in eggs.
3. Spoon evenly into buttered, 1½-quart ring mold. MICROWAVE (high), uncovered, 7–9 minutes, until mixture starts to set on edges. Let stand 5 minutes. Loosen edges lightly with knife if necessary. Unmold. Serve immediately or cool in refrigerator and serve chilled.

CAULIFLOWER SOUP

What a delicious way to increase vegetables in your meals. A sprinkling of cheese adds color to this creamy white soup.

Preparation time: 15 minutes
Microwave time: 27 minutes
Servings: 6–8

½ **cup chopped onion**
1 **tablespoon butter**
1 **large cauliflower, cored and roughly chopped**
2 **cups chicken stock or broth**
1 **cup milk**
¼ **teaspoon ground nutmeg**
½–1 **teaspoon salt**
½ **teaspoon freshly ground pepper**
¼ **cup grated cheddar cheese**

1. Put onion and butter in 3-quart casserole. MICROWAVE (high) 2 minutes until tender. Stir in cauliflower. Cover. MICROWAVE (high) 12–15 minutes, until quite tender, stirring every 4 minutes. Puree in blender or processor.

2. Return puree to casserole. Stir in broth. Cover. MICROWAVE (high) 5–7 minutes, until boiling. Stir in milk, nutmeg, salt, and pepper. MICROWAVE (high) 3 minutes, until heated through. Serve topped with cheese.

TIP: *For a thinner soup, add more chicken broth. Cream, sour cream, or yogurt may be substituted for milk.*

CAULIFLOWER AND BEEF IN BEAN SAUCE

Conventional cooking usually calls for extra liquid such as soy sauce or water with prepared bean sauce. In the microwave, however, natural juices from the beef and cauliflower combine with the bean sauce to create a delicious brown gravy.

Preparation time: 20 minutes
Microwave time: 14 minutes
Servings: 4–6

1 pound boneless sirloin steak
4 tablespoons black bean sauce
1 tablespoon sherry
1 medium cauliflower, cored and cut into flowerets
¼ cup water
1 cup peanuts
2 green onions, white and first 2 inches of green, sliced

1. Trim fat from steak. Cut across grain into ¼- by ½- by 3-inch strips. (Partially frozen meat is easier to cut.) Mix steak, half (2 tablespoons) black bean sauce, and sherry. Let marinate for 10 minutes on counter while you prepare cauliflower.
2. Put cauliflower and water in 2-quart casserole. Cover. MICROWAVE (high) 6–8 minutes, until just tender, stirring twice. Let stand, covered, 3 minutes. Drain. Stir in remaining black bean sauce. Set aside.
3. Put beef in 2-quart rectangular casserole. Do not cover, or moisture will be trapped and the texture will be more like a stew than a stir-fry. MICROWAVE (high) 3–4 minutes until exterior of beef just loses redness, stirring every minute.
4. Stir in peanuts. Stir in cauliflower. Do not cover. MICROWAVE (high) 2 minutes to heat through. Sprinkle with green onions. Serve with rice.

TIP: *Cooked as directed, the interior of the beef will look rare (red) in step 3, then continue to cook while standing and reheating to reach medium-rare. For medium finished beef, cook another minute or two in step 3 until interior of meat turns from red to pink.*

TIP: *Other thick sauces such as oyster sauce may be substituted for the bean sauce.*

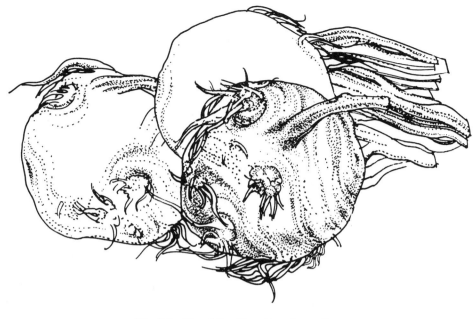

CELERIAC

Despite its odd, round shape and dull-looking exterior, celeriac—also called *celery root* or *knob celery*—is a pleasant-tasting vegetable, a bit like celery with a tang.

Celeriac is related to Pascal celery, the common vegetable used in relish trays. But celeriac is cultivated for its large root instead of stalks.

Its somewhat pungent flavor is evident when the vegetable is paired with potatoes in a smooth puree. Sugar tones down this sharp edge in our recipe for celeriac and pineapple salad and the honey-topped celeriac with carrots.

Use a stainless steel knife when cutting celeriac because iron discolors the white vegetable. To keep slices white, put them in a bowl of cold water with vinegar or lemon juice until ready to cook.

Select roots that are firm, not spongy. The knobby appearance and pungent smell are normal. However, the smoothest knobs will be easier to peel and have less waste.

Store celeriac unwashed in the refrigerator for a week.

CELERIAC AND PINEAPPLE SALAD

Celeriac benefits from a little sweetness, provided here by pineapple chunks.

Preparation time: 10 minutes
Microwave time: 8 minutes
Servings: 4

1 ¾-pound celeriac, peeled and julienned
¼ cup water
½ cup mayonnaise
1 tablespoon fresh lemon juice
1 cup canned pineapple chunks, all but 1 tablespoon syrup drained

1. Put celeriac and water in 1-quart casserole. Cover. MICROWAVE (high) 6–8 minutes, until just tender. Let stand 2 minutes. Drain. Set on counter to cool.
2. Mix mayonnaise, lemon juice, and pineapple juice. Stir into celeriac. Stir in pineapple chunks. Serve immediately or refrigerate, covered, for an hour.

HONEY-TOPPED CELERIAC AND CARROTS

Carrots taste good with celeriac and add color to this simple side dish.

Preparation time: 10 minutes
Microwave time: 10 minutes
Servings: 4

1 ¾-pound celeriac, peeled and julienned
2 carrots, julienned
¼ cup water
3 tablespoons fresh lemon juice
3 tablespoons honey
¼ cup chopped pecans

1. Put celeriac, carrots, and water in 2-quart casserole. Cover. MICROWAVE (high) 7–9 minutes, until just tender. Let stand 2 minutes. Drain.
2. Mix lemon juice and honey in 2-cup measure. Stir in pecans. MICROWAVE (high) 1 minute to slightly soften nuts. Pour over celeriac and carrots. Serve immediately or refrigerate, covered, for an hour.

CELERIAC AND POTATO PUREE

This is a wonderful way to enjoy celeriac. Note that the celeriac needs longer to cook, so it is microwaved first. The exact amounts of the two root vegetables are not critical. I like this ratio of two potatoes to one celeriac.

Preparation time: 20 minutes
Microwave time: 17 minutes
Servings: 6–8

1 ¾-pound celeriac, peeled and cut into ½-inch cubes
½ cup water
2 medium potatoes, peeled and cut into ½-inch cubes
2 tablespoons butter
1 cup milk
½ teaspoon salt
⅛ teaspoon freshly ground pepper
¼ teaspoon ground nutmeg

1. Put celeriac and water in 2-quart casserole. Cover. MICROWAVE (high) 5 minutes. Stir in potatoes. Cover. MICROWAVE (high) 10–12 minutes, until both vegetables are quite tender. Puree in blender or processor.
2. Mix in butter. Whip in milk, salt, pepper, and nutmeg. Serve.

TIP: Add a tablespoon of milk before rewarming.

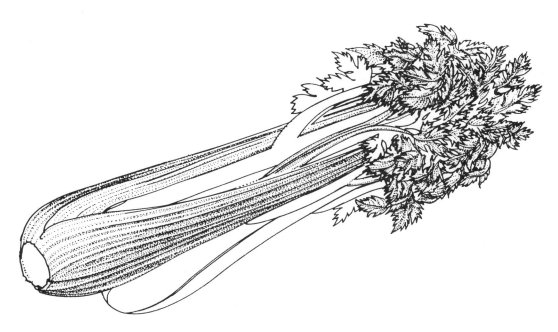

CELERY

Celery is not an ideal vegetable for the microwave because its crisp texture softens less easily than when cooked conventionally. However, if you enjoy crisp celery, this is no problem.

The problem with celery is remembering to use this staple vegetable for something other than raw salads or as a flavoring in soups and sauces. Braised celery can be quite elegant, whether served with just buttered bread crumbs or covered with a fine Mornay sauce.

Waldorf salad, typically served cold, is enhanced by a brief warming in the microwave. And oysters and celery team well in a vegetable-thick stew.

Though high in natural sodium, celery is very low in calories. A cup of celery has a meager nine calories.

The most common variety of celery found in groceries is the light green, Pascal variety, favored for its fine flavor. When talking about celery, a stalk is the same as a bunch. The individual portions are branches or ribs.

Select thick, solid, light green bunches that are crisp enough to break easily. The tiny dark green leaves should be crisp.

Store in an airtight box in the refrigerator for up to two weeks. When ready to use, separate ribs, wash well with a brush, and trim off roots and blemishes.

CELERY AU GRATIN

This simple dish fares well with broiled fish or chicken.

Preparation time: 10 minutes
Microwave time: 12 minutes
Servings: 4

1 1¼-pound bunch celery,
   trimmed and julienned
¼ cup chicken broth
3 tablespoons butter
¼ cup fine bread crumbs

1. Put celery and broth in 2-quart casserole. Cover. MICROWAVE (high) 8–10 minutes, until tender, stirring once. Let stand 3 minutes. Drain.
2. Put butter in casserole. MICROWAVE (high) 1–2 minutes to melt. Stir in bread crumbs. Spoon crumbs over celery. Serve.

CELERY WITH CHEDDAR CHEESE SAUCE

Pale celery looks pretty paired with an orange cheddar cheese sauce. For a monochromatic look, switch to Gruyère cheese for a fine Mornay sauce.

Preparation time: 15 minutes
Microwave time: 16 minutes
Servings: 4

1 1¼-pound bunch celery,
   trimmed and julienned
¼ cup water
3 tablespoons butter
3 tablespoons flour
¼ teaspoon salt
⅛ teaspoon freshly ground
   pepper
1 cup milk, room temperature
1 cup grated sharp cheddar
   cheese

1. Put celery and water in 2-quart casserole. Cover. MICROWAVE (high) 8–10 minutes, until tender, stirring once. Let stand 3 minutes. Drain.
2. Put butter in 4-cup measure. MICROWAVE (high) 40–50 seconds, until melted. Stir in flour, salt, and pepper. Slowly whisk in milk. MICROWAVE (high) 1–2 minutes, until thickened, stirring twice. Stir in cheese. MICROWAVE (high) 2–3 minutes, until cheese melts and sauce is smooth. Pour sauce over celery and serve.

HOT WALDORF SALAD

Brief cooking in the microwave heightens the flavor of celery in traditional Waldorf salad. And because the salad is warm, a scant 2 tablespoons of mayonnaise spreads far enough for four servings.

Preparation time: 10 minutes
Microwave time: 5 minutes
Servings: 4

1½ **cups diced celery**
2 **tablespoons water**
1½ **cups cored, diced, unpeeled red delicious apples**
½ **cup chopped walnuts**
2 **tablespoons mayonnaise**
1 **dozen green seedless grapes, halved**

Put celery and water in 2-quart casserole. Cover. MICROWAVE (high) 3 minutes. Stir in apples and walnuts. Cover. MICROWAVE (high) 2 minutes, until celery and apples are warmed through but still crisp. Stir in mayonnaise and grapes.

CELERY WITH OLIVES AND PINE NUTS

Celery slices are cooked but still crisp in this warm side dish accented by glossy black olives.

Preparation time: 10 minutes
Microwave time: 5 minutes
Servings: 6

4 **cups celery ribs, cut into ½-inch diagonal slices**
2 **tablespoons water**
3 **tablespoons good-quality (extra virgin) olive oil**
1½ **teaspoons dried marjoram**
½ **teaspoon dried oregano**
¼ **teaspoon freshly ground pepper**
¼ **cup pine nuts**
1 **6-ounce can medium pitted black olives, drained**

1. Put celery and water in 2-quart casserole. Cover. MICROWAVE (high) 3–5 minutes, until still slightly crisp. Drain.
2. Mix in rest of ingredients. Serve slightly warm on a bed of lettuce.

OYSTER-CELERY STEW

This is a very thick stew, laden with plenty of celery and mushrooms. For a thinner variety, add a cup or more of milk and adjust the seasoning.

Preparation time: 15 minutes
Microwave time: 17 minutes
Servings: 4

1 1¼-pound bunch celery, trimmed and cut into ¼-inch diagonal slices
2 tablespoons water
½ pound fresh mushrooms, quartered
3 green onions, white and first 2 inches of green, sliced
1 cup half-and-half
1 teaspoon dried thyme
¼ teaspoon salt
⅛ teaspoon freshly ground white pepper
⅛ teaspoon cayenne
1 8-ounce can whole oysters, with juices
2 tablespoons butter (optional)

1. Put celery and water in 2-quart casserole. Cover. MICROWAVE (high) 8–10 minutes, until quite tender.
2. Stir in mushrooms and onions. Cover. MICROWAVE (high) 2–4 minutes, until mushrooms are tender. Stir in half-and-half, thyme, salt, pepper, cayenne, and oysters with juices. MICROWAVE (high) 2–3 minutes to warm through. Serve topped with small pat of butter, if desired.

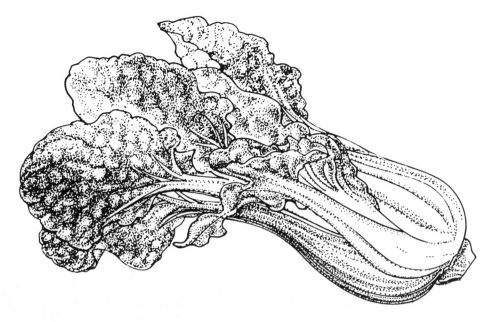

CHARD

A patch of chard strokes a gardener's ego like no other vegetable. Put the seeds in late, and they grow anyway. Forget to water the chard, and it thrives. Pick a plant almost to the bone, and it reappears with vigor. Indeed, one small packet of seeds keeps our family in chard through the summer and long after the trees have shed their autumn leaves.

Growing your own chard is the best way to assure a plentiful supply, for this wonderful green rarely shows up in groceries. If you spot it, take some home and try it in your usual recipes for spinach.

A member of the beet family, chard is also called *spinach beet* or *Swiss chard*. It has a less astringent flavor than spinach, and its thicker leaves take a little longer to cook. Its color remains more vividly green than spinach when cooked.

The thick stems, or *chards* as they are sometimes called, should be cut away and cooked separately because they require a longer cooking time. Save them for braised chards, the first recipe in this chapter.

Select leaves that are crisp and young. There are two chard versions—the more common one with green leaves with white ribs and one with red leaves and red ribs. The ribs should be either clear white or red, with no browning. Avoid yellow or wilted leaves.

Store loosely wrapped in plastic bags for three to five days.

BRAISED CHARDS

Don't throw away the stems when preparing fresh chard. Cook them separately with a bit of butter and pepper.

Preparation time: 5 minutes
Microwave time: 8 minutes
Servings: 4

Stems from 2 bundles (1½ pounds) chard, washed and cut into 3-inch-long julienne strips
¼ cup water
1 tablespoon butter
Freshly ground pepper

Put stems and water in 1-quart casserole. Cover. MICROWAVE (high) 7–9 minutes, until tender. Let stand 2 minutes. Drain. Mix in butter and pepper. Serve.

CHARD WITH TINY ONIONS

You need nothing more than a pat of butter and little white onions for a good-tasting and pretty, green and white dish.

Preparation time: 15 minutes
Microwave time: 14 minutes
Servings: 4

1 tablespoon butter
½ pound small white onions, peeled
1½ pounds (2 bundles) chard leaves, cleaned and roughly chopped

1. Put butter and onions in 3-quart casserole. Cover. MICROWAVE (high) 3–5 minutes, until onions start to get tender, stirring once.
2. Add chard. Cover. MICROWAVE (high) 7–9 minutes, until both chard and onions are tender. Drain. Serve.

TIP: Larger onions, peeled and quartered, may be substituted.

TIP: Swish chard leaves several times in a sink of cold water to clean. Lift out leaves and drain water. Repeat.

TIP: Note that a large, 3-quart casserole is needed to hold chard leaves, which will cook down considerably.

CHARD WITH ANCHOVY-ROQUEFORT DRESSING

Zesty anchovies and Roquefort cheese quickly awaken cooked, mild chard.

Preparation time: 15 minutes
Microwave time: 9 minutes
Servings: 4

1½ **pounds (2 bundles) chard leaves, cleaned and roughly chopped**
3 **anchovy fillets, cut up**
1 **teaspoon minced garlic**
4 **tablespoons fresh lemon juice (about 1½ lemons)**
¼ **teaspoon salt**
⅛ **teaspoon freshly ground pepper**
4 **tablespoons vegetable oil**
3 **ounces room-temperature Roquefort cheese, crumbled**

1. Put chard in 3-quart casserole. Cover. MICROWAVE (high) 7–9 minutes, until tender, stirring once. Drain.
2. In a large bowl, mash anchovies and garlic. Stir in lemon juice, salt, and pepper. Whisk in oil. Beat in Roquefort cheese. Pour over chard. Serve.

TIP: *The Roquefort dressing doesn't need to be heated if the ingredients are at room temperature when you start.*

COLD GREEN SOUP

Unlike spinach, chard remains a vivid green when cooked, providing this cool summer soup with spectacular color. For a special presentation, consider topping each serving with pretty white rose petals or a yellow nasturtium.

Preparation time: 15 minutes
Microwave time: 12 minutes
Servings: 4

½ cup chopped onion
1 tablespoon butter
1 10-ounce bunch fresh chard leaves, cleaned and chopped
2 cups chicken broth
⅛ teaspoon ground nutmeg
½ teaspoon salt
⅛ teaspoon freshly ground pepper
½ cup half-and-half
4 tablespoons sour cream (optional)

1. Put onion and butter in 3-quart casserole. MICROWAVE (high) 1–2 minutes, until tender. Add chard. Cover. MICROWAVE (high) 6–8 minutes, until tender, stirring twice.
2. Stir in chicken broth, nutmeg, salt, and pepper. Puree in blender or processor. Return to casserole.
3. Blend in half-and-half. Cover and refrigerate for 2 hours. Top with sour cream, if desired.

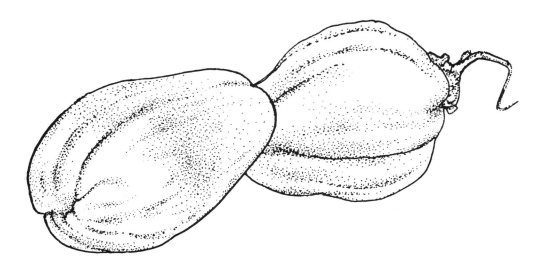

CHAYOTE

The veteran Chicago cabbie could resist no longer. "What are those green things?" he asked as we sped back from bountiful South Water Street market with 20 of the few chayotes available in town that day. His reaction—and the elusive availability—are typical here of this Mexican and South American favorite.

Chayotes are transcending their status as an exotic specialty to become regular cameo guests in the American market, spurred by the interest in Mexican and Southwest American cuisine. But most shoppers, I wager, still don't know what to do with them.

The first stumbling block is the name. Or names. Only the most hip confidently pronounce *chayote* (chah-YO-tay). *Mirliton*, as it is called in Louisiana, sounds like a magic potion. *Chokos* (Australia) and *chocho* (Jamaica) are difficult for an adult to request with a straight face. And *vegetable pear* confuses the botany.

The chayote is a pear-shaped gourd with creamy white to dark green, furrowed skin and a crunchy, pale-green flesh. The larger dark green variety covered with spikes is considered the best but rarely is spotted in the markets. Its skin generally is not eaten, but the almond-shaped seed is prized for its fine, nutty flavor. While the texture is crisp like an apple, its taste more closely resembles cucumbers and zucchini.

Chayotes can be ready to eat in less than 10 minutes with the microwave. The first recipe presents chayote as it is often eaten in Mexico, with just butter and a sprinkle of fresh pepper. But the mild-flavored vegetable marries well with hot salsa or dresses for dinner with a shrimp stuffing (shown on the cover). I doubt, however, that that's what the cabbie did with his chayote later that night.

Select firm, unblemished chayotes, weighing ½ to 1 pound. They don't need to ripen and are ready to eat as sold.

Store lightly wrapped in the refrigerator for three to four weeks.

CHAYOTE WITH BUTTER AND PEPPER

Enjoy this relatively new vegetable in its simplest form as is often done in Mexico, touched with butter and freshly ground pepper.

Preparation time: 5 minutes
Microwave time: 8 minutes
Servings: 4–6

**3 chayotes, peeled, cored, and
   cut into ¼-inch pieces**
¼ cup water
¼ teaspoon salt
3 tablespoons butter
Freshly ground pepper

1. Put chayote in 1-quart casserole with water and salt. Cover. MICROWAVE (high) 6–8 minutes, until just tender. Let stand 2 minutes. Drain.
2. Add butter. MICROWAVE (high) 30 seconds to melt. Stir. Top with freshly ground pepper to taste. Serve.

TIP: To cube or slice fresh chayote, first cut off thin slices from both bumpy ends. Discard ends. Cut rest in half lengthwise. Peel as you would an apple.

    Use a serrated tool (a grapefruit spoon works well) or melon baller to remove white, pithy core and almond-shaped seed. Reserve edible seed. Discard core.

    Turn chayote halves flat side down on cutting board. Cut into slices or cubes.

TIP: The seed has an extraordinary taste, much like a fresh nut just off a tree. If you're impatient, munch it raw. But the flavor deepens when the seed is cooked. Slip it into a dish for the last 2 minutes to cook.

CHAYOTE SLICES WITH BREAD CRUMBS

The gentle flavor of chayote gets dressed with just a drizzle of buttered bread crumbs.

Preparation time: 10 minutes
Microwave time: 10 minutes
Servings: 4–6

2 cups peeled, cored, ¼-inch-sliced chayote, plus seeds
¼ cup water
¼ teaspoon salt
¼ cup butter
3 tablespoons finely ground bread crumbs
1 tablespoon fresh lemon juice

1. Put chayote slices, seeds, water, and salt in 1-quart casserole. Cover. MICROWAVE (high) 7–9 minutes, stirring once, until just tender. Let rest 3 minutes, covered.
2. Remove seeds only and slice into slivers. Drain chayote slices well in colander. Arrange overlapping slices in circle on serving plate.
3. Put butter in 1-cup measure. MICROWAVE (high) 30–40 seconds to melt. Stir in crumbs and lemon juice. MICROWAVE (high) 20 seconds. Spoon over chayote slices. Top with seed slivers.

CHAYOTE IN HOT TOMATO SAUCE

Sweet as it is, chayote can take the heat, like this jalapeño-spiked sauce.

Preparation time: 15 minutes
Microwave time: 26 minutes
Servings: 4–6

2 cups peeled, cored, ¼-inch chayote cubes
¼ cup water
¼ teaspoon salt
1⅓ cups minced onion
1 teaspoon minced garlic
1 teaspoon seeded, minced jalapeño pepper
2 tablespoons oil
2 cups seeded, coarsely chopped fresh tomatoes
1 tablespoon red wine vinegar
2 dashes Worcestershire sauce
¼ teaspoon salt
½ teaspoon sugar
2 tablespoons chopped fresh coriander (optional)

1. Put chayote, water, and salt in 1-quart casserole. Cover. MICROWAVE (high) 6–8 minutes, until just tender, stirring twice. Let stand 2 minutes. Drain. Set aside.
2. Put onion, garlic, jalapeño pepper, and oil in 1½-quart casserole. MICROWAVE (high) 3 minutes, stirring once.
3. Stir in tomatoes, vinegar, Worcestershire sauce, salt, and sugar. MICROWAVE (high), uncovered, 12–15 minutes, until thickened.
4. Reserve a small handful of cooked chayote for garnish. Mix rest into sauce. Top with reserved chayote. Sprinkle with coriander.

CHICKEN-CHAYOTE SALAD

Chameleonlike chayote blends smoothly into this unusual salad.

Preparation time: 10 minutes
Microwave time: 8 minutes
Chilling time: 2 hours
Servings: 4

2 **cups pared, cored, ¼-inch chayote cubes**
¼ **cup water**
¼ **teaspoon salt**
½ **cup mayonnaise**
3 **teaspoons Dijon mustard**
¼ **teaspoon salt**
⅛ **teaspoon freshly ground pepper**
2 **green onions, white and first 2 inches of green, sliced**
2 **cups cooked, skinless, cubed chicken breast**
½ **cup dry-roasted peanuts**

1. Put chayote, water, and salt in 1-quart casserole. Cover. MICROWAVE (high) 6–8 minutes, until just tender, stirring twice. Let stand, covered, 2 minutes. Drain.
2. In 2-quart bowl, blend mayonnaise, mustard, salt, and pepper. Mix in green onions, chicken, peanuts, and cooked chayote. Cover. Refrigerate for 2 hours to blend flavors.

SHRIMP-STUFFED CHAYOTE

Firm, attractive chayote work beautifully as stuffed vegetables. Serve this shrimp-filled version as an appetizer or center of a luncheon plate.

Preparation time: 15 minutes
Microwave time: 11 minutes
Servings: 4

2 medium chayotes
2 tablespoons water
3 tablespoons butter
1 teaspoon minced garlic
2 green onions, white and first 2 inches of green, sliced
2 cups fresh croutons (see Tip)
1 tablespoon chopped pimiento
⅛ teaspoon cayenne
½ teaspoon dried thyme
¼ teaspoon freshly ground black pepper
¼ teaspoon salt
½ teaspoon dried basil
6 ounces (about ½ cup) cooked small shrimp, all but 12 chopped

1. Cut chayotes in half lengthwise. Put on plate with necks pointing inward. Add water to plate. Cover. MICROWAVE (high) 6–9 minutes, rotating once, until skin is just tender. Let stand, covered, 5 minutes.

2. Remove almond-shaped seed and eat or reserve for other use. Discard white, pithy center. Scoop out chayote pulp, leaving ¼-inch shell. Set shells upside down to drain. Dice pulp. Reserve.

3. Put butter, garlic, and green onions in 1-quart casserole. MICROWAVE (high) 2 minutes, stirring once. Add chayote pulp and rest of ingredients except for the 12 whole shrimp. Mix gently.

4. Spoon mixture into chayote shells. Top with reserved whole shrimp. Serve.

TIP: *To make croutons, put 2 tablespoons butter in 8" × 8" × 2" dish. MICROWAVE (high) 30 seconds to melt. Stir in 2 teaspoons snipped parsley. Mix in 2 cups of ½-inch cubed French bread. MICROWAVE (high), uncovered, 3–5 minutes, stirring every minute. Let cool.*

TIP: *This dish travels well as a dinner party contribution. Wrap well in plastic right on the serving platter. Just before reheating, turn back an edge of the plastic to form a vent. MICROWAVE (medium) 3–4 minutes to reheat, turning several times.*

CORN

The revolution started one hot August day in 1950 when Professor John R. Laughnan wandered onto the cornfields of the University of Illinois. A professor of genetics, Laughnan stood among rows of his specially mated hybrids and, on a whim, took a bite.

The corn was sweet. Super sweet. His experiment with an odd, mutant Shrunken 2 gene created a breakthrough in the quality of one of our most popular vegetables.

New, "super" sweet corn developed from the Shrunken 2 gene doesn't have as much starch as regular corn. But it has three times the sugar, which converts to starch at a much slower rate than in traditional corn. The new corn thus starts sweeter and stays sweet in the refrigerator for up to 12 days after picking.

Super sweet corn has been tricky to grow economically on a large scale, farmers say. But Florida now has about 80 percent of its winter crop in this new corn, and it's showing up increasingly in groceries and roadside stands, with names such as Summer Sweet, Butterfruit, Florida Staysweet, Kandy Korn, Ivory and Gold Xtra-Sweet, and How Sweet It Is.

The corn revolution means that the availability of good-quality, fresh corn is unprecedented—and right in time for new microwave technology. The first recipe here is for fresh corn on the cob, cooked right in the husk on the floor of a microwave. The microwave method is faster than starting with a pot of water to boil, and the husk adds an earthy flavor. Although corn right from the garden is best, and new super sweets store well, frozen corn is a good convenience product. Try it in a sweet and spicy maque choux or a whiskey corn pudding.

Select ears of corn with firm, smallish kernels. To test freshness, slash one or two kernels with a knife or fingernail. Regular corn turns from sugar to starch quickly; the liquid inside the kernel thus will be creamy, whitish, and feel a bit sticky. Extremely fresh corn or a super sweet variety will be translucent and feel cleaner. Super sweets also have a little shine, are crisper, and harder to slash. Avoid corn with brownish silk or with dimpled kernels.

Store immediately in the husk in the refrigerator. Non-super sweets should be cooked as soon as possible. Super sweets may last up to ten days in the refrigerator.

CORN ON THE COB

In the time it takes to get a big pot of water to boil, you can have fresh corn on the cob out of the microwave and on the table. Cooking corn right in the husk adds flavor, and the silk just slides away. Soaking in water first will produce a softer texture; I prefer this straight-from-the-stalk method.

Preparation time: 5 minutes
Microwave time: 12 minutes
Servings: 4

4 ears fresh corn, husk on
4 tablespoons butter
Salt

1. Place corn 2 inches apart on microwave oven floor. MICROWAVE (high) 10–12 minutes, until just tender, turning over and rearranging once. Let stand 3 minutes.
2. To husk, pull back leaves carefully to avoid steam. Grab silk and pull sharply. Serve slathered with butter and a sprinkle of salt.

TIP: To cook fresh corn without the husk, wrap individual ears in waxed paper and microwave as above.

TIP: Try the corn without butter. Extra flavor and moistness from this microwave method can help lop off a bit of butter from your diet.

SWEET, SWEET CORN

A little sugar, cinnamon, and butter sweeten a package of frozen corn in a jiffy.

Preparation time: 3 minutes
Microwave time: 5 minutes
Servings: 4

1 10-ounce package frozen corn
1 tablespoon water
1 tablespoon butter
½ teaspoon ground cinnamon
½ teaspoon sugar

Mix all ingredients in a 1-quart casserole. Cover. MICROWAVE (high) 4–5 minutes, stirring twice. Let stand 1 minute, uncovered. Serve.

DOUBLE CHEESE CORN EGGS

A single ear of fresh corn provides a nutlike crunch to this colorful dish.

Preparation time: 10 minutes
Microwave time: 15 minutes
Servings: 4–6

2 cups (3 ounces) shredded
  cream Havarti
1 cup cream-style cottage cheese
¼ cup diced sweet red pepper
¼ cup diced green pepper
¾ cup (1 ear) fresh corn
5 eggs
¼ cup flour
½ teaspoon baking powder

1. In 3-quart bowl, whisk all ingredients together. Pour into 9-inch pie plate.
2. MICROWAVE (medium-high), uncovered, 12–15 minutes, until center is just set, rotating one-quarter turn every 3 minutes. Let stand 3 minutes on counter.

CORN MAQUE CHOUX

"Yes, if you want to make it authentic, you have to use evaporated milk," New Orleans chef and Cajun high priest Paul Prudhomme advised as I researched this Cajun simmered corn dish and adapted it to the microwave using considerably less butter and oil. I usually avoid evaporated milk because to me it tastes like baby formula. But baby, this is good.

Preparation time: 10 minutes
Microwave time: 24 minutes
Servings: 4–6

4 cups fresh or frozen corn kernels
2 tablespoons butter
2 tablespoons vegetable oil
½ cup minced onion
2 tablespoons sugar
½ teaspoon freshly ground white pepper
¼ teaspoon salt
¼ teaspoon cayenne
½ cup evaporated milk
1 egg

1. Mix corn, butter, oil, onion, sugar, white pepper, salt, and cayenne in 1½-quart casserole. Cover. MICROWAVE (high) 6–7 minutes, stirring after 3 minutes.
2. MICROWAVE (high), uncovered, 8–9 minutes, until liquid thickens slightly, stirring three times.
3. Stir in half the evaporated milk (¼ cup). MICROWAVE (medium-high), uncovered, 7–8 minutes, until most of the liquid is absorbed.
4. In a small bowl, whisk remaining milk and the egg until frothy. Stir into corn. Serve hot.

NOTE: Maque choux, literally "false cabbage" in French, is an old Louisiana dish with numerous variations. Originally it was made with a type of Indian corn, eaten cob and all, that tasted somewhat like cabbage. The dish, of course, no longer tastes like cabbage, but the name stuck.

JALAPEÑO CORN BREAD

Quick bread like this corn-and-cheese-enhanced recipe can be ready after just 9 minutes in the microwave. For perfect results, use a ring-shaped casserole or see Tip below.

Preparation time: 15 minutes
Microwave time: 9 minutes
Servings: 6–8

1 cup fresh, canned, or defrosted frozen corn kernels, drained
¼ cup chopped onion
½ cup chopped green pepper
1 tablespoon minced jalapeño pepper
¼ cup oil
1 cup flour
¾ cup cornmeal
1½ teaspoons baking powder
½ teaspoon salt
½ teaspoon chili powder
1 cup milk
2 eggs, beaten
1 cup (4 ounces) shredded cheddar cheese

1. Mix corn, onion, green pepper, jalapeño pepper, and oil in 2-cup measure. Cover. MICROWAVE (high) 2 minutes, stirring once.
2. In a large bowl, mix flour, cornmeal, baking powder, salt, and chili powder. Stir in milk and eggs just until blended. Fold in corn mixture and ⅔ cup cheese, reserving the rest of the cheese.
3. Pour mixture evenly into a 1½-quart ring mold. Leave uncovered. MICROWAVE (high) 6–7 minutes, rotating a quarter turn every 2 minutes, until a toothpick stuck in the middle of batter comes out clean. The top will be a little soft but not sticky. Sprinkle with remaining ⅓ cup cheese. Let stand 5 minutes. Serve warm or cold.

TIP: *The ring-shaped casserole helps prevent a soggy middle. For the same effect, invert a small glass in the center of a 1½-quart baking dish. Pour the batter around the glass. Baking time is the same.*

TIP: *Don't overstir when adding the liquid. Stir gently until just blended.*

TIP: *For a breakfast version, omit the jalapeño peppers.*

WHISKEY CORN PUDDING

I borrow a generous jigger of my husband's best Kentucky bourbon whiskey for this sweet, creamy pudding. Perhaps that's why it smells so good while cooking.

Preparation time: 10 minutes
Microwave time: 18 minutes
Servings: 4–6

1 10-ounce package frozen corn
1 tablespoon cornstarch
1 cup milk
3 tablespoons bourbon whiskey
3 tablespoons sugar
¼ teaspoon salt
⅛ teaspoon freshly ground pepper
3 tablespoons butter
1 egg

1. Put corn in 1-quart casserole. MICROWAVE (high) 5–6 minutes. Drain.
2. Whisk cornstarch and about 4 tablespoons of the milk in 1½-quart casserole. Whisk in rest of milk, whiskey, sugar, salt, and pepper. Add butter. MICROWAVE (high) 3–4 minutes until thickened, whisking every minute.
3. In 2-cup measure or bowl, beat egg. Whisk about 5 tablespoons of the hot mixture, 1 tablespoon at a time, into the egg. Return egg mixture to casserole. Whisk. Stir in corn.
4. MICROWAVE (medium-high), uncovered, 6–8 minutes, until tiny bubbles that start on the edges finally reach the middle and center and stay bubbling about a minute. Rotate a quarter turn every 2 minutes. The center will be soft but finish cooking while standing.
5. Let stand, uncovered on the counter, 5–10 minutes.

TIP: *A good corn pudding in the microwave was one of my first failures. The trick, described above in step 4, is knowing how long to cook so that the center is done but the edges aren't overdone.*

FLOATING CORN SOUP

Invite guests at a casual party to pick up little chunks of fresh corn simmered in this vegetable-laden soup and eat them with their fingers. Whole white hominy adds extra texture.

Preparation time: 20 minutes
Microwave time: 16 minutes
Servings: 6

1 cup finely chopped onion
1 medium carrot, sliced thin
2 ribs celery, chopped
2 medium potatoes, peeled and chopped (about 3 cups)
1 teaspoon salt
3 cups chicken broth
1 14½-ounce can white, whole hominy, rinsed and drained
3 ears fresh, thin corn, cut into 1½-inch chunks
⅛ cup cream
¼ cup chopped green onions

1. Mix onion, carrot, celery, potatoes, salt, and chicken broth in 2-quart casserole. Cover. MICROWAVE (high) 8 minutes, until vegetables are just getting soft.
2. Puree soup a portion at a time in blender or food processor. Return to casserole.
3. Mix in hominy and corn chunks. Cover. MICROWAVE (high) 7–8 minutes, until corn is tender, stirring twice. To serve, add 2 pieces of corn to each filled bowl, drizzle with 1 teaspoon cream, and sprinkle with green onions.

TIP: *A sturdy butcher knife easily cuts thin ears of corn. To cut medium-sized ears, cut partially with a knife, then use two hands to snap off the chunks.*

TIP: *Consider microwaving the soup right in a pretty serving bowl. But before starting, test to see if the bowl is microwave-proof. (See "The Microwave" chapter.)*

TIP: *Serve warm hand towels after dinner to cleanse corn-messy hands. Have 6 damp, rolled towels ready in a dish. MICROWAVE (high) 1–2 minutes, uncovered.*

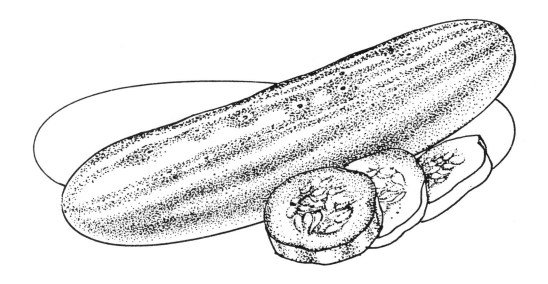

CUCUMBERS

The cucumber, faithful companion to lettuce and tomato salads, transforms into quite a different vegetable once cooked. Its crisp texture softens; its sweet, mild taste strengthens; and its botanic relationship to summer squash becomes more apparent.

Technically, cucumber is a fruit and, like its cousin watermelon, is mostly water—about 95 percent water. It cooks very quickly in the microwave and will exude plenty of moisture.

When selecting cucumbers or their seeds, you'll find three main types: common smooth-skinned, smaller bumpy pickling cucumbers, and long, seedless cucumbers. The last ones, also called "burpless" cucumbers, are the newest on the market, designed to avoid causing stomach problems. I use the common smooth-skinned in these recipes, but the burpless could be substituted.

Cucumbers are a vegetable that I prefer to grow or buy from a farmer's market in summer. Fresh garden cucumbers not only are especially crisp and flavorful, but you can eat them peel and all; bitterness previously associated with the skins has been pretty well bred away.

Most cucumbers purchased in groceries have a sticky, protective wax coating that helps prevent moisture loss. I find the wax impossible to wash off and unappealing to eat. You just have to peel waxed cucumbers.

Select straight, fairly thin cucumbers with clear, dark green skins. Large ones are airy inside and have large seeds. Avoid soft or yellowish ones.

Store loosely wrapped in plastic in the refrigerator for three or four days.

CUCUMBERS WITH DILL

Cucumbers change character when cooked, tasting like sweet, mild summer squash. Try this cucumber, yogurt, and dill combination as a pleasant side dish or as a topping for fish or baked potatoes. It is also good cold.

Preparation time: 5 minutes
Microwave time: 5 minutes
Servings: 4

2 medium cucumbers **¼ cup water** **½ teaspoon salt** **⅓ cup yogurt** **1½ tablespoons fresh lemon juice** **1 teaspoon sugar** **⅛ teaspoon freshly ground white pepper** **1 tablespoon chopped fresh dill** *or* **½ teaspoon dried**	1. Peel cucumbers. Cut in half lengthwise, then into ¼-inch slices. Put cucumbers and water in 1-quart casserole. Cover. MICROWAVE (high) 3–5 minutes, until just tender. Drain. Salt. Continue to drain in colander in sink. 2. Return cucumbers to casserole. Stir in yogurt, lemon juice, sugar, pepper, and dill. Taste and add more salt if necessary. Sauce will be thin; serve with slotted spoon.

TIP: Salting and then draining helps remove much of the water in cucumbers. Excess water would make the yogurt sauce too thin.

TIP: If you can afford the calories, substitute sour cream for yogurt to make a richer, thicker sauce.

TIP: No dill? Try fresh or dried chives.

CUCUMBER-CHICKEN SALAD

Cooked cucumbers blend smoothly with chunks of chicken and fresh apple; a little curry powder provides the zip. Serve warm with fresh corn on the cob and sliced tomatoes or cold on lettuce as a luncheon entree.

Preparation time: 15 minutes
Microwave time: 12 minutes
Servings: 4–6

2 **skinned, boned chicken breast halves**
1 **tablespoon fresh lemon juice**
2 **medium-sized cucumbers**
1–2 **medium-sized red apples (red delicious or empire are good)**
½ **cup mayonnaise**
1 **teaspoon curry powder**
½ **teaspoon salt**
¼ **cup chopped walnuts**

1. Put chicken in 2-quart rectangular casserole. Sprinkle with lemon juice. Cover with waxed paper. MICROWAVE (high) 6–8 minutes, until inside no longer is pink and juices run clear, not pink, turning chicken over after 4 minutes. Let stand, covered, 2 minutes. Leaving broth in casserole, remove chicken, cut into bite-sized pieces, and reserve.
2. Peel cucumbers. Cut lengthwise in half, then lengthwise again into quarters. Seed. Cut into ¾-inch slices (about 2 cups). Core, seed, and cut apples into ¾-inch chunks (about 1 cup); leave skins on for good color.
3. Put cucumbers and apples in casserole with remaining cooking broth from chicken. Cover. MICROWAVE (high) 3–4 minutes, until just tender, stirring once. Let stand 1 minute. Drain. Return to casserole.
4. In a small bowl, blend mayonnaise, curry powder, and salt. Add curry mixture, chicken chunks, and nuts to cucumber mixture. Blend well. Serve.

SPICY CUCUMBER SOUP

Consider it a Bloody Mary with extra vegetables but no vodka, and this colorful soup could become a Sunday brunch favorite. The recipe makes 4 cups; because it is spicy, a ½-cup serving is fine. Serve it hot with rye crisps or cold with bubbly champagne.

Preparation time: 20 minutes
Microwave time: 9 minutes
Servings: 4–8

½ **cup chopped onion**
1 **teaspoon minced garlic**
1 **tablespoon olive oil**
1 **medium-sized green pepper, cored, seeded, and minced**
1 **medium cucumber, peeled, seeded, and minced**
2 **medium tomatoes, peeled, seeded, and chopped**
1½ **cups (2 6-ounce cans) spicy tomato juice**

1. Put onion, garlic, and olive oil in 2-quart casserole. MICROWAVE (high) 1 minute to soften.
2. Stir in green pepper, cucumber, tomatoes, and ¼ cup of spicy tomato juice. Cover. MICROWAVE (high) 5–6 minutes, until vegetables are just tender, stirring once. Stir in remaining tomato juice. MICROWAVE (high) 2 minutes to heat through.

TIP: *Note that only ¼ cup of the tomato juice is added to the vegetables as they cook. Adding more liquid would slow down the cooking process in the microwave.*

CRAB-STUFFED CUCUMBERS

Stuffing and cucumbers are cooked separately, then combined and reheated in this light entree. The portions are small, so serve as part of a buffet or combination platter.

Preparation time: 20 minutes
Microwave time: 11 minutes
Servings: 4

2 medium-sized cucumbers
2 tablespoons fresh lemon juice
2 tablespoons butter
2 green onions, white and first 2 inches of green, sliced
2 tablespoons flour
½ pound sliced fresh mushrooms
½ teaspoon salt
¼ teaspoon freshly ground pepper
1 tablespoon cognac or sherry
2 tablespoons minced fresh parsley
7 ounces frozen crabmeat (or shrimp and crabmeat), defrosted and well drained
2 tablespoons grated Swiss cheese

1. Peel cucumbers. Slice in half lengthwise. Scoop out seeds, leaving canoelike shell. Pat dry with paper towel. Sprinkle with lemon juice. Arrange in 2-quart rectangular casserole.
2. Cover with waxed paper. MICROWAVE (high) 3 minutes, until just starting to get tender but still holding shape well. Drain. Reserve.
3. Put butter and onions in 4-cup measure. MICROWAVE (high) 2 minutes. Stir in flour and mushrooms. Do not cover. MICROWAVE (high) 3 minutes. Stir in salt, pepper, cognac, parsley, and crabmeat.
4. Stuff crab mixture into cucumbers. Cover with waxed paper. MICROWAVE (high) 2 minutes to heat through. Sprinkle with cheese. MICROWAVE (high) 1 minute to melt.

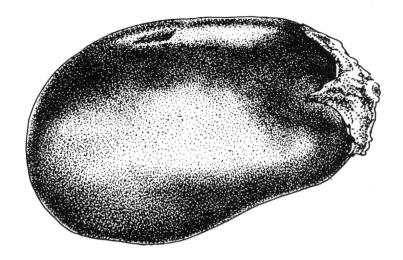

EGGPLANT

Call it *aubergine*, as they do in France, and add a romantic ring to this sultry-colored vegetable typically associated with Mediterranean cooking. Or call it *eggplant* and risk a troubled welcome.

There is precedent for hating eggplant. As members of the genus nightshade, both eggplant and tomatoes were considered inedible in the Middle Ages. Indeed, raw, bitter eggplant still deserves that description.

Cooked eggplant, however, is one of the most exciting vegetables for a creative cook. It's not bitter if cooked properly and readily absorbs herbs and spices. To avoid overcooked surfaces, however, avoid directly salting before cooking in the microwave.

Eggplant appears small and round (which no doubt inspired its English name), long and oval, or even furrowed and pear-shaped. Colors range from white to black. Most common, however, is the shiny purple-black, bulb-shaped eggplant.

Team eggplant with apples and malt vinegar as in the following recipes for an unusually good salad. Go traditional southern Italian with hearty Eggplant Parmesan. Watch it act like meat, especially when teamed with a bit of beef. Or let it go Cajun.

I tend to remove the peel when eggplant is in a sauce or mixed with other vegetables. If you don't mind the sometimes chewy texture, it may be left on. Avoid carbon steel knives when cutting eggplant, as they leave quite unromantic, greyish-black stains.

Select eggplant with glossy, taut skin and a green, not brown cap. It should be heavy for its size. Avoid dark or soft spots.

Store ideally in a dry, 50-degree location. Parts of the refrigerator are too cold, and in summer the kitchen counter is too warm. Frequently the best storage method is to put eggplant in the warmer, or front and bottom area, of the refrigerator for three to four days.

EGGPLANT AND APPLES WITH MALT VINEGAR

Serve this simple but unusual dish warm with pork or cold as the center of a fresh pear salad.

Preparation time: 10 minutes
Microwave time: 6 minutes
Servings: 4

1 medium eggplant, peeled and cubed (about 4 cups)
¼ cup water
¼ teaspoon salt
⅓ cup minced red onion
1 medium red delicious apple, cored and chopped, unpeeled
4 tablespoons malt vinegar
2 tablespoons chopped walnuts

1. Mix eggplant, water, and salt in 2-quart casserole. MICROWAVE (high) 2 minutes. Drain.
2. Mix in onion and apple. Cover. MICROWAVE (high) 3–4 minutes. Drain. Stir in malt vinegar and walnuts.

TIP: *Don't feel guilty about buying a bottle of malt vinegar just for this recipe. Sprinkle it on french fries; dab it on a fresh tomato. The applelike flavor perks up a basic vinaigrette, too.*

EGGPLANT AND BASIL BAKE

So easy and so good. The flavor combination is a natural.

Preparation time: 10 minutes
Microwave time: 13 minutes
Servings: 4

1 medium eggplant (1 pound), peeled and cubed
¼ cup water
¼ teaspoon salt
2 eggs, well beaten
¾ cup grated cheddar cheese
¼ cup roughly chopped fresh basil

1. Mix eggplant, water, and salt in 1½-quart casserole. Cover. MICROWAVE (high) 5 minutes, stirring once. Drain.
2. Blend eggs, cheese, and basil. Stir into eggplant. Cover. MICROWAVE (medium-high) 7–8 minutes, turning dish every 2 minutes. Let stand, covered, 5 minutes.

TIP: *Fresh basil really makes a difference. But if you just don't have any, replace with 1 teaspoon dried basil for flavor and 3 tablespoons roughly chopped fresh spinach for texture.*

EGGPLANT AND BEEF
WITH OYSTER SAUCE

This is a fine example of how beautifully beef can be handled in the microwave. Eggplant and beef strips are cut in the same shape to double the meaty image.

Preparation time: 10 minutes
Microwave time: 10 minutes
Servings: 4–6

½ **pound boneless sirloin steak**
4 **tablespoons oyster sauce**
1 **medium eggplant, peeled and cut into ½- by ½- by 3-inch strips**
¼ **cup water**
¼ **teaspoon salt**

1. Remove fat from steak. Cut across grain into ¼- by ¼- by 3-inch strips. (Partially frozen meat is easier to cut.) Mix steak and half (2 tablespoons) oyster sauce in 2-quart oblong dish. Let marinate while you prepare eggplant.

2. Stir eggplant, water, and salt in 1-quart casserole. Cover. MICROWAVE (high) 6–7 minutes, stirring once, until just tender. Drain. Add remaining 2 tablespoons oyster sauce. Cover. Let stand while beef cooks.

3. In original dish, MICROWAVE the beef (high) 2–3 minutes, stirring once, until beef just loses redness. Do not cover, or beef will cook more like a stew than a stir-fry. Spoon beef, then eggplant and any extra juices over plain rice.

TIP: To make rice, mix 1 cup rice and 2 cups water in 2-quart casserole. Cover. MICROWAVE (high) 5 minutes, then MICROWAVE (medium) 15 minutes.

TIP: To wean away from red meat, slip in more eggplant and less beef each time you make this dish.

"BLACKENED" EGGPLANT

This unusual, light takeoff of cast iron cooking made famous by New Orlean's chef Paul Prudhomme starts with a whole eggplant, partially peeled to make stripes. Roll it in spices and butter and bake in the microwave. The deep purple skin turns almost black, and the exposed portions get drenched in spices. You get the color and the taste—at a fraction of the butter.

Preparation time: 15 minutes
Microwave time: 6 minutes
Servings: 4–6

1 large eggplant
3 tablespoons butter
3 tablespoons prepared Cajun spice mix

1. Wash eggplant. Slice off top and bottom. Use potato peeler to remove ¾-inch strips of peel lengthwise, leaving a striped eggplant.
2. Put butter in pie pan. MICROWAVE (high) 40 seconds to melt. Mix in spices. MICROWAVE (high) 1 minute, until bubbly hot.
3. Turn eggplant in spice mixture to coat all sides. Place eggplant in pan. MICROWAVE (high) 4–5 minutes, turning every minute. Let stand 5 minutes.
4. Set eggplant on serving platter. Spread top with remaining butter-spice mixture. Present whole at table, then slice into circles. Scoop a little butter mixture onto flat side of each circle as you serve.

TIP: *To make your own Cajun spice, mix ¾ teaspoon sweet paprika, ½ teaspoon dried thyme, ¼ teaspoon dried oregano, ¼ teaspoon garlic powder, ¼ teaspoon onion powder, 1 teaspoon salt, ½ teaspoon freshly ground pepper, and ¼ teaspoon ground red peper (cayenne).*

SPINACH-STUFFED EGGPLANT

This beautiful green-flecked dish is elegant enough to serve as a dinner centerpiece.

Preparation time: 20 minutes
Microwave time: 22 minutes
Servings: 4–6

1 10-ounce package frozen chopped spinach
1 medium eggplant
¼ cup water
¼ teaspoon salt
¾ cup sliced mushrooms
3 tablespoons chopped onion
1 clove garlic, minced
2 tablespoons butter
1 teaspoon salt
⅛ teaspoon freshly ground pepper
2 tablespoons flour
½ cup cream

1. Put unwrapped spinach in 1-quart casserole. MICROWAVE (high) 4–5 minutes, until defrosted. Drain. Set aside.
2. Cut eggplant in half lengthwise. Scoop out pulp, leaving ¼-inch shell. Reserve shells.
3. Chop pulp coarsely. Mix pulp, water, and ¼ teaspoon salt in 4-quart casserole. Cover. MICROWAVE (high) 3–5 minutes, until pulp is just tender. Drain.
4. Add drained spinach, mushrooms, onion, garlic, butter, 1 teaspoon salt, and pepper to drained eggplant. Cover. MICROWAVE (high) 3–5 minutes. Stir. Add flour. Stir. Add cream.
5. Put shells on microwave-proof serving dish. Fill shells with mixture. Cover with waxed paper. MICROWAVE (high) 6–7 minutes, until shell exterior is just soft.

TIP: *To carve a neat shell, first use a knife to follow the oval shape ¼ inch within the split shell. Scoop out pulp with a spoon.*

TIP: *The eggplant shell serves as a natural insulator, keeping this dish warm while you finish dinner.*

TIP: *Frozen spinach in a box also can be defrosted right in its paper package. Pierce the box several times, place on a plate, and MICROWAVE (high) 5–6 minutes. Let stand.*

EGGPLANT UNDER BLUE CHEESE SAUCE

This lovely dish just melts under the fork. Serve it as an appetizer or as a side dish to simply prepared fish.

Preparation time: 30 minutes
Microwave time: 18 minutes
Servings: 4

3 tablespoons butter
3 tablespoons flour
¼ teaspoon salt
⅛ teaspoon freshly ground pepper
1 cup milk, room temperature
3 ounces blue cheese, crumbled
2 cups finely chopped mushrooms
¼ cup finely chopped onion
2 tablespoons butter
2 tablespoons water
½ teaspoon salt
1 medium eggplant (1 pound), peeled and cut into ¾-inch slices
2 tablespoons snipped parsley

1. Put 3 tablespoons butter in 4-cup measure. MICROWAVE (high) 40–50 seconds to melt. Stir in flour, ¼ teaspoon salt, and pepper. MICROWAVE (high) 30–45 seconds to cook flour. Slowly whisk in milk. MICROWAVE (high) 1–2 minutes, until just thickened, stirring twice. Stir in cheese. MICROWAVE (high) 2–3 minutes, until cheese is melted. (See Tip.)

2. Put mushrooms in 1-quart casserole. Cover. MICROWAVE (high) 3 minutes, stirring after 1 minute. Drain. Return to casserole. Add onion and 2 tablespoons butter. Cover. MICROWAVE (high) 2 minutes or until onions are tender.

3. Put water and ½ teaspoon salt in 9-inch pie plate. Overlap eggplant slices in a circle on the plate. Cover. MICROWAVE (high) 5–6 minutes, turning once, until eggplant is just tender. Drain.

4. Place eggplant slices on serving dish. Spread mushroom mixture evenly on the slices. Reheat sauce if necessary. Pour over eggplant. Sprinkle with parsley.

TIP: *The sauce (step 1) can be made ahead, covered, and refrigerated. To reheat, MICROWAVE (medium) until warmed through, adding a little milk if too thick.*

TIP: *Microwaving time varies in step 2 depending on how finely you chop the onions. Taste and feel as you cook.*

EGGPLANT PARMESAN

Generously topped with cheese, eggplant assumes a satisfying, meatlike role.

Preparation time: 45 minutes
Microwave time: 17 minutes
Servings: 6–8

1 teaspoon salt **2 small eggplants, peeled and cut into ⅜-inch slices** **2 eggs** **2 tablespoons water** **1 cup bread crumbs** **2 tablespoons chopped fresh oregano *or* 1 teaspoon dried** **1½ cups shredded mozzarella cheese** **½ cup grated Parmesan cheese** **1 15-ounce can tomato sauce**	1. Salt eggplant. Set in colander to drain 30 minutes; pat dry. 2. Beat eggs with water. Dip eggplant slices in egg mixture, then in bread crumbs. Place in 12″ × 8″ pan, overlapping edges. 3. MICROWAVE (high) 11–15 minutes, until skin is tender, rearranging slices and rotating dish after half the cooking time. 4. Sprinkle with oregano, three-fourths of the mozzarella, and half the Parmesan. Spoon sauce over. Top with remaining cheeses. Cover. 5. MICROWAVE (high) 1½–2 minutes or until cheeses melt.

TIP: Because the eggplants won't be drained after cooking, extra time is needed to salt and drain them before starting.

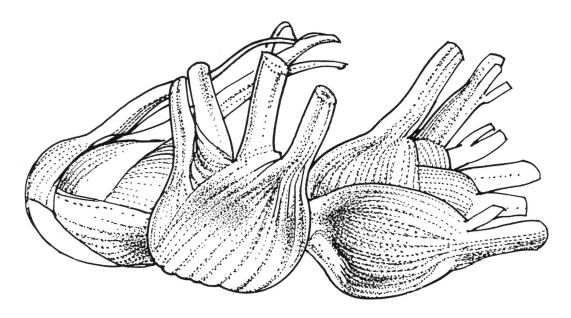

FENNEL

Fennel is a vegetable I discovered only a few years ago while searching a produce department for fresh dill. The leaves on a fennel plant resemble delicate, feathery dill, which I wanted to mix with fresh carrots.

I nibbled the fennel leaves, liked the licoricelike flavor, and brought it home to use bulb and all with carrots. What a fun way to rediscover a vegetable that is traced back to the gardens of Thomas Jefferson, who had the seeds imported from Italy, and before that to the Greeks, who used it as a full-flavored but low-calorie, weight-reducing aid.

As its fernlike foliage suggests, fennel, also called *Florentine fennel*, *sweet fennel*, or *finocchio*, is related to celery, carrots, and parsley. Its foliage is edible and makes a fine garnish, but the vegetable is prized mostly for its white bulb that grows above the ground. Fennel seeds, used particularly in sausages and soups, come from a related herb.

Look for fennel from early fall to early spring. Its unusual, sweet licorice or anise flavor mellows as it cooks and it makes a particularly distinctive accompaniment to fish and tomatoes. Save some choice slices to serve raw with Parmesan cheese or chevre and a sweet, red dessert wine.

Fennel leaves may be dried and stored in an airtight container to make tea. And while still fresh, a bed of aromatic fennel leaves is reputed to scare fleas off a suffering household pet—a side benefit I haven't yet confirmed.

Select crisp, compact bulbs with fresh, green foliage. Avoid yellowed or limp foliage. A bulb that spreads at the top is overmature.

Store loosely wrapped in the refrigerator for three or four days.

FENNEL WITH CARAWAY SEEDS

Try this simple fennel dish with pork chops, sausage, or duck. Note that caraway seeds are softened right in the casserole—no need to dirty another bowl.

Preparation time: 5 minutes
Microwave time: 10 minutes
Servings: 3–4

1 **fennel (1½ pounds with leaves)**
2 **tablespoons water**
1 **tablespoon butter**
1 **teaspoon caraway seeds**
¼ **teaspoon salt**
⅛ **teaspoon freshly ground white pepper**

1. Trim thin stalks, reserving some of the edible leaves for garnish. Cut bulb in half. Discard outer layer if woody. Leave core to hold layers intact. Cut bulb into thin slices.
2. Put fennel slices and water in 2-quart casserole. Cover. MICROWAVE (high) 7–9 minutes, until tender, stirring twice. Let stand, covered, 2 minutes. Drain. Return to casserole.
3. Push fennel to side. Put butter in cleared space. MICROWAVE (high) 1 minute to melt. Stir caraway seeds into butter to soften and develop flavor. Mix into fennel. Stir in salt and pepper.

TIP: Chopped chives may be substituted for caraway seeds.

FENNEL AND TOMATOES AU GRATIN

This is a very pretty side dish of tender fennel topped with tomato slices, golden buttered crumbs, and a sprinkling of green fennel leaves.

Preparation time: 15 minutes
Microwave time: 14 minutes
Servings: 6

2 fennel bulbs
3 tablespoons butter
1 teaspoon salt
¼ teaspoon freshly ground pepper
2 medium tomatoes, cut into ¼-inch slices
⅓ cup fine bread crumbs

1. Trim thin stalks, reserving some of the edible leaves for garnish. Cut bulbs in half. Discard outer layers if woody. Leave cores to hold layers intact. Cut bulbs into thin slices.
2. Put sliced fennel and 1 tablespoon of the butter in 2-quart rectangular casserole. Cover. MICROWAVE (high) 7–9 minutes, until tender, stirring twice. Sprinkle with half (½ teaspoon) salt and half (⅛ teaspoon) pepper. Top with overlapping tomato slices.
3. Put remaining butter (2 tablespoons) in 2-cup measure. MICROWAVE (high) 1 minute to melt. Stir in bread crumbs.
4. Sprinkle bread crumbs over tomatoes. Cover with waxed paper. MICROWAVE (high) 3–4 minutes to warm through. Sprinkle with remaining salt, pepper, and reserved fennel leaves.

FENNEL WITH ANCHOVY-GARLIC DRESSING

Cooked, chilled fennel topped with a zesty anchovy dressing makes an unusual salad.

Preparation time: 15 minutes
Microwave time: 9 minutes
Chilling time: 1 hour
Servings: 4–6

2 **fennel bulbs**
¼ **cup water**
3 **anchovy fillets, cut up**
1 **teaspoon minced garlic**
4 **tablespoons fresh lemon juice**
2 **tablespoons wine vinegar**
¼ **teaspoon salt**
⅛ **teaspoon freshly ground
   pepper**
4 **tablespoons vegetable oil**

1. Trim thin stalks. Cut bulbs in half. Discard outer layers if woody. Leave cores to hold layers intact. Cut bulbs into thin slices.
2. Put fennel slices and water in 2-quart casserole. Cover. MICROWAVE (high) 7–9 minutes, until tender, stirring twice. Let stand, covered, 2 minutes. Drain. Refrigerate for at least 1 hour.
3. In a large bowl, mash anchovies and garlic. Stir in lemon juice, vinegar, salt, and pepper. Beat in oil. Spread over fennel and serve.

RED SNAPPER WITH FENNEL AND TOMATOES

Fennel slices finish cooking atop the snapper fillets, allowing the vegetable flavor to permeate the fish.

Preparation time: 15 minutes
Microwave time: 22 minutes
Servings: 4

2 tablespoons butter
1 large or 2 small to medium fennel bulbs, trimmed and sliced thin; reserve leaves for garnish
2 tablespoons minced shallots
1 10½-ounce can plum tomatoes, drained and quartered
1 teaspoon salt
1 pound ½-inch-thick snapper fillets
1 tablespoon fresh lemon juice

1. Put butter in 2-quart casserole. MICROWAVE (high) 45 seconds to 1 minute to melt. Stir in fennel slices and shallots. Do not cover. MICROWAVE (high) 6–8 minutes, until almost tender, stirring once.
2. Add tomatoes. Do not cover. MICROWAVE (high) 2–4 minutes. Stir in salt.
3. Arrange fish fillets skin side down in 2-quart rectangular casserole with thickest portions to outside. Sprinkle with lemon juice. Cover with waxed paper. MICROWAVE (high) 2 minutes.
4. Turn fish over. Top with fennel mixture. Cover with waxed paper. MICROWAVE (medium-high) 6–7 minutes or until fish flakes when pressed with finger, rotating dish once. Serve topped with fennel leaves.

TIP: *Other lean fish such as cod, flounder, haddock, halibut, perch, sole, or turbot may be substituted for snapper. Defrost frozen fish overnight in refrigerator.*

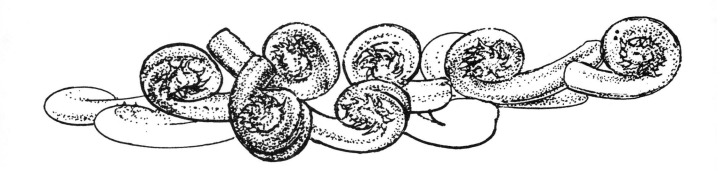

FIDDLEHEAD FERNS

You don't have to fly to exotic places to find a new culinary star. The backwoods of Maine, New Hampshire, and Vermont will do just fine.

Here, in the dampness of spring and intermittent sunshine, ostrich ferns break through the soil and prepare to unfurl their lacy green foliage. But if you snip the budding fern while it is still coiled tightly, you have a fiddlehead fern: a local treat turned celebrity.

Fiddleheads, so called because they resemble the scrolled head of a violin, cook up like asparagus and have a similar but nuttier flavor. They are seasonal and expensive. Look for the New England supply in specialty produce shops in May; some southern fiddleheads are available in April, and later Canadian crops in June and July.

Take care if you pick them yourself that you know your varieties of ferns; not all fern fronds are considered suitable to consume.

Select trim, tightly coiled, deep green fiddleheads about 1½ inches in diameter; paperlike husks may be still attached.

Store loosely wrapped in the refrigerator for two or three days.

FIDDLEHEAD AND CHEESE APPETIZERS

The nutty flavor of barely cooked fiddlehead ferns marries well with sharp cheddar cheese. Microwave fiddleheads briefly, then place each on a shredded cheese–covered cracker. The cheese gets just sticky enough to hold the fiddlehead steady. Don't be tempted to cover the fiddleheads with cheese; you want to show off their pretty, unusual shape.

Preparation time: 15 minutes
Microwave time: 5 minutes
Servings: 24 appetizers

1 pound fiddlehead ferns, stems trimmed to 1 inch, brown furry covering removed
2 tablespoons water
1 cup grated cheddar cheese
24 firm crackers

1. Wash fiddleheads. Put fiddleheads and water in 1-quart casserole. Cover. MICROWAVE (high) 3–4 minutes, until just tender, stirring once. Drain.
2. Divide cheese onto crackers. Top each with 1 or 2 fiddleheads. Arrange 8 at a time around edge of 9-inch plate. Do not cover. MICROWAVE (high) 15 seconds, just to soften cheese. Repeat with remaining fiddleheads.

MARINATED FIDDLEHEAD SALAD

Fiddlehead ferns are cooked briefly, then marinated in a mustard vinaigrette. Serve with sliced fresh tomatoes, mushrooms, and green onions.

Preparation time: 10 minutes
Microwave time: 4 minutes
Marinating time: 2 hours
Servings: 4

1 pound fiddlehead ferns, stems trimmed to 1 inch, brown furry covering removed
¼ cup water
1 shallot, minced
2 tablespoons red wine vinegar
¼ teaspoon salt
⅛ teaspoon freshly ground pepper
6 tablespoons olive oil
1 tablespoon Dijon mustard

1. Wash fiddleheads. Put fiddleheads and water in 1-quart casserole. Cover. MICROWAVE (high) 3–4 minutes, until just tender, stirring once. Drain.
2. In 4-cup measure, mix shallot, vinegar, salt, and pepper. Whisk in oil, then mustard. Mix in fiddleheads. Cover and let marinate in refrigerator for at least 2 hours. Drain. Use extra marinade to toss tomatoes or other salad ingredients.

FIDDLEHEAD EGGS

Fiddleheads' delicate flavor calls for quiet, soft accompaniment. Scrambled eggs, topped with fiddleheads, do the job admirably.

Preparation time: 10 minutes
Microwave time: 6 minutes
Servings: 2–4

½ **pound fiddlehead ferns, stems trimmed to 1 inch, brown furry covering removed**
2 **tablespoons water**
1 **green onion, white and first 2 inches of green, sliced**
1 **tablespoon butter**
4 **eggs**
2 **tablespoons milk**
1 **tablespoon chopped fresh tarragon** *or* **½ teaspoon dried**

1. Wash fiddleheads. Put fiddleheads and water in 1-quart casserole. Cover. MICROWAVE (high) 2–3 minutes, until just tender, stirring once. Drain. Reserve.
2. Put green onion and butter in 1-quart round casserole. MICROWAVE (high) 1 minute. Stir. Use fork to beat in eggs and milk. MICROWAVE (high) 1½ minutes. Move outer, cooked portion to inside. MICROWAVE (high) 1 minute, until almost set but still glistening. Stir in tarragon.
3. Place eggs on serving dish. Arrange cooked fiddleheads on top.

Spicy Cucumber Soup
Baby Vegetables: Sunburst Squash and Green and Yellow Zucchini with Lime Butter
Rosemary Green Beans
Princess Pattypans

Chicken Breasts Stuffed with Watercress
Snow Peas with Shrimp and Cashews

Spaghetti Squash with Basil
Marinated Mushrooms
Zucchini-Chicken Nachos
Toasted Pumpkin Seeds

Duxelles-Stuffed Cabbage
Whiskey Corn Pudding
Spinach Lasagna

GARLIC

Now here is a gal with a past. From earliest records in Asia Minor, through Egypt, India, and into Europe, garlic has been revered, feared, and methodically pressed into action.

Its potent cloves could—according to lore—dispel evil spirits and cure bloodshot eyes, athlete's foot, baldness, and the plague. Rub it on a poisonous bite. Stick it in a painful ear. Stuff a vampire's mouth for good. Or, if your love life needs a breath of fresh air, mix garlic with fresh coriander and wine for a surefire aphrodisiac. Or so they used to say.

Technically, garlic is a member of the lily family, sharing the same genus with onions, leeks, and shallots. For cooking, it typically serves as an herb, flavoring meats and vegetables. But to encourage its use beyond a flavoring, I've elevated garlic to a separate vegetable in this book.

Bake a whole head of garlic in the microwave to serve with roasts. Puree garlic with potatoes for a distinctive soup. Or let softened chunks of garlic serve as a meat substitute on top of spaghetti. The flavor may surprise you. Raw garlic is pungent, but it mellows to an almost nutty flavor when baked.

Do note the first tip in this chapter for an easy way to peel garlic. It may be the most useful tip in this book. A brief sojourn in the microwave loosens garlic's paperlike covering so that the cloves pop right out. Do heed the times I've worked out. Too short a stint doesn't loosen the covering; too long in the microwave, and the whole head of garlic will explode into a sticky mess (believe me).

When you are using the microwave to loosen garlic peels, the garlic warms and loses some of its pungency and its crisp texture. The technique isn't suitable for garlic that will be used raw, as in a Caesar salad dressing. But it is perfect when you need to peel two whole heads for garlic soup or cooked sauces.

One problem the microwave cannot solve is how to rid garlic's distinctive smell from hands and fingers. The most convenient solution for fingers is to rub on lemon juice and salt, then rinse with cold water. For your breath, the antidote is a sprig of fresh parsley.

Select plump, firm heads with white or purplish paperlike covering intact. Elephant garlic, a larger variety with cloves the size of a Brazil nut, is milder in flavor, easier to peel, and more expensive.

Store in a cool, dry, well-ventilated place. Do not refrigerate. Garlic keeps well up to a month. You can use one clove at a time.

ROASTED GARLIC

An elegant touch for roast chicken or game, these whole garlic cloves need less than a minute in the microwave. Use the scant teaspoon of butter or none at all.

Preparation time: 3 minutes
Microwave time: 2 minutes
Servings: 4

1 teaspoon butter
16 garlic cloves (about 1 head), peeled (see Tip), ends trimmed

Put butter in 1-quart casserole. MICROWAVE (high) 30 seconds to melt. Stir in garlic. Cover. MICROWAVE (high) 30 seconds to 1 minute, until tender. (If you did not use technique below for peeling, add 30 more seconds.) Serve.

TIP: Use this great technique to peel garlic, whether the garlic is intended for a microwave or conventional cooking recipe:

Put the whole head of garlic in the microwave. MICROWAVE (high) 45 seconds, turning the head upside down after half the time. Let stand 1 minute to cool. Squeeze the papery skin, and the garlic cloves will pop out.

For individual cloves, put on plate or paper towel. MICROWAVE (high) 30 seconds. Let stand and remove skins as above.

GARLIC SOUP

Garlic mellows as it cooks, as this unusual soup demonstrates. Still, there is enough pungent flavor that not even salt is needed here. Without the half-and-half, the soup has a rough, peasant dish charm that you may prefer.

Preparation time: 15 minutes
Microwave time: 21 minutes
Servings: 4

2 heads (30 cloves) garlic, peeled (see Tip in Roasted Garlic recipe) and crushed
¼ cup minced onion
2 tablespoons butter
2 cups grated potato (about 2 medium)
1 carrot, grated
2 cups chicken broth
½ cup half-and-half
⅛ teaspoon freshly ground pepper

1. Put garlic, onion, and butter in 2-quart casserole. MICROWAVE (high) 3–5 minutes, until tender. Add potatoes and carrots. Cover. MICROWAVE (high) 7–9 minutes, until potatoes and carrots are tender, stirring once. Add chicken broth. Puree in blender or processor.

2. Return soup to casserole. MICROWAVE (high) 6–7 minutes, until boiling. Stir in half-and-half and pepper.

GARLIC AND MUSHROOMS WITH PASTA

Chunks of whole garlic and quartered mushroom caps make an unusual and welcome topping for pasta.

Preparation time: 15 minutes
Microwave time: 7 minutes
Servings: 4

2 whole heads garlic (about 30 cloves), peeled (see Tip in Roasted Garlic recipe)
½ pound fresh mushrooms, stems chopped, caps quartered
4 tablespoons olive oil
¼ cup red wine
1 pound cooked vermicelli (see Tip)
2 tablespoons chopped fresh basil

1. Reserve half (about 15) of the whole garlic cloves. Chop the rest. Put chopped garlic, chopped mushroom stems, and olive oil in 2-quart casserole. MICROWAVE (high) 2 minutes, stirring once.
2. Stir in the whole garlic cloves, mushroom cap quarters, and wine. MICROWAVE (high) 4–5 minutes, until vegetables are tender, stirring once. Toss into pasta. Sprinkle with basil.

TIP: Because large amounts of water take long to boil in the microwave, it is faster to make pasta the conventional way, on the stove.

GREENS

As I stood at the demarcation line between our homes, I recall that as a youth I felt the same way. "Befriend the lovely dandelion," our young neighbor's very demeanor suggests, as she coaxes tender spring leaves. "Grow and multiply," her gentle hands coo.

"Kill them," I say. And I defend my line with spray and spade.

Squatting for dandelion greens lacks the ring of foraging for mushrooms. And the long-rooted puffs of a flower are no asset to a yard. It's best to get such greens at the store or from someone else's yard.

The most common varieties of leafy food known as greens are dandelion greens, mustard greens, turnip and beet tops, and collards, also known as kale. Spinach and chard, which have their own chapters in this book, also may be substituted in the recipes.

Beet tops have a slightly sweet taste, and mustard greens—my favorite—have a pleasant, peppery bite that makes you feel that you're eating something very healthful. Which you are, indeed.

Greens are high in calcium and iron, plus vitamins A and C and fiber. They should be washed just before using, and the water that clings will be enough to cook them in the microwave. The small amount of water and quick cooking help to preserve nutrients.

To wash fresh greens, swirl them in a sink of cold water, then lift out the greens, leaving soil behind. Drain the sink and repeat. Greens are inexpensive, so buy a lot. What looks like a huge bouquet of fresh leaves cooks down considerably.

Select greens that are crisp and small for the variety. Avoid limp or yellowed leaves.

Store unwashed, loosely wrapped in plastic, in the refrigerator for two or three days.

COOKED-UP GREENS

"Cooked-up greens." That is the standard way to describe this traditional southern dish. Cooking is faster in the microwave, but the ingredients are the same: pork fat or bacon, a bunch of greens, and hot sauce.

Preparation time: 10 minutes
Microwave time: 13 minutes
Servings: 4

¼ pound bacon (about 5 strips), cut into 1-inch pieces
2 bunches (1½ pounds) kale, mustard, or other greens, washed, stems removed, cut into 1-inch strips
12 shakes Tabasco sauce
⅛ teaspoon freshly ground pepper

1. Put bacon in 3-quart casserole. MICROWAVE (high) 2–3 minutes, until bacon starts to curl up but is not crisp. Drain. Return bacon to casserole.
2. Mix in greens. Cover. MICROWAVE (high) 8–10 minutes, stirring every 3 minutes. Drain. Mix in Tabasco sauce and pepper.

MUSTARD GREENS SOUP

I like the natural nippy taste from mustard greens in this soup. A milder version can be made by substituting spinach or chard.

Preparation time: 10 minutes
Microwave time: 18 minutes
Servings: 4

1 bunch (¾ pound) mustard greens, cleaned, stems removed, chopped into 1-inch strips
½ cup chopped onion
1 tablespoon butter
2 cups chicken broth
½ 15-ounce can white beans, drained and rinsed
¼ teaspoon salt
⅛ teaspoon freshly ground pepper

1. Put greens in 3-quart casserole. Cover. MICROWAVE (high) 6–8 minutes, stirring after 3 minutes. Drain in colander.
2. Put onion and butter in the 3-quart casserole. MICROWAVE (high), uncovered, 2–3 minutes, until onions are tender. Add chicken broth. Cover. MICROWAVE (high) 4 minutes, until boiling. Stir in greens, beans, salt, and pepper. MICROWAVE (high) 2–3 minutes to heat through. Serve.

SAUSAGE AND ROSEMARY GREENS

Served with corn bread and apple juice or beer, this dish makes a fine light supper.

Preparation time: 10 minutes
Microwave time: 18 minutes
Servings: 4

½ **pound bulk sausage, formed into 4 patties**
2 **bunches (1½ pounds) greens, washed, stems removed, cut into 1-inch strips**
1 **teaspoon dried rosemary, crushed**

1. Place sausage patties around edge of serving plate. Cover with waxed paper. MICROWAVE (high) 2–3 minutes, until outside is no longer pink, rotating dish once. Turn patties over. MICROWAVE (high) 2–3 minutes, until interior no longer is pink, rotating dish once. Drain. Set aside to keep warm.
2. Put greens in 3-quart casserole. Cover. MICROWAVE (high) 8–10 minutes, stirring every 3 minutes. Drain.
3. Mix in rosemary. Place sausage on top of greens on a serving plate. To reheat, cover with waxed paper and MICROWAVE (high) 1–2 minutes. Let stand 1 minute.

GREENS WITH VINEGAR AND MINT

The double tang from vinegar and fresh mint leaves pairs well with stronger greens like kale and mustard.

Preparation time: 10 minutes
Microwave time: 10 minutes
Servings: 4

2 **bunches (1½ pounds) greens, washed, stems removed, cut into 1-inch strips**
1–2 **tablespoons vinegar**
2 **tablespoons roughly chopped fresh mint leaves**

1. Put greens in 3-quart casserole. Cover. MICROWAVE (high) 8–10 minutes, stirring every 3 minutes. Drain.
2. Mix in vinegar and mint leaves. Serve.

GREENS AND CHEESE PIE

This hearty, main-course pie is a good way to slip in extra vegetables. Chop the greens fine for a prettier-looking pie slice.

Preparation time: 20 minutes
Microwave time: 18 minutes
Servings: 6

 1 bunch (¾ pound) greens,
   washed, stems removed, cut
   into 1-inch slices
 3 green onions, white and first
   2 inches of green, sliced
 ½ cup snipped parsley
 3 slices bacon, diced, cooked,
   and drained
1½ cups creamed cottage cheese
 ½ teaspoon fennel seed
 ¼ teaspoon salt
 ¼ teaspoon freshly ground
   pepper
 2 eggs, beaten
 1 prepared 9-inch pie crust (see
   Tip)
 ¼ cup grated Parmesan cheese

1. Put greens in 3-quart casserole. Cover. MICROWAVE (high) 6–8 minutes, stirring after 3 minutes. Drain. Chop greens.
2. In 3-quart casserole, stir chopped greens, onions, parsley, bacon, cottage cheese, fennel, salt, and pepper. Cover with waxed paper. MICROWAVE (high) 2–3 minutes to heat through. Stir in eggs. Pour mixture into pie crust.
3. Place pie atop inverted dinner plate. MICROWAVE (high), uncovered, 5–7 minutes, until all but very center is firm to the touch, rotating pie once. Sprinkle with cheese. Let stand 5 minutes so pie center finishes cooking and firms.

TIP: *Add ⅛ teaspoon either ground almonds or ground cinnamon to dry ingredients in favorite pastry recipe. This helps provide good color to microwave pastry and tastes good, too.*

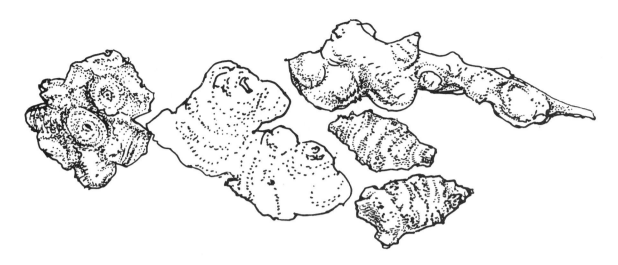

JERUSALEM ARTICHOKES

Jerusalem artichokes are neither from Jerusalem nor artichokes. The name is an interesting twist of linguistics for a tuber that indeed tastes similar to globe artichokes.

A species of sunflower that produces underground tubers, the vegetable is native to North America and was introduced to European settlers by Indians. In Italy, the vegetable became known as *girasole*, or turning toward the sun, which sunflowers do. As living languages are wont to do, *girasole* began sounding like *Jerusalem* in English.

The artichoke label is closer to the truth. Jerusalem artichokes not only taste like globe artichokes, but the cooked tuber has a firm and slightly threadlike texture, very similar to cooked artichoke bottoms. It is remarkable to consider that this delicacy—appreciated as such in Europe—has been relegated to stock feed in this country.

A one-pound bag of Jerusalem artichokes, or sunchokes as they have been currently renamed, includes 8 to 10 tubers and will serve four people.

The first recipe in this chapter gives you a taste of Jerusalem artichokes at their finest, just drizzled with lemon juice. The mild, sweet flavor blends well with mushrooms and eggs for a special breakfast dish. Or try them with peak-flavor tomatoes and good olive oil in Jerusalem Artichokes Provençale.

To keep a fine light color, drop Jerusalem artichokes in a solution of water with lemon juice as you peel them. And if the vegetable is new to you, test your tolerance with a small portion. It produces a particularly foul gas in some people; others in the same family, however, may be unaffected.

Select firm, tan roots that are as smooth as possible. The smoothness makes them easier to peel.

Store loosely wrapped in the refrigerator for two to three weeks.

JERUSALEM ARTICHOKES WITH LEMON JUICE

Crunchy chips of Jerusalem artichokes with just a drizzle of lemon juice make a wonderful snack, as well as side dish.

Preparation time: 15 minutes
Microwave time: 5 minutes
Servings: 4

1 pound Jerusalem artichokes, peeled and cut into ¼-inch slices
¼ cup water
4 tablespoons fresh lemon juice (about 1 lemon)
2 tablespoons minced fresh parsley

Put Jerusalem artichokes and water in 2-quart casserole. Cover. MICROWAVE (high) 4–5 minutes, until just tender. Let stand, covered, 2 minutes. Drain. Drizzle with lemon juice and sprinkle with parsley. Serve.

TIP: *If cutting Jerusalem artichokes ahead of time, dip in lemon juice to prevent discoloration.*

BAKED JERUSALEM ARTICHOKES

The small vegetables can be microwaved whole like new potatoes. Top with butter and minced parsley or serve with the following mustard dressing.

Preparation time: 20 minutes
Microwave time: 6 minutes
Servings: 4

1 **pound Jerusalem artichokes, peeled**
2 **tablespoons water**
½ **teaspoon minced garlic**
1 **green onion, white and first 2 inches of green, sliced**
2 **tablespoons minced fresh parsley**
¼ **cup sour cream**
½ **cup mayonnaise**
2 **heaping tablespoons Dijon mustard**

1. Put Jerusalem artichokes around edges of dish or pie plate. Use fork to pierce each one several times. Add water to bottom of plate. Cover. MICROWAVE (high) 4–6 minutes, until just tender, rotating dish halfway after 2 minutes. Drain.
2. To make dressing, mix remaining ingredients in bowl.

TIP: *The dressing tastes best if left at room temperature to blend for a half hour.*

EGGS WITH JERUSALEM ARTICHOKES AND MUSHROOMS

It takes only a handful of Jerusalem artichokes to add interest and great taste to scrambled eggs. Note that the Jerusalem artichokes and mushrooms are cooked until quite tender before adding the eggs so that the vegetables blend, rather than crunch.

Preparation time: 10 minutes
Microwave time: 9 minutes
Servings: 2–4

½ **cup peeled, ¼-inch-cubed Jerusalem artichokes**
½ **cup quartered, medium-sized mushroom caps**
2 **tablespoons butter**
4 **eggs**
1 **tablespoon minced fresh tarragon** *or* ¼ **teaspoon dried**
⅛ **teaspoon salt**

1. Put Jerusalem artichokes, mushrooms and half (1 tablespoon) of the butter in a 1-quart round casserole. MICROWAVE (high) 5–6 minutes, until quite tender, stirring twice. Add remaining butter. MICROWAVE (high) 1 minute. Stir.
2. Whisk in eggs and tarragon. MICROWAVE (high) 1½ minutes. Stir, gently chop up cooked eggs portion, and push uncooked portion toward outside. MICROWAVE (high) 30 seconds. Eggs should be almost set but still moist. Sprinkle on salt. Stir and serve.

TIP: Wash the casserole right away and the bits of egg will come off easily.

JERUSALEM ARTICHOKES PROVENÇALE

Jerusalem artichokes themselves taste wonderful, but add good-quality olive oil, a couple ripe tomatoes, and shiny black olives, and the dish becomes memorable.

Preparation time: 20 minutes
Microwave time: 11 minutes
Servings: 4

1 pound Jerusalem artichokes, peeled and cut into ¼-inch slices
¼ cup water
4 tablespoons olive oil
1 teaspoon minced garlic
2 medium tomatoes, seeded and chopped (skins may be left on)
1 tablespoon fresh lemon juice
¼ teaspoon salt
⅛ teaspoon freshly ground pepper
1 tablespoon chopped fresh basil *or* ½ teaspoon dried
1 cup sliced black olives (half of a 6-ounce jar)

1. Put Jerusalem artichokes and water in 2-quart casserole. Cover. MICROWAVE (high) 4–5 minutes, until just tender. Let stand, covered, 2 minutes. Drain.
2. Put olive oil and garlic in 4-cup measure. MICROWAVE (high) 1 minute to soften. Stir in tomatoes, lemon juice, salt, pepper, and basil. MICROWAVE (high) 3–5 minutes, until tomatoes soften and mixture starts to look like a thick sauce. Mix tomato mixture, Jerusalem artichokes, and olives in serving dish. Serve.

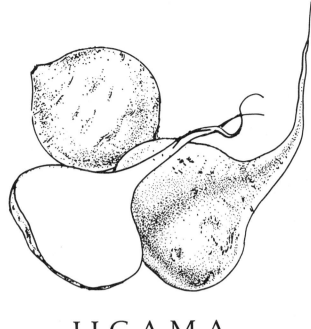

JICAMA

Stuffed in a produce department among snappy snow peas, elegant asparagus, or big, juicy tomatoes, jicama is just not a jewel that catches your eye. As large as a grapefruit, with tough, leathery brown skin, jicama looks like a giant turnip in a trench coat.

But what a surprise awaits. Inside its easily peeled skin is crisp, white meat with a light, slightly sweet flavor similar to that of water chestnuts. In Mexico and other parts of Central America and South America it often is eaten raw, with just a squirt of lime juice. When cooked, it keeps its crunchy texture and its sweetness increases.

Jicama is a legume that grows underground. In Chinese markets, it is known as *yam bean*. But it is marketed here under the Spanish name *jicama* (HEE-kah-mah).

Jicama serves as a starch in climates too warm to grow the Irish potato. But it shares many of the virtues of potatoes. It is low in calories, very low in sodium, but fairly high in vitamin C and potassium.

Peel and slice half a jicama to enjoy raw, perhaps as a chip substitute with Tomatillo Salsa (see index for recipe). The rest will keep for a couple of days in the refrigerator and not discolor.

Select firm, heavy jicama. Avoid any that are soft, spongy, or showing signs of mold.

Store in the refrigerator. Wash just before using.

JICAMA AND SHRIMP RUMAKI

This popular hors d'oeuvre usually is made with water chestnuts. However, jicama has a similarly crisp texture and mild flavor, is less expensive, and is easier to cut up. Shrimp is added at the end because shrimp takes less time to cook than bacon.

Preparation time: 30 minutes
Microwave time: 5 minutes
Servings: 60 appetizers

60 small to medium-sized shrimp, fresh or frozen and defrosted
½ cup teriyaki sauce
1 medium jicama
1 pound bacon slices, cut in thirds (60 strips)

1. Mix shrimp and teriyaki sauce in bowl. Let marinate for 10 minutes.
2. Peel jicama. Cut into ¼-inch slices, then into 1-inch squares.
3. Wrap a piece of bacon around a jicama square and secure with toothpick, piercing jicama and leaving a little room at end where the shrimp will go later. Repeat, using all of bacon. Put 12 wrapped tidbits on paper towel–lined plate. Cover with paper towels. MICROWAVE (high) 4 minutes until bacon is almost crisp.
4. Thread a shrimp on end of each toothpick. MICROWAVE (high) 1 minute, until shrimp is pink and bacon crisp. (This is enough time for small shrimp. If your shrimp are larger, microwave longer, checking every 15 seconds so that you don't overcook the shrimp.) Transfer immediately to serving plate. Serve.

HOT JICAMA SLAW

Red cabbage gives this warm salad a pretty light purple color. Green cabbage may be substituted.

Preparation time: 15 minutes
Microwave time: 6 minutes
Servings: 4

2 cups shredded red cabbage
¼ cup water
2 cups peeled, julienned jicama
½ cup sour cream
2 heaping tablespoons Dijon mustard

1. Put cabbage and water in 2-quart casserole. Cover. MICROWAVE (high) 3 minutes to slightly soften cabbage. Add jicama. Cover and MICROWAVE (high) 3 minutes until just tender. Drain.
2. In small bowl, combine sour cream and mustard. Mix dressing into jicama and cabbage. Serve.

JICAMA-CRANBERRY SAUCE

This version of homemade cranberry sauce has a little less sugar than most recipes, a jolt of lemon juice, and some crunch from jicama. Serve it warm or cold with a big holiday turkey or everyday pork chops.

Preparation time: 15 minutes
Microwave time: 8 minutes
Servings: 4 cups

2 cups (10 ounces) fresh or frozen cranberries
2 cups peeled, ½-inch cubed jicama
¾ cup sugar
2 tablespooons fresh lemon juice
1 tablespoon grated lemon zest

Mix all ingredients in 2-quart casserole. Cover with waxed paper. MICROWAVE (high) 6–8 minutes, until cranberries pop open and sauce thickens, stirring twice.

JICAMA AND SHRIMP SOUP

Although jicama usually is associated with Mexican-style cooking, the crisp vegetable fits right into this light, Oriental-style soup.

Preparation time: 20 minutes
Soaking time: 30 minutes
Microwave time: 12 minutes
Servings: 4

1 cup dried black mushrooms
1 small jicama, peeled and cut into 2-inch julienned strips (1-2 cups)
4 cups chicken broth
12 ounces fresh or defrosted frozen shrimp
1 green onion, white and first 2 inches of green, sliced

1. Cover dried mushrooms with boiling water and soak 20–30 minutes to reconstitute. Carefully lift out mushrooms without stirring water so that any sand or grit is left behind. Squeeze mushrooms dry. Cut off tough stems. Cut caps in half or in quarters, if large. Strain soaking broth and add up to 1 cup to soup in addition to chicken broth, if desired.
2. Put jicama, chicken broth, and mushroom broth, if desired in 2-quart casserole. Cover. MICROWAVE (high) 7–9 minutes until boiling.
3. Add mushrooms. Cover. MICROWAVE (high) 2 minutes or until broth boils again. Add shrimp. Cover. MICROWAVE (high) 1 minute. Serve, sprinkling each serving with green onions.

TIP: *A can of drained mushrooms may be substituted for the dried black mushrooms; diced, cooked chicken may replace the shrimp.*

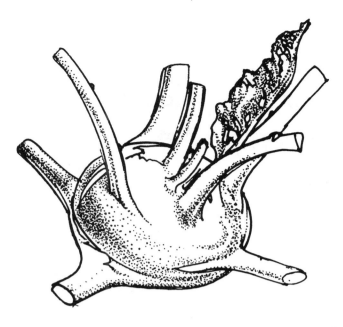

KOHLRABI

Although kohlrabi is well known in Mediterranean countries, it gets little notice here. But those who enjoy turnips also will like the pleasantly sharp, turniplike flavor of kohlrabi.

The name is a combination of two German words: *kohl* (cabbage) and *rabi* (turnip), chosen because of its cabbagelike leaves and turniplike taste. The edible portion is a round bulb that grows above ground. It may be substituted for turnips in recipes. And, like turnips, its perky flavor softens and sweetens when cooked.

To clean kohlrabi, cut off the greens and save for other recipes for greens or spinach. Trim the thin spikes, which may be eaten raw or cooked. Unless the kohlrabi is very tender, the round bulb needs to be peeled lightly. Kohlrabi then is ready to be sliced or chopped according to the recipe.

Four kohlrabi, two to three inches in diameter, will make about 2 cups slices.

Select kohlrabi with small to medium, light green or purple, firm bulbs and fresh, crisp-looking leaves. Avoid large, woody, cracked bulbs or yellowed leaves.

Store loosely wrapped in a plastic bag in refrigerator for a week. Remove the leaves and store separately in a covered container in the refrigerator.

KOHLRABI WITH CREAM AND THYME

Fresh kohlrabi needs little more than a bit of cream and some fresh thyme.

Preparation time: 10 minutes
Microwave time: 12 minutes
Servings: 4

4 medium (2- to 3-inch-diameter) kohlrabi, peeled and julienned
½ cup half-and-half
1 tablespoon fresh thyme *or* 1 teaspoon dried
¼ teaspoon salt
⅛ teaspoon freshly ground white pepper

1. Put kohlrabi and half-and-half in 2-quart casserole. Cover. MICROWAVE (high) 3–5 minutes, stirring once.
2. Uncover to let cream thicken. MICROWAVE (high) 5–7 minutes, until just tender. Stir in thyme, salt, and pepper.

TIP: Even though kohlrabi would just fit in a 1-quart casserole, use the larger 2-quart casserole so that the moisture will evaporate quicker.

KOHLRABI WITH CURRY SAUCE

Kohlrabi's sharp bite teams well with curry.

Preparation time: 10 minutes
Microwave time: 13 minutes
Servings: 4

4 medium (2- to 3-inch-diameter) kohlrabi, peeled and julienned
½ cup water
2 tablespoons butter
2 tablespoons flour
1 teaspoon curry powder
¼ teaspoon salt
⅛ teaspoon freshly ground white pepper
1 cup milk

1. Put kohlrabi and water in 2-quart casserole. Cover. MICROWAVE (high) 6–8 minutes, until just tender, stirring twice. Drain.
2. Put butter in 4-cup measure. MICROWAVE (high) 1 minute to melt. Blend in flour, curry powder, salt, and pepper. Whisk in milk. MICROWAVE (high) 3–4 minutes to thicken. Pour sauce over kohlrabi.

KOHLRABI SOUP

Kohlrabi joins carrots, potatoes, and tomatoes in this vegetable-rich soup.

Preparation time: 30 minutes
Microwave time: 20 minutes
Servings: 4–6

½ cup minced onion
1 tablespoon butter
1 cup chopped carrots
1 cup peeled, cubed potatoes
4 medium 2- to 3-inch-diameter) kohlrabi, peeled and cubed
1 14½-ounce can tomatoes, with juice
1 bay leaf
1 cup beef broth
1 cup diced ham
¼ teasoon salt
⅛ teaspoon freshly ground pepper
2–3 teaspoons Worcestershire sauce

1. Put onion and butter in 2-quart casserole. MICROWAVE (high) 2 minutes, stirring after 1 minute. Stir in carrots, potatoes, and kohlrabi. Cover. MICROWAVE (high) 6 minutes, until tender, stirring once.

2. Add tomatoes and break each in half with spoon. Stir in bay leaf, beef broth, ham, salt, and pepper. MICROWAVE (medium) 10–12 minutes to develop flavor. Remove bay leaf. Add Worcestershire sauce to taste.

KOHLRABI WITH PORK

A little pork enhances a side dish of cubed kohlrabi. Sausage may be substituted for the ground pork; if the sausage is highly spiced, omit fennel and taste before adding salt and pepper.

Preparation time: 20 minutes
Microwave time: 16 minutes
Servings: 4–6

⅓ **pound ground pork**
½ **cup minced onion**
1 **teaspoon minced garlic**
¼ **teaspoon fennel seeds**
4 **medium (2- to 3-inch-diameter) kohlrabi, peeled and diced**
¼ **cup cream**
½ **teaspoon salt**
¼ **teaspoon freshly ground pepper**

1. Put pork in 2-quart casserole. MICROWAVE (high) 2–3 minutes, until no longer pink, breaking up and stirring twice. Drain all but 2 tablespoons fat.
2. Stir in onion, garlic, and fennel seeds. MICROWAVE (high) 3–5 minutes, until onions soften, stirring once.
3. Stir in kohlrabi. Do not cover because you want moisture from onions to evaporate. MICROWAVE (high) 6–8 minutes, until tender, stirring twice. Stir in cream, salt, and pepper.

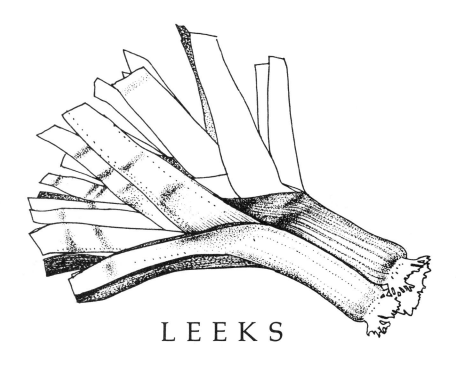

LEEKS

The young grocery clerk turns and pauses. She needs to type a code into the computer to identify and weigh the overflowing pile of long, deep green and creamy white vegetables.

Long before computers, the Welsh chose this vegetable to stand as their national emblem. Centuries before that, Egyptians and Romans sold bundles of the long, firm vegetable in open markets.

Currently, backyard gardeners in Europe pride themselves on just how tall they can urge the plant to grow. And in this country, in spring and again in September through November, young grocery clerks are introduced to this new, "old" vegetable.

"Leeks?" she wagers. Yes, leeks they are—and a vegetable worth meeting.

A mild member of the onion family, leeks add flavoring to stuffings or soups or simply stand alone. Indeed, when the supply of spring asparagus wanes, slender leek stalks topped with buttered crumbs traditionally provide a humble substitute in many European countries. They are not usually eaten raw.

To prepare leeks, chop off root end and dark green leaves. Only the white portion is used for cooking, although the tough green tops may be used to flavor soups.

Unless leeks are being used whole (not recommended in the microwave because the stalks cook unevenly), split leeks in half lengthwise. Run under faucet to clean, carefully separating stalk sections to reveal and remove dirt.

A few precautions are necessary to cook leeks well in the microwave. Remove

144

and discard the outermost layer because this slightly tough layer will become tough in the microwave.

If appropriate for the recipe, separate the outer, white portion and inner, light green portion. Arrange the white portion on the outside of the casserole so that it cooks more in the microwave. Put the more tender green portions in the inside so that they won't overcook.

Ideally, use chopped leeks in the microwave; this reduces problems of uneven cooking. Do not overcook leeks, or they will be mushy.

Select firm but pliable, straight stalks, reasonably free from dirt for easier cleaning. Avoid dried-out, yellowed, or wilted leaves.

Store loosely wrapped in plastic in the refrigerator for about a week. Wash just before using.

LEEKS WITH GRATED CHEESE

Apple juice gives extra flavor to leeks, which are topped with Swiss cheese.

Preparation time: 10 minutes
Microwave time: 7 minutes
Servings: 4

4 medium-sized leeks
¼ cup apple juice
¼ cup grated Swiss cheese

1. Cut off root ends of leeks. Trim all but 2 inches of green. Slice in half lengthwise; if large, cut again into 4 lengths. Wash well under running water, separating stalk sections to remove dirt.
2. Separate thicker, white outer stalk sections and more tender, green inner sections into two groups. Julienne both groups.
3. Arrange white, outer sections to outside and green, inner sections to inside of 2-quart rectangular casserole. Add apple juice. Cover with plastic wrap, turned back at corner to form vent. MICROWAVE (high) 3–5 minutes, until tender, gently stirring white and green portions separately once. Drain.
3. Sprinkle with cheese. Do not cover. MICROWAVE (high) 2 minutes to melt cheese. Serve.

LEEKS VINAIGRETTE

Prepare leeks as in Leeks with Grated Cheese, but use ¼ cup water instead of apple juice, and omit cheese. Toss with ¼ cup vinaigrette (see Index), cover, and refrigerate. Drain and serve in salad with hard-boiled eggs.

LEEKS WITH DUXELLES AND BLUE CHEESE

Prepare leeks as in Leeks with Grated Cheese, but use ¼ cup water instead of apple juice, and omit Swiss cheese. Spoon on ¼ cup Duxelles (see "Mushrooms" chapter), then sprinkle with 2 tablespoons crumbled blue cheese. MICROWAVE (high) 45 seconds to melt cheese slightly.

BAKED APPLES WITH LEEKS AND SAUSAGE

Baked apples work beautifully in the microwave, and they are more than dessert fare, as this recipe demonstrates. Microwave these leek- and sausage-stuffed apples first and let them cool a little while you prepare waffles for brunch. Or present them on a platter around a golden roast chicken or goose.

Preparation time: 20 minutes
Microwave time: 12 minutes
Servings: 4

4 tart apples (Granny Smith are good)
¼ pound bulk sausage
1½ cups chopped leeks (1 medium leek)
½ teaspoon dried sage
¼ teaspoon salt
¼ teaspoon freshly ground pepper
½ cup fresh bread cubes (1 slice bread)
2 tablespoons butter
4 tablespoons red wine or apple juice

1. Core and hollow out apples, leaving ½-inch shell but being sure not to cut through bottoms. Peel a thin strip around the center of each to keep the skins from splitting. Set apples aside.
2. Put sausage and leeks in 2-quart casserole. MICROWAVE (high) 4–5 minutes, until sausage no longer is pink, stirring and breaking up with fork twice. Break up sausage well with fork. Stir in sage, salt, pepper, and bread cubes.
3. Stuff apples with leek mixture. Put on round dish. Top each apple with ½ tablespoon butter and 1 tablespoon wine or apple juice.
4. Cover. MICROWAVE (high) 6–7 minutes, until tender but still holding shape, rotating dish once.

GILA'S EXTRA-CREAMY VICHYSSOISE (LEEK AND POTATO SOUP)

If you can wait until this soup has chilled for several hours in the refrigerator, you'll have a lovely vichyssoise, an elegant first course to serve in chilled cups. Piping hot from the microwave, it is a more humble-sounding but equally delicious leek and potato soup, terrific with crusty French bread and white wine.

Preparation time: 20 minutes
Microwave time: 24 minutes
Chilling time: 3 hours
Servings: 4–6

3 tablespoons butter
3 large or 4 medium-sized leeks, white portions only, cleaned and chopped (about 4 cups)
3 medium potatoes, peeled and sliced thin (about 3 cups)
3 cups chicken stock or broth
8 ounces cream cheese, softened
1 cup half-and-half
1 teaspoon salt
⅛ teaspoon freshly ground white pepper
⅓ cup finely chopped chives *or* 1 tablespoon dried

1. Put butter and leeks in 3-quart casserole. Cover. MICROWAVE (high) 7–9 minutes, stirring every 2 minutes. Stir in potatoes and ½ cup chicken broth. Cover. MICROWAVE (high) 9–11 minutes, until vegetables are very tender, stirring twice.

2. Add remaining chicken broth. Cover. MICROWAVE (high) 4–5 minutes until boiling. Let stand, covered, 3 minutes.

3. Process cream cheese in food processor (with steel blade) or blender until fluffy. Gradually add half-and-half (pulsing, with processor) until well mixed. Remove to a bowl and reserve.

4. Puree leek mixture in processor or blender. Return to casserole. Whisk in cream cheese mixture, salt, and pepper. Chill, covered, in refrigerator at least 2 hours. Serve in chilled bowls, sprinkled with chives.

TIP: Taste the soup before serving cold. Salt loses its impact in cold foods, and you may want to add more.

TIP: To serve hot, whisk in cream cheese mixture, salt, and pepper as directed. Cover. MICROWAVE (high) 5–7 minutes, until hot but not boiling. Sprinkle with chives and serve.

TIP: To soften cream cheese, remove foil wrap, place on a plate, and MICROWAVE (medium) 1 minute.

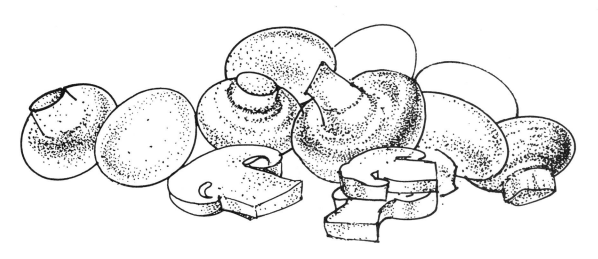

M U S H R O O M S

"Bring the marinated mushrooms," she says. "Period." There is no room for negotiation. No "thank you" for the new vegetables offered for Thanksgiving dinner: broccoli in oyster sauce, broccoli with hot peppers and garlic, peas with figs and apple butter, peas with prosciutto and cream.

"Sure, bring those, too," she softens. "And the mushrooms."

Ordinarily, it is not that simple. By conventional methods, mushrooms must be marinated in a large stockpot, which is then out of commission for three days. And during those days, mushroom samples disappear by the handful. But insistent hostesses—and a microwave—are great inspiration.

The three-day process for my favorite marinated mushrooms recipe is reduced to 30 minutes in the microwave and 1 hour on the counter. And none of my mushroom fans were the wiser.

The elegant mushroom technically is a fungus, enjoyed as a luxury food since the days of the Roman Empire. In the 19th century, mushrooms were developed on a commercial basis, and white button mushrooms now are available all year.

In larger markets, you'll also find slender, pin-shaped enoki mushrooms, broad-capped oyster mushrooms, trumpet-shaped chanterelles, meaty shiitake, seasonal fresh morels, and dried porcini (cèpes) and Chinese black mushrooms.

Mushrooms give off a lot of moisture when cooked and turn darker in color. This is an asset in soups and sauces. For other dishes, where you want to keep juices to a minimum and to keep a lighter color, do not cover when cooking in the microwave.

Select firm white button mushrooms. Fresh, medium-sized mushroons will have a little netting connecting the cap to stem. Avoid mushrooms that have opened wide to expose brown gills; they are past their prime. Avoid brown spotted or soggy mushrooms.

Store unwashed, loosely wrapped in refrigerator for up to five days. Do not leave tightly wrapped in plastic wrap or the mushrooms will start to decay. Wipe clean with a damp paper towel or rinse very quickly under the faucet. Do not soak.

MUSHROOMS WITH TARRAGON

This simple mushroom recipe can be varied by adding different herbs such as basil, marjoram, or oregano or by thickening into a sauce.

Preparation time: 10 minutes
Microwave time: 7 minutes
Servings: 4–6

2 tablespoons butter
1 tablespoon fresh tarragon *or* ½ teaspoon dried
1 pound fresh mushrooms, wiped clean and quartered

Put butter in 2-quart casserole. MICROWAVE (high) 1 minute to melt. Stir in tarragon, then mushrooms. Do not cover. MICROWAVE (high) 4–6 minutes, until mushrooms are tender and let out juices, stirring twice. Drain if desired.

TIP: To thicken juices, blend in 2 tablespoons flour after mushrooms have cooked for 4 minutes. Microwave 1–2 minutes, until sauce thickens, stirring once.

TIP: Mushrooms have a lot of moisture that they will let out as they cook. For this reason, you generally do not add extra liquid when microwaving mushrooms and do not cover. Butter, olive oil, or wine may be used for flavoring, however.

TIP: If the mushroom juices (about ⅓ cup per pound of mushrooms) aren't needed in the recipe, save for soups or gravies.

TIP: Use this basic recipe to note how a pound of quartered mushrooms cook in the microwave. After 3 minutes, the mushrooms are al dente, with a still-firm bite. At 4 minutes, they start to let out juices but still are fairly firm. By 5 to 6 minutes, the mushrooms are getting soft and have developed a richer flavor and more juices. Cook them to 9 minutes, and they are quite soft. After 9 minutes, the texture and flavor won't change much.

You can't really overcook mushrooms, and they reheat well.

DUXELLES

Duxelles may sound fancy on a menu, but it is simply chopped mushrooms, cooked with onions or shallots. It is a handy way to use leftover mushroom stems, tastes great atop other vegetables such as eggplant or leeks, and stores well in a covered jar in the refrigerator.

Preparation time: 10 minutes
Microwave time: 8 minutes
Servings: 1½ cups

½ **pound mushrooms, chopped fine (about 2 cups)**
2 **teaspoons minced shallots**
2 **tablespoons butter**
¼ **teaspoon salt**
⅛ **teaspoon freshly ground pepper**

1. Put mushrooms in 1-quart casserole, MICROWAVE (high) 3 minutes, stirring after 1 minute. Drain about half the liquid.
2. Add shallots and butter. MICROWAVE (high) 4–5 minutes, until almost all the moisture has evaporated. Season with salt and pepper to taste.

TIP: When adding butter to an already filled casserole, push the other food to the side so that the microwaves have a clear shot at the butter. Stir once it melts.

MUSHROOM SAUCE

A handy trick to have up your sleeve, homemade mushroom sauce enlivens plain hamburgers, a grilled steak, or just a bowl of rice.

Preparation time: 5 minutes
Microwave time: 8 minutes
Servings: 1½ cups

2 **tablespoons butter**
¼ **pound fresh mushrooms, wiped clean and sliced**
3 **tablespoons flour**
1 **cup beef broth or stock**
⅛ **teaspoon freshly ground pepper**
Salt (optional)
1 **tablespoon sherry (optional)**

1. Put butter and mushrooms in 1-quart casserole. Do not cover. MICROWAVE (high) 3 minutes, until mushrooms let out juices, stirring after 1½ minutes. Blend in flour. Add broth and stir well.
2. Do not cover. MICROWAVE (high) 4–5 minutes, until sauce thickens, stirring twice. Taste. Add pepper and salt and sherry if desired.

TIP: Taste before adding salt, particularly if using canned broth, which may contain a lot of salt.

BLUE CHEESE–STUFFED MUSHROOMS

Stuffed mushroom appetizers are easier in the microwave than in a conventional oven because you can make or reheat them right on serving plates. They can be stuffed ahead of time and finished in the microwave just before serving.

Preparation time: 20 minutes
Microwave time: 7 minutes
Servings: 24

24 medium-sized or large mushrooms
1 tablespoon butter
1 tablespoon minced garlic (about 3 small cloves)
⅓ cup crumbled blue cheese
⅓ cup fine bread crumbs
2 green onions, white and first 2 inches of green, chopped fine
½ teaspoon salt
¼ teaspoon freshly ground pepper
2–3 tablespoons chopped fresh parsley

1. Wipe mushrooms clean. Snap out stems. Reserve caps. Chop stems.
2. Put chopped stems, butter, and garlic in 2-quart casserole. MICROWAVE (high) 2 minutes, until tender, stirring once to distribute butter. Mix in blue cheese. Mix in bread crumbs, green onions, salt, and pepper.
3. Stuff caps lightly with stem mixture. Arrange caps on plate or 2-quart rectangular casserole, making sure mushrooms don't touch. (You will need to do this in two or three batches.) Do not cover. MICROWAVE (high) 4–5 minutes until heated through. Sprinkle with parsley and serve.

TIP: *If the stems are long, you will have a little stuffing left over. Save and reheat to top other vegetables such as baked tomatoes or fresh green beans.*

TIP: *Stuffed mushrooms freeze and reheat well. Freeze on a sturdy paper plate, covered with plastic wrap. MICROWAVE (medium) until heated through.*

MUSHROOM SOUP

In these days of canned convenience foods, this rich, beef stock–based, homemade mushroom soup may be an unusual treat.

Preparation time: 20 minutes
Microwave time: 19 minutes
Servings: 4

½ **cup minced onions**
2 **tablespoons butter**
1 **pound fresh mushrooms,**
   wiped clean and sliced
2 **tablespoons flour**
2 **cups beef stock or broth**
1 **cup cooked rice or barley**
¼ **cup cream**
1 **tablespoon chopped fresh basil**
   or ½ **teaspoon dried**
¼ **teaspoon salt**
⅛ **teaspoon freshly ground**
   pepper

1. Put onions and butter in 3-quart casserole. MICROWAVE (high) 2–3 minutes, until tender, stirring once. Stir in mushrooms. MICROWAVE (high) 8–10 minutes, until mushrooms are tender and have released juices, stirring twice. Blend in flour.
2. Stir in beef stock and rice or barley. Cover to help reheat quickly. MICROWAVE (high) 5–6 minutes, to low boil. Stir in cream, basil, salt, and pepper.

MARINATED MUSHROOMS

When I waitressed for a summer at Anthony's Pier 4 in Boston, I became addicted to the restaurant's brine-soaked mushrooms. A friend in Boston, Deane McCraith, helped create a very similar recipe, which has become one of my standard party buffet dishes. The original recipe calls for marinating the mushrooms for three days. However, a stint in the microwave reduces that time to about 30 minutes. Also, the original recipe calls for 4 tablespoons of Accent (monosodium glutamate), which does make it taste better, but I have eliminated it for health reasons.

Preparation time: 30 minutes
Microwave time: 32 minutes
Marinating time: 1 hour
Servings: 2 quarts

4 pounds medium-sized fresh mushrooms, wiped clean
1 cup vegetable oil
2 cups wine vinegar
1 tablespoon chopped red onion
4 tablespoons sugar
4 tablespoons salt
½ teaspoon pressed garlic .
½ teaspoon freshly ground white pepper
½ teaspoon freshly ground black pepper
⅛ teaspoon red pepper flakes
⅛ teaspoon dried oregano

1. Mix half the mushrooms (2 pounds) and all the rest of the ingredients in a 3-quart casserole. MICROWAVE (high) 12–16 minutes, until liquid simmers, stirring twice. Let cool and marinate on counter 30 minutes.

2. Use slotted spoon to remove marinated mushrooms, leaving liquid in casserole. Add second half of mushrooms. Repeat microwave cooking and cooling. Store drained mushrooms covered in refrigerator for several weeks.

MUSHROOM-STUFFED GYROS

You hardly miss the meat in this vegetable-stuffed pocket sandwich.

Preparation time: 30 minutes
Microwave time: 7 minutes
Servings: 4

1 teaspoon minced garlic
¼ cup chopped onion
2 tablespoons butter
1 pound mushrooms, wiped
  clean and quartered
2 tablespoons flour
1 teaspoon dried oregano
¼ teaspoon salt
⅛ teaspoon freshly ground
  pepper
½ cup plain yogurt
⅓ cup chopped cucumber
1 tablespoon fresh thyme *or*
  ½ teaspoon dried
4 6-inch pocket bread rounds
1 medium tomato, chopped
1 small onion, sliced thin

1. Put garlic, onion, and butter in 2-quart casserole. MICROWAVE (high) 2 minutes. Stir in mushrooms. Do not cover. MICROWAVE (high) 3 minutes, until mushrooms are tender but not yet releasing juices.
2. Blend in flour. Stir in oregano, salt, and pepper. MICROWAVE (high) 2 minutes to cook flour and blend flavors.
3. Combine yogurt, cucumber, and thyme in 2-cup measure or bowl.
4. Cut bread in half vertically. Open to form a pocket. Spoon mushrooms into each pocket. Top with yogurt mixture, then tomatoes and onions.

TIP: To warm bread, place in overlapping circle on plate. Cover. MICROWAVE (high) 1 minute.

MUSHROOM-BEEF STEW

This stick-to-the-ribs, hearty dish tastes wonderful on a chilly winter day.

Preparation time: 40 minutes
Microwave time: 1 hour, 13 minutes
Servings: 4

1 cup chopped onions
1 teaspoon dried thyme
1 tablespoon vegetable oil
1½ pounds boneless beef chuck, cut into ½-inch cubes
2 tablespoons flour
1 pound medium-sized mushrooms, caps halved, stems chopped
1 cup grated carrots
½ cup uncooked rice
½ teaspoon salt
¼ teaspoon freshly ground pepper
4 cups beef broth or stock

1. Mix onions, thyme, and oil in 3-quart casserole. MICROWAVE (high) 3–5 minutes, until tender, stirring once.
2. Coat beef with flour. Mix into onions. Cover. MICROWAVE (high) 6–8 minutes, until meat turns from red to barely pink inside, stirring once.
3. Stir in mushrooms, carrots, rice, salt, pepper, and half (2 cups) of the beef broth. Cover. MICROWAVE (high) 8–10 minutes, until boiling. Stir. Cover. MICROWAVE (medium) 45–50 minutes, until beef is tender, stirring twice. Stir in last 2 cups of broth. Reheat if necessary. Serve.

TIP: *Large amounts of liquid actually slow down the cooking process in the microwave, so the final 2 cups of broth are added at the end.*

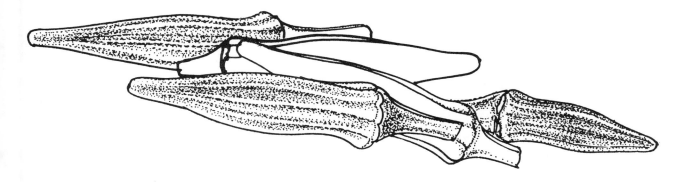

OKRA

S-L-I-M-E. That is thy middle name, fond okra. Without it, what would cement chicken to rice in a bowl of gumbo? With it, who can sell a plate of boiled okra north of the Mason-Dixon line?

Actually, the microwave can. Perhaps it is the small amount of water needed to cook up a batch, but whole okra cooked in a microwave is delightfully crisp, without the stickiness that many people dislike. Its flavor certainly is inoffensive, mild and "green"-tasting, as easy to enjoy as fresh green beans or Chinese pea pods.

Savored particularly in the warm climates of Africa, India, Greece, and our own Deep South, an okra pod resembles a legume. It belongs, however, to the Hibiscus genus and is closely related to cotton.

Many recipes for okra take advantage of the sap okra exudes when sliced. You'll see and appreciate this in the following chicken gumbo recipe. Also, okra's mild flavor plays base to a spicy salsa, or it teams quietly with a pile of black-eyed peas. But most attractive to those of refined taste or stubborn fear is my microwave skid-free okra salad. No slime.

Select small pods, 1½ to 2 inches long. The freshest and most tender have a velvetlike exterior.

Store for up to two days in the refrigerator, unwashed, dry, and loosely wrapped. Wash just before cooking. Handle carefully, for okra bruises easily, blackening within a few hours.

SKID-FREE OKRA SALAD

This slightly tart vinaigrette works well with okra. There is no stickiness if you use small, fresh, whole okra and are careful not to overcook them.

Preparation time: 10 minutes
Microwave time: 6 minutes
Chilling time: 1 hour
Servings: 4

1 pound whole fresh okra, stem ends snapped off but not cut
¼ **cup water**
¼ **teaspoon salt**
3 **tablespoons oil**
3 **tablespoons vinegar**
¼ **teaspoon salt**
⅛ **teaspoon freshly ground pepper**
2 **green onions, white part and first 2 inches of green, sliced**

1. Put okra, water, and salt in 1½ quart casserole. Cover. MICROWAVE (high) 5–6 minutes, until tender, stirring once. Let stand 1 minute. Drain.
2. In a 1-cup measure or bowl, whisk oil, vinegar, salt, and pepper. Gently toss with okra. Refrigerate, covered, for at least 1 hour. Serve sprinkled with green onions.

OKRA WITH SALSA

Tomatoes and okra team naturally in this dish, which can be served warm or cold.

Preparation time: 15 minutes
Microwave time: 21 minutes
Servings: 4–6

1⅓ cups onion
1 teaspoon minced garlic
1 teaspoon seeded, minced jalapeño pepper
2 tablespoons oil
2 cups seeded, coarsely chopped fresh tomatoes
1 tablespoon red wine vinegar
¼ teaspoon salt
1 pound whole fresh okra, stem ends snapped off but not cut

1. Put onion, garlic, jalapeño pepper, and oil in 1½-quart casserole. MICROWAVE (high) 3 minutes, stirring once.
2. Stir in tomatoes, vinegar, and salt, MICROWAVE (high), uncovered, 10–12 minutes, until sauce starts to thicken.
3. Stir in okra. Cover. MICROWAVE (high) 5–6 minutes, until okra is just tender, stirring once. Let stand, covered, 1 minute. Serve warm or refrigerate, covered, for 2 hours.

TIP: *Whole fresh okra look best in this dish. Frozen or sliced fresh okra may be substituted, but the consistency will be thicker and somewhat sticky.*

OKRA WITH BLACK-EYED PEAS

My husband's Texas heritage requires a big bowl of black-eyed peas to herald in good fortune on New Year's Day. Black-eyed peas with okra makes a good variation well within the spirit of the South. Frozen okra works well in this dish, but don't be tempted to substitute canned black-eyed peas for the superior texture from dried peas. The microwave reduces the soaking time for these dried whole legumes from overnight to just one hour.

Preparation time: 10 minutes
Microwave time: 31 minutes
Standing time: 1 hour
Servings: 6–8

4 strips bacon, roughly diced
1 teaspoon minced garlic
¼ teaspoon cayenne
⅛ teaspoon freshly ground black pepper
½ teaspoon salt
1 cup dried black-eyed peas, rinsed and sorted
2 cups water
1 10-ounce package frozen okra
¼ cup water

1. Mix bacon, garlic, cayenne, black pepper, salt, peas, and 2 cups water in 3-quart casserole. Cover. MICROWAVE (high) 10 minutes. Stir. MICROWAVE (medium) 10–12 minutes, until you can bite through one pea easily. Let stand, covered, 1 hour, until tender. Drain, reserving 1 cup cooking broth.

2. About 10 minutes before the black-eyed peas are ready, put frozen okra and ¼ cup water in 1-quart casserole. Cover. MICROWAVE (high) 5–6 minutes, stirring after 3 minutes, until heated through. Let drain in colander in sink for 1 minute.

3. Add okra to peas. Add the cup of reserved broth from the peas. Mix. MICROWAVE (high) 2–3 minutes, until warmed through. Serve warm.

TIP: Use the drip technique (step 2) in other recipes to remove some of the stickiness from okra sap. It takes a full minute in a colander for the sap to drip away like honey. Don't bother to rinse cooked, sliced okra. The sap foams up like liquid soap into a sticky mess that only aggravates the situation.

CHICKEN GUMBO

Gumbo is okra at its pinnacle. Its sometimes cursed sap stars as the flavorful glue in this slightly spicy, stick-to-the-ribs soup.

Preparation time: 20 minutes
Microwave time: 28 minutes
Servings: 4–6

1½ **pounds chicken thighs (4 small)**
 1 **cup chopped onions**
 1 **cup diced green pepper**
 1 **cup diced celery**
 1 **teaspoon minced garlic**
 ⅛ **teaspoon cayenne**
 ¼ **teaspoon salt**
 ⅛ **teaspoon freshly ground pepper**
1½ **cups sliced fresh okra (about ½ pound)**
 2 **tablespoons flour**
 2 **cups chicken broth**

1. Place chicken along sides of 2½-quart casserole, with thickest portions to outside. Cover with plastic wrap, leaving vent at one corner. MICROWAVE (high) 5–7 minutes, until no longer pink, turning over once and putting thinner portion to outside. Let stand, covered, 2 minutes. Lift out to cool on a plate, leaving juices in casserole.
2. Add onions, green pepper, celery, garlic, cayenne, salt, pepper, and okra to casserole. Cover. MICROWAVE (high) 5–6 minutes, until vegetables are just tender, stirring once. Stir in flour.
3. Remove skin from chicken. Discard skin. Remove meat from bones and shred with fingers. Add meat plus any extra juices from the plate to the vegetables. Add chicken broth.
4. MICROWAVE (medium-high) 12–15 minutes, uncovered, until gumbo thickens to consistency of thin cream. Serve over rice.

TIP: I prefer the heartier flavor of dark chicken meat in this gumbo, but white chicken breasts can be substituted. Use just one cut at a time, either thighs or breasts, for more uniform shapes and even microwave results.

TIP: Chicken skins add flavor, keep the meat moist, and are easier to remove after the initial cooking (step 1). However, for lower fat content, you may remove and discard skins before cooking.

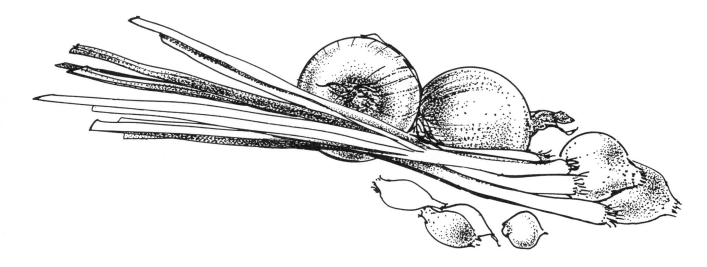

ONIONS

An onion is an onion. Right?

Wrong. Residents of Georgia long have touted their mild, sweet Vidalia onions. Hawaiians boast of Maui onions. And in Washington state, the Walla Walla reigns supreme.

The same onion will taste sweeter or sharper, depending on soil and weather conditions, a climate disparity that invites acute allegiances among onion producers and consumers.

Thanks to good transportation, this boasting and smart promotion add up to good seasonal buys. If you favor mildly sweet onions, look for Vidalias in late May through July, Mauis in mid-May through mid-September and again in November through January, and Walla Wallas in late June through mid-August.

Soft, sweet onions are a richly flavored but low-calorie accompaniment to many entrees. A medium onion has only 38 calories; green onions, a mere 3 calories each. Onions also have an anticoagulant that may help prevent heart attacks.

Green onions, also called *scallions*, are actually small onions. If allowed to grow, they would develop into large onions. Next in size come pearl or button onions, wonderful for creaming.

Regular boiling onions, about 1½ to 2 inches in diameter, are all-purpose. Large Spanish or Bermuda onions provide the most dramatic rings.

Onions are cooked first in many microwave dishes to develop flavor and then impart good taste to whatever is added next. Because they have significant moisture, little extra liquid is needed, but butter or olive oil often is added for flavor.

Traditionalists will relish how quickly the microwave produces a fine, classic onion soup. Experiment with onions and raspberries or my favorite tart apple-onion sauce.

Select green onions that have crisp, dry, bright green tops and firm, white bottoms; avoid those that are wilted. Select dry onions that are dry and firm, with parchment covering intact. Avoid those that are sprouting or have moisture at the top; the moisture indicates rot, which starts at the center and works outward.

Store green onions loosely wrapped in the refrigerator for three to four days. Store dry onions in a cool, dry, well-ventilated area—not in the refrigerator, which is too humid and cold.

CREAMED ONIONS

This traditional accompaniment to holiday meals is made even easier in the microwave. The sauce is a basic white sauce with nutmeg.

Preparation time: 20 minutes
Microwave time: 15 minutes
Servings: 4

1 **pound creaming (small white) onions, peeled**
¼ **cup water**
2 **tablespoons butter**
2 **tablespoons flour**
¼ **teaspoon salt**
⅛ **teaspoon freshly ground white pepper**
¼ **teaspoon ground nutmeg**
1 **cup milk**

1. Put onions and water in 2-quart casserole. Cover. MICROWAVE (high) 6–8 minutes, stirring once. Drain.
2. Put butter in 4-cup measure. MICROWAVE (high) 1 minute to melt. Stir in flour, salt, pepper, and nutmeg until smooth. Whisk in milk. MICROWAVE (high) 5–6 minutes, until thick, stirring after 1½ minutes, then every 2 minutes. Pour sauce over onions and mix.

TIP: *Although the recipe yields only 1 cup of sauce, the 4-cup measure is needed to avoid spill-overs as the sauce boils.*

FRESH ONION RINGS WITH BASIL

Sweet onions, cooked until just soft, then tossed with olive oil and basil, make a wonderful accompaniment to almost any dish.

Preparation time: 5 minutes
Microwave time: 5 minutes
Servings: 4

2 medium onions
2 tablespoons water
1 tablespoon olive oil
1 tablespoon minced fresh basil
  or **1 teaspoon dried**
1/8 teaspoon salt

1. Peel onions. Cut into 1/4-inch slices. Separate into rings.
2. Put onions and water in 1-quart casserole. Cover. MICROWAVE (high) 4–5 minutes, until just tender, stirring once. Drain. Toss with olive oil, basil, and salt.

TIP: *Red wine may be substituted for water.*

CURRIED ONION RINGS

Prepare onions as in Fresh Onion Rings with Basil recipe, but omit olive oil, basil, and salt. Stir in 1/4 cup sour cream mixed with 1 teaspoon curry powder. Serve over fish or chicken.

TART APPLE–ONION SAUCE

Apples and onions make wonderful companions for stuffings, so why not try them together in a sauce? I combined a sweet fresh onion with tart Granny Smith apples to make this unusual, onion-enhanced applesauce. It is sweet and fresh-tasting, wonderful with pork.

Preparation time: 20 minutes
Microwave time: 14 minutes
Servings: 2–3 cups

1 **medium onion, peeled and minced**
2 **pounds tart apples (4 large ones; Granny Smith are good), peeled, cored, and sliced**
¼ **cup water**
1 **tablespoon fresh lemon juice**
2 **tablespoons sugar**

Put onion, apples, water, and lemon juice in 2-quart casserole. Cover. MICROWAVE (high) 12–14 minutes, until very tender, stirring three times. Stir in sugar. Serve as is, chunky style, or puree in blender or processor.

RASPBERRY ONIONS

I paused between excitement and skepticism the first time I saw such combinations on "nouvelle cuisine" menus. But this strange-sounding duet is a winner. To save time (and expense), fresh crushed raspberries are replaced with a dab of raspberry preserve. But a garnish of fresh berries makes this an impressive side dish.

Preparation time: 5 minutes
Microwave time: 7 minutes
Servings: 3–4

1 **large onion, peeled and sliced thin**
2 **tablespoons water**
2 **tablespoons raspberry preserve**
Fresh whole raspberries (for garnish, optional)

1. Put onion slices and water in 1-quart casserole. Cover. MICROWAVE (high) 5 minutes, until almost tender, stirring once. Drain.
2. Brush on raspberry preserve. Do not cover. MICROWAVE (high) 2 minutes, until onions are tender. Garnish with fresh raspberries if desired; serve the whole berries at room temperature or MICROWAVE (high) 30 seconds.

CLASSIC ONION SOUP

Classic onion soup requires about 1½ hours of slow cooking by conventional methods. The microwave delivers a fine soup in half the time. Note that onions do turn a golden brown and caramelize in the microwave when cooked long enough.

Preparation time: 20 minutes
Microwave time: 44 minutes
Servings: 4

**2 large Spanish onions, peeled
    and sliced thin
3 tablespoons butter
2 tablespoons flour
½ cup sugar
4 cups beef stock or broth
¼ cup white wine (optional)
Salt
Freshly ground pepper
4 thin slices French bread,
    toasted
1 cup grated Swiss cheese**

1. Put onions and butter in 2-quart casserole. Do not cover. MICROWAVE (high) 25–30 minutes, until browned, stirring every 5 minutes.
2. Blend in flour and sugar. Stir in stock or broth and wine, if desired. Do not cover. MICROWAVE (high) 12–14 minutes, until soup boils and thickens, stirring twice. Taste. Add salt and pepper if desired. Ladle soup into bowls. Top each with toasted bread, then cheese.

TIP: *The amount of salt and pepper needed will depend on the stock or broth used. Good homemade stock is best. However, good-quality canned broth is available. Since canned products typically contain added salt, taste your soup before adding more.*

SAUSAGE-STUFFED ONIONS

Sausage is cooked first to make sure that it is thoroughly done, then stuffed into hollowed-out onions. Fresh bread cubes absorb some of the fine juices; an egg helps hold everything together.

Preparation time: 30 minutes
Microwave time: 17 minutes
Servings: 4

½ **pound bulk pork sausage**
4 **large onions, peeled**
1 **cup coarsely chopped fresh mushrooms**
1 **cup fresh bread cubes (from 2 slices bread)**
1 **egg, lightly beaten**
¼ **cup finely chopped fresh parsley**
2 **tablespoons chopped fresh thyme *or* 1 teaspoon dried**
1 **cup chicken broth**

1. Put sausage in 2-quart casserole or bowl. MICROWAVE (high) 2–3 minutes, until pink color is almost gone, stirring and breaking up meat with spoon twice. Drain. Return to casserole.
2. Slice off top quarter of each onion, plus a thin slice from bottom to allow onion to sit flat; reserve cut portions. Hollow center of each onion, leaving ¾-inch-thick shell; reserve centers.
3. Chop reserved onion slices and centers. Add to sausage. Add mushrooms. Do not cover. MICROWAVE (high) 3–4 minutes, until pork no longer is pink and vegetables are soft. Stir in bread cubes, egg, parsley, and thyme.
4. Arrange onions in 2-quart rectangular casserole. Fill with sausage mixture. Pour broth over onions. Cover. MICROWAVE (high) 8–10 minutes, until onions are tender, rotating dish once. Let stand, covered, 3 minutes. Baste with broth. Serve.

ONION PIE

Serve this sweet yet hearty pie with a salad as a light lunch or as an impressive accompaniment to roast pork or turkey.

Preparation time: 15 minutes
Microwave time: 31 minutes
Servings: 4–6

1 **prepared pie crust, uncooked (see Tip in recipe for Greens and Cheese Pie)**
3 **large onions, sliced thin**
2 **teaspoons chopped garlic**
1 **tablespoon butter**
3 **tablespoons olive oil**
3 **tablespoons sherry**
1 **tablespoon fresh thyme** *or* ½ **teaspoon dried**
½ **teaspoon salt**
⅛ **teaspoon freshly ground pepper**
3 **tablespoons flour**
3 **strips bacon, diced**

1. Prick bottom and sides of pie crust. Put pie plate on inverted dinner plate. MICROWAVE (high) 4–5 minutes, turning pie one quarter turn after 3 minutes, until crust is just dry. Cool.
2. Put onions, garlic, butter, and olive oil in 3-quart casserole. MICROWAVE (high) 3 minutes, stirring once. Stir in sherry, thyme, salt, and pepper. Cover. MICROWAVE (high) 12–15 minutes, until onions are tender.
3. Mix in flour. MICROWAVE (high) 1 minute to blend. Spoon onion mixture into cooled pie shell. Top with bacon. Place pie on inverted dinner plate. MICROWAVE (high) 5–7 minutes, until bubbly hot and bacon is cooked. Serve warm.

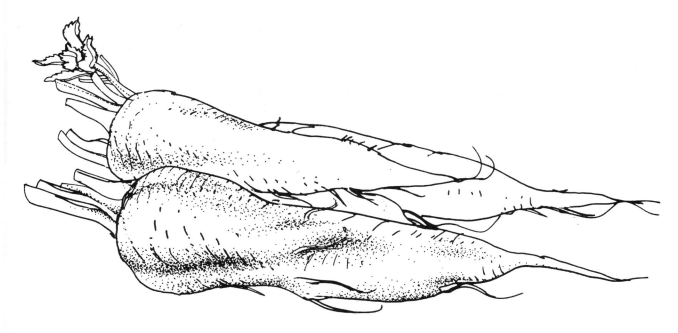

P A R S N I P S

Parsnips are annoying vegetables. Not pungent or foul enough to be called nasty. Just annoying. They look like large white carrots but lack a carrot's fine sweet flavor. They function like potatoes, but lack the upbringing to serve as quiet backdrops for sweet butter and fine herbs. Their harsh, nutty flavor needs attention.

Yet it is unfair to eliminate parsnips from our round-up. Parsnips were a major source of carbohydrates in Europe before they were replaced by potatoes in the 1600s. And there are those who yet love this root vegetable.

Still, my best plan of attack for parsnips is to hit them hard with herbs and spices. Purists likely will love the straightforward recipes for parsnips with butter and cinnamon and parsnips puree.

For my taste, however, douse the rascals quickly with brandy and macadamia nuts. Now that way, parsnips taste good.

Select small to medium, smooth, firm parsnips. Large ones tend to be woody.

Store in original plastic bag or wrap in plastic and keep refrigerated one to two weeks. When preparing, remove woody cores from larger parsnips for more even cooking.

PARSNIPS WITH BUTTER AND CINNAMON

Two tablespoons of butter are a minimum here. Try this dish with cod for a traditional meal from England.

Preparation time: 10 minutes
Microwave time: 7 minutes
Servings: 4–6

1 pound parsnips, peeled and julienned
¼ cup water
2 tablespoons butter
¼ teaspoon ground cinnamon
½ teaspoon sugar
¼ teaspoon salt
⅛ teaspoon freshly ground pepper

1. Put parsnips and water in 1-quart casserole. Cover. MICROWAVE (high) 5–7 minutes, until tender, stirring once. Let stand, covered, 2 minutes. Drain.
2. Stir in butter, cinnamon, sugar, salt, and pepper. Serve.

CURRIED PARSNIPS

This sweet curry works well with parsnips, teamed with broiled chicken and brown rice.

Preparation time: 10 minutes
Microwave time: 9 minutes
Servings: 4–6

1 pound parsnips, peeled and cut into diagonal slices
¼ cup water
3 tablespoons butter
1 teaspoon curry powder
1 teaspoon brown sugar
¼ cup slivered almonds

1. Put parsnips and water in 2-quart casserole. MICROWAVE (high) 5–7 minutes, until tender, stirring twice. Let stand 2 minutes. Drain.
2. Put butter, curry powder, brown sugar, and almonds in 2-cup measure. MICROWAVE (high) 1–2 minutes, stirring once. Mix gently into parsnips.

TIP: *For efficient microwave cooking, use the correct-size containers. Julienned or circular sliced parsnips work well in a 1-quart casserole. Larger diagonal slices require more room and more stirring to cook evenly, so use a 2-quart casserole.*

CREAMED PARSNIPS WITH FINE HERBS

Parsnips benefit from a good bath in cream or half-and-half. This dish is cooked a little more after the half-and-half is added to help the sauce thicken and cling.

Preparation time: 10 minutes
Microwave time: 10 minutes
Servings: 4–6 servings

1 pound parsnips, peeled and cut into ¼-inch-thick rounds
¼ cup water
½ cup half-and-half
½ teaspoon dried tarragon
1 tablespoon minced fresh parsley
2 green onions, white and first 2 inches of green, sliced
¼ teaspoon salt
⅛ teaspoon freshly ground pepper

1. Put parsnips and water in 1-quart casserole. Cover. MICROWAVE (high) 6–8 minutes, until tender, stirring once. Let stand, covered, 2 minutes. Drain.

2. Mix in remaining ingredients. MICROWAVE (medium-high), uncovered, 1–2 minutes to thicken, stirring often so cream doesn't boil. Serve.

TIP: *I prefer parsnip circles, rather than julienned strips, with this dish so that the cream clings better. Note that circles require a minute more in the microwave than julienned strips.*

TIP: *For more even cooking in the microwave, try to cut pieces the same size. Circles from the thicker, stem portion of the parsnip may need to be cut in half.*

PARSNIP PUREE

Try this classic dish with a beef roast and fresh brussels sprouts.

Preparation time: 15 minutes
Microwave time: 10 minutes
Servings: 4–6

1 **pound parsnips, peeled and cut into ¼-inch slices, cores removed**
½ **cup water**
1 **cup milk**
1 **tablespoon butter**
¼ **teaspoon ground allspice**
¼ **teaspoon ground nutmeg**
¼ **teaspoon salt**
⅛ **teaspoon freshly ground pepper**

1. Put parsnips and water in 1-quart casserole. Cover. MICROWAVE (high) 8–10 minutes, until tender enough to pierce easily with fork. Let stand 2 minutes. Drain. Puree in blender or processor.
2. Blend in milk. Mix in butter, allspice, nutmeg, salt, and pepper. Serve with extra pat of butter on top, if desired.

TIP: *You need to cook parsnips longer than usual to make a smooth puree. Cook until parsnips are fork-tender.*

BRANDIED PARSNIPS WITH MACADAMIA NUTS

This is a favorite. Parsnips and macadamia nuts share a hearty sweetness, and brandy, well, cures anything.

Preparation time: 10 minutes
Microwave time: 9 minutes
Servings: 4–6

1 **pound parsnips, peeled and sliced**
2 **tablespoons butter**
2 **tablespoons brown sugar**
2 **tablespoons brandy**
¼ **cup ground macadamia nuts**

1. Mix parsnips, butter, brown sugar, and brandy in 1-quart casserole. Cover. MICROWAVE (high) 7–9 minutes, until tender, stirring every 2 minutes. Let stand, covered, 2 minutes.
2. Mix in half the nuts (⅛ cup) to absorb juices. Sprinkle with remaining nuts. Serve.

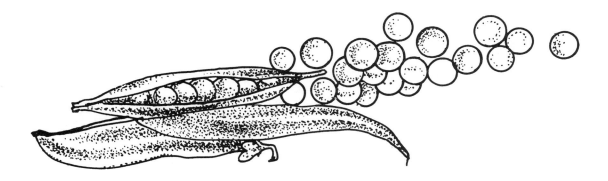

PEAS

Snitching plump English peas from the garden, then eating them raw in a teepee hideaway, is one of my earliest culinary escapades—and one that spoils you for life.

Garden-fresh peas are extraordinarily fine. The pods open with a snap to reveal just-firm, sugar-sweet peas that don't taste as good a few hours later. Like traditional corn, sugar in peas rapidly turns to starch once the vegetable is picked. And once you become hooked on garden-fresh peas, fresh whole peas sold in the market just can't compare.

When peas in our garden are gone, I bypass the starchy offerings in the grocery and switch to frozen peas. Try different brands until you find one in which the peas are fairly small yet firm and sweet. These can be very acceptable.

Because of their round shape, peas are ideal for cooking in the microwave. Just taste and look as you cook. Peas turn a brighter green when cooked. Take care not to overcook them.

For peas with edible pods, see "Snow Peas" chapter.

Select bright green pea pods with well-formed peas. Overmature peas will bulge and form ridges on the pods. Avoid yellow or limp pods and overmature peas that have sprouted.

Store loosely wrapped in the refrigerator for up to two days. Use as soon as possible.

PEAS WITH MINT

This is a good basic recipe for peas in the microwave, even without the classic addition of mint. Peas taste fresher (that is, more like good raw peas) when cooked only four to five minutes and served with only a little butter or no butter at all.

Preparation time: 15 minutes
Microwave time: 6 minutes
Servings: 4

2 cups shelled fresh peas (2 pounds in pods)
¼ **cup water**
1 tablespoon butter
2 tablespoons chopped fresh mint *or* 1 teaspoon dried

1. Put peas and water in 1½-quart casserole. Cover. MICROWAVE (high) 4–6 minutes, stirring once. Drain.
2. Stir in butter and mint. Serve.

TIP: Frozen peas may be substituted. Before cooking, run them under water to remove ice crystals. Stir an extra time while cooking.

TIP: Add salt to taste at end of cooking.

PEAS WITH MUSHROOMS AND NUTMEG

This is a good way to add interest to peas and stretch one box of frozen peas to serve six. Mushrooms are added first because they take longer to cook. Flour and butter combine with the mushroom juices to create a sauce.

Preparation time: 10 minutes
Microwave time: 7 minutes
Servings: 4–6

½ **pound fresh mushrooms, caps quartered, stems sliced** ¼**-inch thick**
2 tablespoons butter
2 tablespoons flour
¼ **teaspoon salt**
½ **teaspoon ground nutmeg**
1 10-ounce box frozen peas, rinsed to remove frost

1. Put mushrooms and butter in 1½-quart casserole. Do not cover. MICROWAVE (high) 3 minutes, until mushrooms start to let out juices, stirring twice.
2. Blend in flour, then salt and nutmeg. Stir in peas. Cover. MICROWAVE (high) 3–4 minutes, stirring once.

PEA SOUP

Carrots and tomatoes make this pea soup a pretty deep orange, instead of green. Puree only half of the soup for a chunky look. For a very smooth soup, soak the peas overnight in water before cooking.

Preparation time: 20 minutes
Microwave time: 1 hour, 15 minutes
Servings: 6

1 cup split peas, rinsed and sorted
2 cups peeled, cubed potato (1 medium)
1 cup chopped carrot (1 medium)
½ cup chopped onion
4 cups water
1 14-ounce can peeled tomatoes, with juices
½ teaspoon dried basil
1½ teaspoons salt
¼ teaspoon freshly ground pepper
½ cup cubed boneless ham (optional)

1. Mix all ingredients in 4-quart casserole. Cover. MICROWAVE (high) 14–16 minutes, until boiling. Stir. Cover. MICROWAVE (medium) 55 minutes to 1 hour, until peas are tender, stirring every 15 minutes.
2. Puree half of the soup in blender or processor. Mix puree back into the rest of the soup. Add hot water to thin, if desired.

TIP: Lentils may be substituted for the split peas.

PEAS WITH PROSCIUTTO AND CREAM

Pretty red strips of prosciutto make this dish festive, as well as great-tasting.

Preparation time: 10 minutes
Microwave time: 11 minutes
Servings: 6–8

¼ **cup minced onion**
2 **cups heavy cream**
2 **cups fresh peas or 2 10-ounce boxes frozen, rinsed to rid peas of frost**
¼ **pound thinly sliced prosciutto, julienned**

1. Put onions and cream in 2-quart casserole. MICROWAVE (high) 5–6 minutes, until cream starts to bubble.
2. Stir in peas. MICROWAVE (high) 4–5 minutes, until peas are just tender, stirring once. Stir in prosciutto. Serve.

TIP: *Microwave time will vary depending on the temperature of ingredients. If cream comes right from the refrigerator and the peas are frozen, more time will be needed. Room-temperature cream with fresh peas need less time. Lift out a pea to check for doneness after 4 minutes and then every minute.*

PEAS WITH FIGS AND APPLE BUTTER

This rich, sweet side dish teams well with crisp roast duck or a handsome pork roast.

Preparation time: 20 minutes
Standing time: 30 minutes
Microwave time: 18 minutes
Servings: 6–8

2 cups (14 ounces) dried figs
3 cups water
2 tablespoons fresh lemon juice
1 tablespoon honey
2 tablespoons fresh thyme *or* 1 teaspoon dried
4 cups fresh peas *or* 4 10-ounce boxes frozen
½ cup water
½ cup prepared apple butter
Fresh parsley sprigs, for garnish

1. Put figs and 3 cups water in 2-quart casserole. Cover. MICROWAVE (high) 9–11 minutes, until tender when pierced with fork, stirring after 5 minutes. Stir in lemon juice, honey, and thyme. Let stand, covered, 30 minutes.
2. Drain figs, reserving ½ cup liquid. (Strain to reserve as much of the thyme as possible or add more thyme.) Trim away fig stems; cut figs into quarters.
3. Put peas and ½ cup water in a 2-quart casserole. Cover. MICROWAVE (high) 5–6 minutes, until just tender, stirring twice. Drain.
4. Put ½ cup reserved fig juice and the apple butter in 4-cup measure. MICROWAVE (high) 1 minute to heat. Stir in figs. Combine figs and peas in a serving dish. Garnish with parsley.

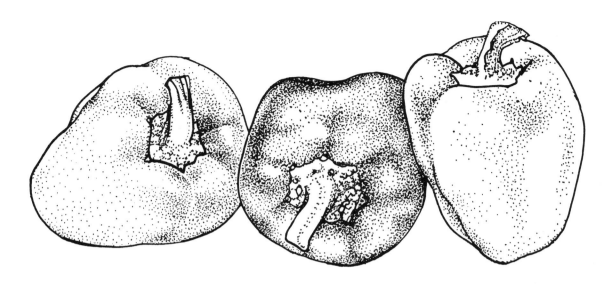

PEPPERS

Remember when a sweet red pepper seemed exotic, a colorful alternative to ordinary green? Who would have envisioned peppers in yellow and even black? But these are the remarkable choices now available to shoppers.

Beautiful tulip-yellow and extraordinary black—actually deep purple—peppers on grocery shelves hail from Holland, which helps explain the high prices attached to these novelties. The flavors are a bit milder and sweeter than those of green varieties. And although yellow peppers hold their color well, black ones fade to green when cooked.

As gardeners know, red peppers are more mature versions of green. That is, they are the same pepper allowed to ripen on the vine from green to red. Red peppers are sweeter, softer, and more perishable than green, which helps explain why they are more expensive than green.

The word *pepper* can be confusing. Sweet peppers, also called *bell peppers*, are not related to black peppercorns used for seasoning; these are dried berries of a shrub that thrives in Asia. Chili peppers, though botanically related, are prized for their hot spiciness; cayenne is made from dried chili peppers. Paprika is made from dried sweet red peppers.

Select firm, smooth, shiny peppers that are heavy for their size. Odd-shaped peppers are fine to eat, just more difficult to cut neatly. When selecting peppers for stuffing, choose ones that are the same size and have square bottoms so that they stand up well. Avoid soft, cracked peppers.

Store loosely wrapped in the refrigerator for up to five days. Use red peppers as soon as possible.

PEPPERS IN OLIVE OIL

One of the simplest and best ways to enjoy sweet green peppers is with olive oil and fresh basil. Save the tops and use later for Chopped Green Peppers, also in this chapter.

Preparation time: 10 minutes
Microwave time: 8 minutes
Servings: 4–6

4 green peppers
1 small onion, sliced thin
2 tablespoons olive oil
2 tablespoons fresh basil *or* 1 teaspoon dried

1. Slice off tops of peppers; save for another use. Remove core and white membrane. Julienne peppers.
2. Put peppers, onion, and olive oil in 2-quart casserole. Cover. MICROWAVE (high) 6–8 minutes, until tender, stirring after 3 minutes. Stir in basil. Let stand, covered, 2 minutes.

CHOPPED GREEN PEPPERS

This is an economical way to use the tops and bumpy bottoms of fresh sweet peppers left over from other dishes. Save the leftover fresh pepper parts, loosely wrapped in the refrigerator, for up to three days. You may, of course, just chop up one or two large peppers. Note that it is not necessary to peel the tomato for this dish.

Preparation time: 15 minutes
Microwave time: 5 minutes
Servings: 4

1½ cups chopped green peppers
(tops from 4 large)
¼ cup chopped onion
½ teaspoon minced garlic
2 tablespoons vegetable oil or
olive oil
1 tomato, seeded and chopped
1 tablespoon fresh marjoram *or*
½ teaspoon dried
2 teaspoons fresh oregano *or* ¼
teaspoon dried
¼ teaspoon salt
⅛ teaspoon freshly ground
pepper

Mix green peppers, onion, garlic, and oil in 1-quart casserole. Cover. MICROWAVE (high) 3–4 minutes, until just tender, stirring once. Stir in remaining ingredients. Do not cover. MICROWAVE (high) 1 minute, until warmed through but before tomatoes release juices.

STEAK PEPPERS

The trick here is a little steak sauce, added to cooked peppers.

Preparation time: 5 minutes
Microwave time: 7 minutes
Servings: 4

4 green peppers, seeded and cut
into 1-inch chunks
¼ cup water
3 tablespoons steak sauce

Put peppers and water in 2-quart casserole. Cover. MICROWAVE (high) 6–7 minutes, until tender but still slightly crisp, stirring once. Drain well so that the water won't dilute the steak sauce. Mix in steak sauce.

CHILLED RED PEPPER SOUP

This brilliantly colored soup is inspired by Princess Marie-Blanche de Broglie, who teaches cooking in her native Normandy. The butter and leeks are traditional elements of cooking in this northern part of France; the sweet red peppers and basil are modern influences.

Preparation time: 30 minutes
Microwave time: 16 minutes
Chilling time: 2 hours
Servings: 6–8

4 sweet red peppers
2 cups chopped leeks (3–4 medium leeks), white portion only
2 tablespoons butter
4 cups chicken stock or broth
2 tablespoons chopped fresh basil *or* 1 teaspoon dried, plus 8 small whole basil leaves, for garnish
1 cup sour cream
¼ teaspoon freshly ground white pepper
Salt

1. Slice off top and bottom of 1 red pepper. Remove and discard core, seeds, and white membrane. Using about one half of the pepper, slice 30 very thin strips; reserve strips for garnish.
2. Chop remainder of pepper. Core, seed, and chop other peppers.
3. Put chopped peppers, leeks, and butter in 3-quart casserole. Cover. MICROWAVE (high) 10–12 minutes, until quite tender, stirring after 3 minutes. Stir in 1 cup chicken stock and basil. Cover. MICROWAVE (high) 3–4 minutes, until boiling. Puree in blender or processor.
4. Return pureed peppers to casserole. Stir in remaining chicken stock, sour cream, and white pepper. Taste. Add salt as needed. Refrigerate, covered, for at least 2 hours. Garnish with red pepper strips and fresh basil leaves.

STUFFED GREEN PEPPERS

When made in the microwave, green peppers don't need to be precooked before they are stuffed. In fact, they stay a brighter green and retain a just-crisp texture if you don't. The filling does get precooked, however, to assure that the meat is done.

Preparation time: 20 minutes
Microwave time: 21 minutes
Servings: 4

4 medium to large sweet green peppers
1 pound hamburger–ground pork mix (¾ pound ground beef to ¼ pound ground pork)
½ cup chopped onion
1 teaspoon minced garlic
1 cup cooked rice
1 teaspoon salt
¼ teaspoon freshly ground pepper
2 tablespoons chopped fresh basil *or* 2 teaspoons dried
½ teaspoon dried oregano
2 cups Tomato Sauce (see index)
½ cup grated cheddar cheese

1. Slice off stem end of green peppers. Remove seeds and white membrane. Rinse.
2. Put ground meat, onion, and garlic in 2-quart rectangular casserole. MICROWAVE (high) 5–6 minutes, until meat no longer is pink, stirring and breaking up with fork twice. Drain. Break up again with fork. Mix in rice, salt, pepper, basil, and oregano.
3. Stuff peppers with meat mixture. Place in 2-quart casserole, separating peppers as much as possible. Pour Tomato Sauce over peppers.
4. Cover with waxed paper. MICROWAVE (high) 3 minutes. MICROWAVE (medium) 10–12 minutes, until just tender. Let stand, covered, 2 minutes. Sprinkle with cheese.

ROSEMARY-LAMB WITH PEPPERS

Tomatoes and lamb are cooked on high just long enough to get hot, then on medium to keep the meat tender. Green peppers are added toward the end to keep them slightly crisp.

Preparation time: 20 minutes
Microwave time: 23 minutes
Servings: 6

½ cup chopped onion
1 teaspoon minced garlic
1 tablespoon butter
1 14½-ounce can tomatoes, with juices
1½ pounds boneless lamb, cut into 1-inch cubes
1 tablespoon dried rosemary, crushed
1 6-ounce can tomato paste
3 green peppers, cored, seeded, and cut into chunks
½ teaspoon salt
¼ teaspoon freshly ground pepper
Dash Tabasco (optional)

1. Put onion, garlic, and butter in 3-quart casserole. MICROWAVE (high) 1 minute to soften. Stir in tomatoes, lamb, rosemary, and half the tomato paste. Cover. MICROWAVE (high) 6–8 minutes, until almost boiling, stirring twice.

2. Stir in green peppers. Cover. MICROWAVE (medium) 10–12 minutes, until lamb and peppers are tender. Stir in remaining tomato paste, salt, pepper, and Tabasco. Do not cover. MICROWAVE (medium) 2 minutes to thicken.

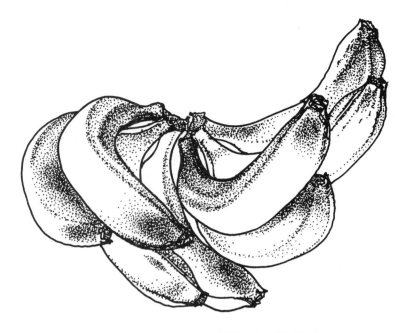

P L A N T A I N

Plantains are a staple food of the tropics, where they are boiled with fish, baked with lime, fried into chips, mashed, stewed—almost anything, it seems, except sliced over cold cereal for breakfast.

A close relative to the sweet banana, plantains technically are fruit. However, they function as a starchy vegetable, much like a potato, and because of their heavy starch content are always served cooked.

Plantains look like bananas—oversized, overripe bananas. But don't let the color fool you. Their skin turns from green to yellow and finally to black before they are fully ripened. Inside, the light yellow fruit remains firm and gets sweeter as the skin darkens. Once cooked, ripe plantain turns a light, golden orange and tastes much like a banana.

Unripe or green plantains are used in cooking, particularly for frying; their green skin is easier to peel if you first cut them in chunks, then peel around the pieces. Fully ripened plantain has skin that is very black, maybe even a little moldy, and easy to peel. Use a paring knife to peel any skin that sticks.

Select clear-skinned, unbruised plantains. It takes at least a week to develop from yellow to black-ripe, so pick those that already are turning black.

Store unwrapped on the counter to ripen at room temperature up to three weeks. Do not refrigerate.

PLANTAIN WITH LIME

One of the simplest ways cooked plantains are enjoyed in the tropics is with a dash of lime juice. The plantains here are microwaved with butter, then served with lime wedges. They make an unusual side dish with pork or poultry.

Preparation time: 5 minutes
Microwave time: 6 minutes
Servings: 4

3 tablespoons butter
2 black-ripe plantains, peeled and halved lengthwise
1 lime, quartered

1. Put butter in 2-quart casserole. MICROWAVE (high) 1–2 minutes to melt.
2. Arrange plantains cut side down in butter. Cover with waxed paper. MICROWAVE (high) 3–4 minutes, until plantains are just tender and deepen to a yellow-orange color. Let stand, covered, 2 minutes. To serve, arrange plantains and lime quarters on plate; spoon remaining butter over plantains.

PLANTAINS WITH CINNAMON AND SUGAR

Naturally sweet plantains make wonderful desserts, such as this cinnamon-topped version.

Preparation time: 5 minutes
Microwave time: 7 minutes
Servings: 4

4 tablespoons butter
2 black-ripe plantains, peeled and cut into ½-inch diagonal slices
1½ teaspoons sugar
¼ teaspoon ground cinnamon

1. Put butter in 2-quart rectangular casserole. MICROWAVE (high) 1–2 minutes to melt. Stir in plantains to coat. Cover with waxed paper. MICROWAVE (high) 3–4 minutes, until plantains are tender and darken to yellow-orange color.
2. Use slotted spoon to remove plantains to serving dish, leaving butter in casserole. Add sugar and cinnamon to casserole. MICROWAVE (high) 30–45 seconds to blend. Pour cinnamon-butter mixture over plantains.

PINEAPPLE PLANTAIN PIE

No need for pastry crust—mashed plantain forms its own pie-shaped dessert, topped with crushed pineapple and coconut.

Preparation time: 15 minutes
Microwave time: 15 minutes
Servings: 6–8

3 black-ripened plantains, peeled and cut into 1-inch slices
1 20-ounce can unsweetened, crushed pineapple, drained, with juices reserved
3 tablespoons butter
¼ cup half-and-half
2 tablespoons brown sugar
¼ teaspoon ground nutmeg
⅓ cup sweetened shredded coconut

1. Put plantain and ¼ cup pineapple juice in 2-quart casserole. Cover with waxed paper. MICROWAVE (high) 6–7 minutes, until quite tender, stirring twice.
2. Mash in butter, half-and-half, brown sugar, and nutmeg. Spread mashed plantain mixture evenly on bottom and up sides of 9-inch pie plate.
3. Spread drained pineapple evenly over bottom of pie. Sprinkle with coconut. Cover with waxed paper. MICROWAVE (high) 7–8 minutes, until heated through. Let cool slightly before serving.

PLANTAIN-SALMON PATTIES

Mashed plantains help to bind these salmon patties together and give them a sweet flavor that your guests may find difficult to identify. Serve them for brunch with scrambled eggs or for supper with buttered noodles and broccoli.

Preparation time: 20 minutes
Microwave time: 10 minutes
Servings: 4

3 green onions, white and first 2 inches of green, sliced
½ teaspoon minced garlic
1 tablespoon butter
2 black-ripened plantains, peeled and cut into 1-inch slices
1 7¾-ounce can salmon or tuna
½ teaspoon ground marjoram
2 tablespoons minced fresh parsley
2 tablespoons finely chopped almonds
1 teaspoon salt
¼ teaspoon freshly ground white pepper
2 eggs, lightly beaten
2 tablespoons fresh lemon juice
1 lemon, quartered

1. Put onions, garlic, and butter in 2-quart casserole. MICROWAVE (high) 1 minute to soften.
2. Add plantains. MICROWAVE (high) 3 minutes, until quite tender and darkened to yellow-orange color. Mash.
3. Mash in salmon, marjoram, parsley, almonds, salt, and pepper. Stir in eggs and lemon juice. Taste and adjust seasonings if desired.
4. In same 2-quart casserole, form mixture into four oblong patties, arranging so patties do not touch. Cover with plastic wrap, turned back to form a vent. MICROWAVE (high) 5–6 minutes, until edges start to get dry. Let stand, covered, 3 minutes. Use spatula to remove patties onto serving platter or plates. Serve with lemon wedges.

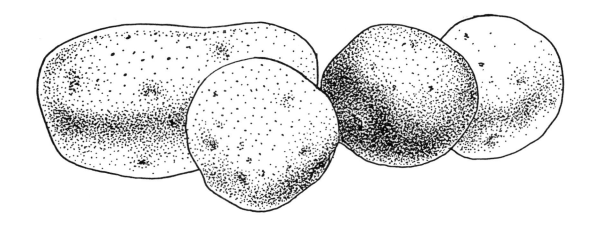

POTATOES

Humble potatoes—salt of the earth and shadow to meat—hardly seem the stuff of which heroes are made. But lowly potatoes have been reborn in this era of healthful eating.

Potatoes, we discover, are not fattening, evil fare. It is the fat in which they are fried or the cream toppings we add that contribute poundage. In their unadorned state, potatoes are low in fat, low in sodium, and high in potassium and carbohydrates—which means excellent and inexpensive eating. A medium potato has about 100 calories.

The common Irish potato is a member of the nightshade family, along with eggplant, peppers, and tomatoes. Because they store well, potatoes are available all year.

New potatoes, which appear in spring, may be red-skinned or white-skinned and are excellent when cooked with just a little butter in the microwave. (Small red potatoes that you find in winter likely have been stored; these are not "new" potatoes but small all-purpose ones.) Choose long russet-colored potatoes for baking whole. Yellow Finnish potatoes hold up particularly well in salads. Round red-skinned or white-skinned potatoes are all-purpose, although white are better for mashing.

Select firm, dry, relatively smooth potatoes for easier peeling. Avoid those with cuts or greenish spots, which come from storage in light.

Store unwashed and unwrapped in a dry, dark spot for several weeks. Do not refrigerate.

NEW POTATOES WITH BUTTER AND LEMON

Removing just a strip of peel from each potato is decorative, eliminates the need to pierce the potatoes, and helps them absorb a buttery flavor.

Preparation time: 10 minutes
Microwave time: 11 minutes
Servings: 4–5

12–15 small new potatoes
  2 tablespoons butter
  ¼ teaspoon salt
  ⅛ teaspoon freshly ground pepper
  1 tablespoon grated lemon zest

1. Use potato peeler to remove small strip of skin around each potato. Put potatoes and butter in 2-quart casserole, smallest potatoes in center. Cover. MICROWAVE (high) 9–11 minutes, until just tender, stirring after 3 minutes.
2. Stir in salt, pepper, and lemon zest. Let stand, covered, 3 minutes.

YOGURT-AND-DILL-STUFFED POTATOES

A big cooked potato is very healthful, if you watch the filling. This yogurt version tastes great and won't bust the diet. Save the sliced tops from these stuffed potatoes and use the next day for the Potato-Top Pizza recipe that follows.

Preparation time: 10 minutes
Microwave time: 16 minutes
Servings: 4

4 medium-sized white baking potatoes
⅓ cup skim milk
½ cup yogurt
¼ teaspoon salt
1 tablespoon fresh dill *or* ½ teaspoon dried dill

1. Wash potatoes well. Prick tops with fork. Put potatoes on corners of paper towel. MICROWAVE (high) 10–12 minutes, until potatoes are just soft, turning towel 180 degrees after 6 minutes. Let stand 3 minutes.
2. Slice ¾-inch top from each potato; reserve for another use. Scoop out center and mash with milk, yogurt, salt, and half the dill (1½ teaspoons). Spoon back into shells. (Recipe can be made to this point a day ahead. Add an extra 30 seconds per potato to reheat time.)
3. Place potatoes on serving plate. MICROWAVE (high) 2–4 minutes, until heated through, rotating plate once. Sprinkle with remaining dill.

TIP: *Note the use of a paper towel to help turn whole potatoes quickly in the microwave. No problem remembering which way you turned which potato and no burnt fingers.*

POTATO-TOP PIZZA

Tasty, economical, and quick. These snacks can be made ahead, wrapped, and stored in the refrigerator for a couple of days before cooking.

Preparation time: 5 minutes
Microwave time: 3 minutes
Servings: 4

4 **top slices, about ¾ inch thick, from baked whole potatoes**
4 **tablespoons spaghetti sauce**
4 **tablespoons shredded mozzarella cheese**
½ **teaspoon dried oregano**

1. Place potato tops flat side up on serving dish or in rectangular 2-quart casserole. Spread evenly with spaghetti sauce. Cover with waxed paper. MICROWAVE (high) 2–3 minutes to heat through.
2. While still hot, sprinkle with cheese and oregano. Serve.

TIP: *If you have a leftover whole baked potato, cut slices from both the top and bottom to use for potato pizza. Dice the middle portion and add to a cold vegetable salad or a hot soup.*

POTATOES VESUVIO

The inspiration for this dish is Chicken Vesuvio, a popular specialty in Chicago Italian restaurants. Chicken is supposed to be the star on the platter, but many of us reach first for the wonderful garlic- and olive oil–laden potatoes. Conventional roasting gives the potatoes a browned finish; leaving the skins on does a similar trick in this microwave adaptation.

Preparation time: 10 minutes
Microwave time: 10 minutes
Servings: 4

2 **tablespoons minced garlic**
4 **tablespoons olive oil**
2 **large potatoes, washed, unpeeled, cut into ¼-inch slices**
½ **teaspoon salt**
⅛ **teaspoon freshly ground black pepper**
½ **teaspoon dried oregano**

1. Put garlic and half (2 tablespoons) of the olive oil in 2-quart casserole. MICROWAVE (high) 1 minute, until tender, stirring once. Stir in potatoes. Cover. MICROWAVE (high) 7–9 minutes, until centers are just tender, stirring twice. Let stand, covered, 3 minutes.
2. Stir in salt, pepper, and oregano. Drizzle with remaining olive oil. Serve.

HOT GERMAN POTATO SALAD

A zesty German version of potato salad. Serve it with juicy bratwurst and dark beer.

Preparation time: 15 minutes
Microwave time: 17 minutes
Servings: 6

4 large yellow potatoes
4 strips bacon, diced
2 tablespoons minced shallots
2 tablespoons apple juice
3 tablespoons cider vinegar
1 teaspoon dry mustard
1 teaspoon salt
1 egg, well beaten
2 green onions, white portion and first 2 inches of green, sliced

1. Scrub potatoes and prick several times with fork. Put potatoes on corners of paper towel. MICROWAVE (high) 10–12 minutes, until potatoes are just soft, turning towel 180 degrees after 6 minutes. Let stand 3 minutes. Peel, cut in half lengthwise, and slice.

2. Put bacon and shallots in 4-cup measure. MICROWAVE (high) 4–5 minutes, stirring once, until bacon is cooked. Stir in apple juice, vinegar, mustard, and salt. MICROWAVE (high) 1 minute to blend.

3. Beat a teaspoon of hot bacon mixture into egg. Beat egg into hot marinade until well mixed. Pour over potatoes. Mix well. Sprinkle with green onions.

TIP: If potatoes are not uniform in size, cook together until the smaller ones are tender. Remove smaller ones. Cook the larger ones longer, checking every minute, until tender.

NIÇOISE SALAD

Canned tuna never had it so romantic! Serve this lovely salad for lunch or a light supper when red potatoes and fresh green beans are at their prime.

Preparation time: 10 minutes
Microwaving time: 10 minutes
Cooling time: 2 hours
Servings: 4

2 cups green beans, cut into
   1½-inch pieces
¼ cup water
½ teaspoon salt
2 cups ¼-inch sliced red potatoes
   with skins on
½ cup pitted black olives,
   preferably Mediterranean-
   style
6 tablespoons olive oil
¼ teaspoon dry mustard
2 tablespoons white wine
   vinegar
2 medium tomatoes, quartered
6 thin slices Bermuda onion,
   separated into rings
   Lettuce
1 hard-boiled egg, peeled and
   quartered
1 6½-ounce can tuna, drained
   and broken into chunks
8 canned anchovy filets, drained
2 tablespoons chopped fresh
   tarragon *or* 1 teaspoon dried
   tarragon

1. Put beans, water, and salt in 2½-quart casserole. Cover. MICROWAVE (high) 2 minutes. Stir in potatoes. Cover. MICROWAVE (high) 6–8 minutes, until just tender. Drain. Return to casserole.
2. Mix in olives, olive oil, mustard, and vinegar. Cover. Refrigerate at least 2 hours.
3. Add tomatoes and onions. Toss gently to mix. Serve on lettuce with eggs and tuna, topped with crossed anchovies and sprinkled with tarragon.

TIP: *Don't use the microwave to hard-cook eggs in the shell. The built-up heat will cause the shells to explode. To hard-cook an egg, break 1 large egg into a greased custard cup. Pierce yolk with fork. Cover with plastic wrap. MICROWAVE (medium) 1¼ minutes, until yolk is set. Let stand, covered, 1 minute.*

DIRTY POTATOES

This was not the intended name for this fine-tasting mashed potatoes dish, but the description is appropriate. The good flavors develop from mushrooms, wine, and tarragon; the appearance is speckled grey. Garnish with fresh tarragon or parsley, serve in a pretty bowl, and assure guests that Dirty Potatoes tastes better than it looks.

Preparation time: 10 minutes
Microwave time: 25 minutes
Servings: 6

½ **cup chopped onion**
½ **pound finely chopped fresh mushrooms**
4 **tablespoons butter**
1 **teaspoon dried tarragon**
¼ **cup white wine**
¼ **teaspoon salt**
⅛ **teaspoon freshly ground pepper**
3 **large white potatoes, peeled and cut into 1-inch by 2-inch chunks**
¼ **cup water**
1 **cup milk**

1. Put onion, mushrooms, and half (2 tablespoons) of the butter in 2-quart casserole. MICROWAVE (high), uncovered, 2 minutes. Stir in tarragon, wine, salt, and pepper. MICROWAVE (high) 5–7 minutes, until vegetables are very tender, stirring once. Set aside to keep warm.
2. Put potatoes and water in 2-quart casserole. Cover. MICROWAVE (high) 14–16 minutes, until very tender, stirring twice. Let stand, covered, 3 minutes.
3. Add rest of the butter (2 tablespoons) to potatoes. Mash. Add mushroom mixture with its liquor and milk. Whip until fluffy. Add more milk if too thick.

TIP: *Note that there is not enough water left to drain after the potatoes are cooked in the microwave. No valuable nutrients going down the drain, either.*

PUMPKINS

Today there is no poetry for the pumpkin. No odes to a sensual form, laments for a harvest gone by.

Inelegant and bumbling, these flushed-orange squash roll into town each autumn, face the world as grinning jack-o'-lanterns, then return to their destiny as mute cans of pumpkin puree on grocery shelves. What a shame.

Fresh pumpkin is marvelous, cooked *al dente* with tarragon or quickly stirred with mounds of whipped cream into a memorable, *real* pumpkin pie.

True, asking a child to dine on jack-o'-lantern is like requesting that he eat his pet. But these huge, stringy, thin-flavored squash are not the best for cooking, anyway.

Seek smaller, 2- to 3-pound versions called *pie pumpkins, cheese pumpkins,* or *sugar pumpkins*. A whole pumpkin cooks up in about 20 minutes in the microwave. Once it is cooked, it is easy to scrape away the stringy insides with a spoon, then use the flesh for fresh pumpkin recipes.

Newest on the scene are mini-pumpkins or Jack-Be-Littles. Too tiny to provide valuable eating, they serve as creative containers for a bit of soup.

The first question for many cooks is what to do with pumpkin seeds, so the first recipe here is for toasted seeds. And for the hard to impress, try the creamy, chestnut-pumpkin soup, studded with porcini mushrooms—nothing bumbling about it.

Select firm, umblemished pumpkins that are heavy for their size. Seek small, 2- to 3-pound pie pumpkins, cheese pumpkins, or sugar pumpkins.

Store pumpkins in a dry, cool (50-degree), well-ventilated area for up to a month or a week at cool room temperature. Do not refrigerate whole pumpkins, or they will suffer chilling injury. Wrap cut pieces in plastic and store in the refrigerator.

TOASTED PUMPKIN SEEDS

When faced with a fresh pumpkin, your first question probably will be what to do with the seeds. No need to leave them for hours in a low-temperature oven; the microwave delivers crisp, browned pumpkin seeds in just 15 minutes. This recipe includes directions for adding butter and salt, but frankly I prefer the simple taste of plain, toasted seeds, which stay fresh for days, uncovered, in a pretty earthenware bowl. Nibble a few after step 1 and decide yourself.

Preparation time: 10 minutes
Microwave time: 12 minutes
Servings: 1 cup

1 cup pumpkin seeds
1 tablespoon butter
½ teaspoon salt

1. Wash seeds well. Drain and pat dry. Put a double layer of paper towels in a 2-quart rectangular casserole. Spread seeds evenly on top. MICROWAVE (high) 10–12 minutes, until toasty and dry, stirring twice. A few seeds may harmlessly pop out of the casserole while cooking; just sweep them up later. Let stand 5 minutes.
2. Put butter in 2-cup measure. MICROWAVE (high) 30 seconds to melt. Add seeds to butter in measuring cup. Stir. Spread on plate. Salt.

TIP: *Smaller squash seeds may be toasted the same way but will need a minute or two less time cooking.*

TIP: *Be sure to wash the seeds well, or they will stick to the paper towels like glue. If you goof up here, just wrap it up, throw in the towel, and do a better job next time.*

TARRAGON PUMPKIN MASH

As pumpkins hit high season in early October, tarragon is among the last of the herbs still beckoning from our summer garden. This recipe is a nice change from the more traditional pairing of pumpkin and nutmeg.

Preparation time: 15 minutes
Microwave time: 18 minutes
Servings: 6–8

1 pumpkin, about 2½ pounds
½ cup milk
2 tablespoons butter
1 tablespoon chopped fresh
   tarragon *or* **½ teaspoon dried**
¼ teaspoon salt
⅛ teaspoon freshly ground
   pepper

1. Use fork to pierce ¼-inch-deep holes all over pumpkin. Set on side on plate. MICROWAVE (high) 16–18 minutes, until skin is soft, turning pumpkin over and rotating plate a quarter turn every 4 minutes. Let stand 5–10 minutes.
2. Cut pumpkin in half. Remove seeds and stringy center. Spoon out flesh. Mash. Mash in milk, then butter, tarragon, salt, and pepper.

PUMPKIN-CHESTNUT
SOUP-IN-THE-SHELL

Save this for when you have time to fuss in the kitchen and need a knock-'em-dead first course. The recipe was inspired by Carolyn Buster, chef/owner of the award-winning The Cottage restaurant just south of Chicago, who made a similar presentation when invited to tout American cuisine in Montreal. Buster's version incorporates about $40 worth of porcini mushrooms, 3 cups of cream, and an hour at the stove. It tastes a bit better than mine. But then, this recipe cost $3.49 worth of porcini mushrooms, 1 cup of cream, and 37 minutes in the microwave.

Preparation time: 30 minutes
Microwave time: 37 minutes
Servings: 6–8

½ **ounce dried porcini mushrooms**
1 **cup hot water**
2 **tablespoons butter**
½ **cup diced onion**
1 **teaspoon minced garlic**
2 **cups diced fresh pumpkin**
1½ **cups diced celery**
½ **cup diced carrots**
½ **pound fresh button mushrooms, chopped**
1½ **tablespoons minced fresh parsley**
¼ **teaspoon ground allspice**
¼ **teaspoon freshly ground white pepper**
2 **cups chicken broth**
2 **cups beef broth**
1 **15-ounce can chestnut puree**
1 **cup heavy cream**
3 **tablespoons cognac**
Salt to taste

1. Soak porcini mushrooms in the hot water in a small bowl for at least 15 minutes.
2. Put butter, onion, and garlic in 3-quart casserole. MICROWAVE (high) 2–3 minutes, until tender. Add pumpkin, celery, carrots, mushrooms, parsley, allspice, and pepper. Cover. MICROWAVE (high) 10–15 minutes, until vegetables are tender, stirring every 4 minutes.
3. Strain porcini mushrooms, reserving the mushrooms and adding the 1 cup of soaking liquor to the vegetable casserole.
4. Add chicken and beef broths to casserole. Cover. MICROWAVE (high) 10 minutes. Stir in chestnut puree. Cover. MICROWAVE (high) 5 minutes, until chestnut is incorporated.
5. Cool slightly. Puree in blender or processor. Stir in porcini mushrooms, cream, cognac, and salt to taste. MICROWAVE (high) 3–4 minutes to heat through, but do not boil. Serve hot in pumpkin shells. (See following Tip.)

TIP: To make pumpkin serving shells, cut off the top of each pumpkin and scoop out the seeds and stringy center. A 2-pound pumpkin will hold about 1½ cups of soup. Mini-pumpkins will hold about ⅓ cup if you scoop out the flesh, leaving a ¼-inch shell. Replace tops.

PUMPKIN PIE GRAND MARNIER

I love the squashlike texture of this fresh pumpkin pie, so unlike pies made with a can of pumpkin puree.

Preparation time: 10 minutes
Chilling time: 3 hours

2½ **cups mashed cooked pumpkin (see note below)**
1 **14-ounce can condensed milk**
3 **tablespoons Grand Marnier**
1 **cup whipping cream, whipped**
1 **baked 9-inch pastry shell (see note below)**

Mix together pumpkin, condensed milk, and Grand Marnier. Fold in whipped cream. Pour into baked shell. Chill 3 hours.

NOTE: For cooked, mashed pumpkin, follow recipe for Tarragon Pumpkin Mash but eliminate milk, butter, and herbs.

For pastry shell, make favorite recipe for single crust, adding ¼ teaspoon ground almonds or cinnamon to dry ingredients for color. Prick bottom and sides. Place pie plate on inverted dinner plate. MICROWAVE (high) 3 minutes. Rotate pie a quarter turn. MICROWAVE (high) 1½ minutes until just dry. Cool.

R A D I C C H I O

With its fine burgundy color and fancy price tag, radicchio (rah-DEEK-kee-oh) ranks with Sophia Loren and Ferrari as one of our classiest Italian imports.

Upscale restaurants were the first to adopt radicchio, using its unusual color to spark salad plates. And groceries in major urban markets now carry imported or lately even domestically grown radicchio. Best supplies are in winter and spring.

Radicchio is a variety of chicory favored in Italy. Its color ranges from dark green to pink, but the most popular imported version is deep red Verona, with white ribs and veins. It is about the size of a small head of lettuce.

Radicchio has a slightly bitter taste that is quite refreshing when the vegetable is served raw in a mixed salad. But this pleasant bitterness can become too strong when the vegetable is cooked in the microwave.

The best test, I find, is to taste radicchio raw. Older, already bitter heads of radicchio become unpleasantly bitter when cooked. Don't use them. Younger, only slightly bitter heads remain pleasant to the taste. When in doubt, serve radicchio raw and use the microwave to help you whip up a dressing.

Select firm, compact heads that are heavy for their size. Leaves should be crisper than Bibb lettuce but less crisp than iceberg. Avoid limp or browned leaves.

Store loosely wrapped in the refrigerator for up to a week.

SIMMERED RADICCHIO

Quick simmering turns radicchio into almost a different vegetable. Its red color fades to brownish-red, and its subtle bitterness deepens. I find that chicken broth tempers the bitterness more than water or olive oil. Start with fresh, young radicchio that is pleasantly bittersweet when raw. Serve with equally assertive game or other red meats.

Preparation time: 5 minutes
Microwave time: 4 minutes
Servings: 3–4

1 head radicchio
¼ cup chicken stock or broth
⅛ teaspoon salt
⅛ teaspoon freshly ground
**   pepper**

Remove core and outer leaves of radicchio if withered. Slice into long shreds. Put shreds and chicken stock in 2-quart casserole. Do not cover. MICROWAVE (high) 3–4 minutes, until just wilted. Drain. Taste. Add salt and pepper, or to taste.

RADICCHIO WITH WARM ANCHOVY DRESSING

Crisp radicchio leaves form natural little cups, great for holding a dab of dressing such as this anchovy-spiked version.

Preparation time: 15 minutes
Microwave time: 1 minute
Servings: 4

1 head radicchio
3 anchovy fillets, cut up
1 teaspoon minced garlic
4 tablespoons fresh lemon juice
**   (about 1 lemon)**
2 tablespoons wine vinegar
¼ teaspoon salt
⅛ teaspoon freshly ground
**   pepper**
4 tablespoons vegetable oil

1. Remove core from radicchio. Separate into individual leaves. Rinse well, dry, and store in airtight container or between linen towels to crisp in refrigerator. Just before serving, arrange on plate.
2. In a large bowl, mash anchovies and garlic. Stir in lemon juice, vinegar, salt, and pepper. MICROWAVE (high) 1 minute. Beat in oil. Toss or brush radicchio with dressing.

RADICCHIO WITH
CAPER-HOLLANDAISE SAUCE

Yes, you can make a fine hollandaise in the microwave. Just keep the power on medium and your whisking wrist agile. The creamy sauce nicely fills crisp cups made by radicchio leaves.

Preparation time: 15 minutes
Microwave time: 4 minutes
Servings: 4

1 head radicchio
2 tablespoons minced shallots
½ cup butter
1 tablespoon fresh lemon juice
¼ teaspoon salt
4 egg yolks
2 tablespoons drained capers

1. Remove core from radicchio. Separate into individual leaves. Rinse well, dry, and store in airtight container or between linen towels to crisp in refrigerator. Just before serving, arrange on plate.
2. Put shallots and butter in 1-quart casserole. Do not cover. MICROWAVE (high) 2 minutes to melt butter and soften shallots. Whisk in lemon juice and salt. Let cool slightly.
3. Whisk in egg yolks. MICROWAVE (medium) 1½ minutes, whisking every 30 seconds, until sauce thickens. Stir in capers. Dab a little hollandaise in each radicchio leaf.

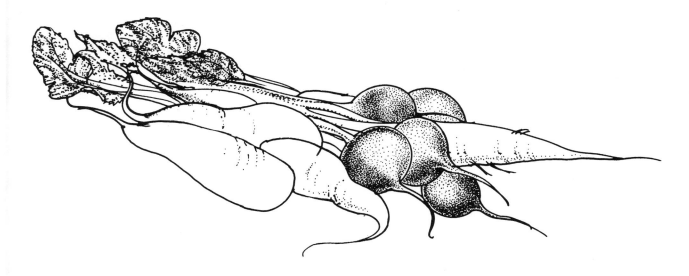

R A D I S H E S

The first time you see a plate of cooked whole radishes you may not recognize the familiar salad ingredient. Fresh radishes transform into almost another vegetable when cooked: from bright red to delicate pink, from sharply flavored to quite mellow.

A member of the cabbage family, radishes may be round or oblong, and typically have a bright red exterior and crisp, white interior. Large, round black radishes with white interior may be found in Russian and Polish markets; large, white, sweet daikon radishes favored in Oriental cooking are now fairly common in major markets.

Select very firm, medium-sized, crisp radishes. Avoid those with cuts. If purchasing with tops attached, look for crisp tops; these are more expensive because they are harvested by hand, but you know that the best-looking ones are fresh.

Store loosely wrapped in the refrigerator for up to a week. Cut off the green tops before storing, or the radishes will age faster.

BAKED WHOLE RADISHES

Radishes take on a milder flavor and lighter color when cooked. Serve as a garnish around a roast or to spark a vegetable platter.

Preparation time: 5 minutes
Microwave time: 5 minutes
Servings: 4

8 ounces (2 cups) whole radishes, stems trimmed ¼ cup water 1 tablespoon butter ¼ teaspoon salt ⅛ teaspoon freshly ground white pepper	Put radishes and water in 1-quart casserole. Cover. MICROWAVE (high) 3–5 minutes, until just tender, stirring after 1½ minutes. Drain. Stir in butter, salt, and pepper.

TIP: *Radishes start to sputter after about 1½ minutes (that is why the recipe suggests stirring them), but I've never had one explode and find piercing unnecessary.*

RADISH CONFETTI

Grated sweet carrots and sharp radishes not only taste great together but make a strikingly colorful side dish. Because the vegetables are grated so fine, no water is needed—just a dab of butter. Salt and pepper aren't missed at all.

Preparation time: 15 minutes
Microwave time: 3 minutes
Servings: 4

8 ounces (2 cups) grated fresh radishes . 2 medium carrots, grated 1 tablespoon butter 2 tablespoons fresh dill *or* 1 teaspoon dried	Put radishes, carrots, and butter in 1-quart casserole. Cover. MICROWAVE (high) 2–3 minutes, until just tender. Stir in dill.

MICRO SHABU SHABU

Genuine shabu shabu—a sort of Japanese fondu—doesn't lend itself to the microwave. But the very last step, in which you drink the broth in which you have cooked various meats and vegetables, can be imitated. The final touch to shabu shabu is grated daikon radish. The version here is light; serve as an appetizer or part of lunch.

Preparation time: 15 minutes
Microwave time: 10 minutes
Servings: 4

1 chicken breast, skinned, boned, and cut into bite-sized strips
4 cups chicken stock or broth
3 ounces bean threads
½ cup shredded daikon (white radish)
1 green onion, white and first 2 inches of green, sliced

Put chicken and broth in 2-quart casserole. Cover. MICROWAVE (high) 8–10 minutes, until boiling. Stir in bean threads. Let stand, covered, 5 minutes. Top with daikon and green onion. Serve.

TIP: *Bean threads, a pleasantly mild-tasting soybean product, are clear, almost plastic-looking when cooked. Look for plastic-wrapped packages in the Oriental food section of major grocery stores.*

RUTABAGAS

"You should have seen her," giggled a friend. "She had a big knife and big eyes and was trying to figure out how to cut that thing."

The neighbors' 10-year-old daughter had graciously accepted a spare rutabaga, but then she was stumped. And no wonder.

Heavy, somber, and sometimes thickly waxed, a large rutabaga resembles a small fortress, impenetrable and downright unfriendly. But pare away that exterior, and a chunk of humble, friendly eating awaits.

Erroneously lumped with the turnip, and even called *yellow turnip*, a rutabaga is a separate vegetable that does indeed resemble the turnip. Both have a potatolike texture and slightly sharp taste, rutabaga being the sweeter. In England, rutabaga answers to the name *swede*; in Scotland, it is *neeps* and traditionally paired with haggis and whiskey.

A handful of cubed rutabaga is essential in an old-fashioned stew like the rutabaga ragout that follows. A very satisfying taste combination—rutabagas and cheddar cheese—was inspired one day by simply smelling the vegetable as it cooked and cooed for something sharp and tangy.

I find it easier to trim a rutabaga as you do a pineapple. Chop off the bottom to create a stable base, lop off the top, and set upright. Use a large knife to slice away vertical strips of skin, following the contour of the vegetable. The trimmed rutabaga then can be sliced as desired.

Select generally smooth, firm, and round or moderately elongated vegetables that are heavy for their size. Avoid those with skin punctures or deep cuts. Late winter storage rutabagas purchased in stores may have a wax coating used to prevent loss of moisture. The wax cuts away easily with the peeling.

Store as you would white potatoes, at cool room temperature in a dry, well-ventilated spot, or up to a week in the refrigerator.

RUTABAGA WITH THYME

An alternative to potatoes, this simple preparation marries well with a handsome roast pork or chicken.

Preparation time: 10 minutes
Microwave time: 14 minutes
Servings: 4–6

1 tablespoon butter
2 tablespoons chopped onion
1½ pounds rutabagas, peeled and cubed
¼ cup water
1 tablespoon butter
½ teaspoon dried thyme
¼ teaspoon salt
⅛ teaspoon freshly ground pepper

Put butter and onion in 2-quart casserole. MICROWAVE (high) 1–2 minutes, until tender. Add rutabagas and water. Cover. MICROWAVE (high) 10–12 minutes, until almost tender, stirring once. Let stand 2 minutes. Drain. Stir in butter, thyme, salt, and pepper. Serve.

RUTABAGA AND CARROT PUREE

Rutabaga pairs well with other root vegetables such as carrots, potatoes, and turnips. This recipe uses milk, but cream or sour cream may be substituted.

Preparation time: 15 minutes
Microwave time: 12 minutes
Servings: 6–8

1 pound rutabagas, peeled and diced
1 pound carrots, peeled and diced
½ cup water
1 cup milk
1 tablespoon chopped fresh dill
or ½ teaspoon dried

1. Put rutabagas, carrots, and water in 2-quart casserole. Cover. MICROWAVE (high) 10–12 minutes, until tender, stirring every 4 minutes. Let stand, covered, 2 minutes. Drain.
2. Puree in blender or processor. Stir in milk and dill. Serve.

TIP: *Change the proportion of rutabagas to carrots for a stronger flavor of either vegetable.*

RUTABAGAS WITH CHEESE SAUCE

Rutabagas need a couple more minutes in the microwave if they are julienned, rather than cubed, but look more attractive served julienned with a cheese sauce. Take care; these french fry look-alikes tend to get snatched from the bowl on the way to the dinner table.

Preparation time: 15 minutes
Microwave time: 20 minutes
Servings: 4–6

1½ **pounds rutabagas, peeled and julienned**
¼ **cup water**
2 **tablespoons butter**
2 **tablespoons flour**
1 **cup milk**
¼ **teaspoon salt**
⅛ **teaspoon freshly ground pepper**
½ **cup grated sharp cheddar cheese**

1. Put rutagabas and water in 2-quart casserole. Cover. MICROWAVE (high) 10–12 minutes, until just tender, stirring every 3 minutes. Let stand 2 minutes. Drain.
2. Put butter in 4-cup measure. MICROWAVE (high) 40–50 seconds to melt. Blend in flour until smooth. Slowly whisk in milk. MICROWAVE (high) 1–3 minutes to thicken, stirring every minute. Stir in salt, pepper, and cheese. MICROWAVE (high) 3–4 minutes, until thick, stirring every minute. Pour cheese sauce over rutabagas.

RUTABAGA RAGOUT

Fresh tomatoes are added at the end of cooking to give a fresh fillip to this rich, hearty ragout. Like most stews, it tastes better the next day.

Preparation time: 25 minutes
Microwave time: 1 hour, 18 minutes
Servings: 6–8

1 **cup chopped onions**	

1 **cup chopped onions**
1 **teaspoon caraway seeds**
1 **tablespoon oil**
1½ **pounds boneless beef chuck, cut into ½-inch cubes**
2 **tablespoons flour**
2 **cups peeled, cubed rutabagas**
1 **cup diced celery**
1½ **cups (1 medium) peeled, cubed potato**
2 **cups beef broth**
½ **teaspoon salt**
¼ **teaspoon freshly ground pepper**
2 **ripe tomatotes, peeled, seeded and chopped**

1. Mix onions, caraway seeds, and oil in 3-quart casserole. MICROWAVE (high) 3–5 minutes, until tender, stirring once.
2. Coat beef with flour. Mix into onions. Cover. MICROWAVE (high) 6–8 minutes, until meat turns from red to barely pink inside, stirring once.
3. Stir in rutabagas, celery, potato, beef broth, salt, and pepper. Cover. MICROWAVE (high) 8–10 minutes, until boiling. Stir. Cover. MICROWAVE (medium) 45–50 minutes, until beef is tender, stirring twice. Stir in tomatoes. MICROWAVE (medium) 5 minutes. Let stand, covered, 10 minutes.

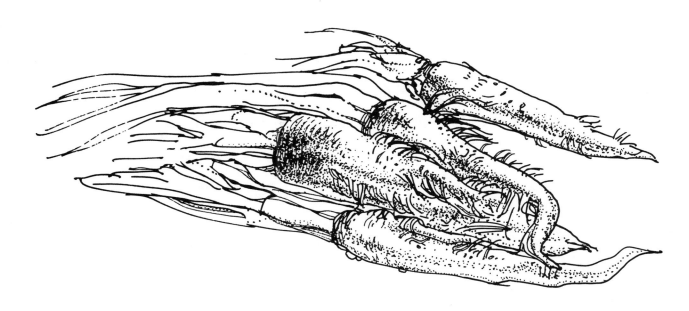

SALSIFY

If you are not familiar with salsify, try it at least to determine if it rates its nickname: *oyster plant* or *vegetable plant*. By reputation, this old-fashioned vegetable tastes like oysters. I find this a puzzlement but have created an unusual recipe using both salsify and oysters so that you can be judge.

A member of the daisy family, salsify roots are slender and typically 8 to 10 inches long. The exterior is greyish-white, the interior a creamy white. Black salsify or scorzonera (skort-suh-NAIR-ah) has a black exterior. Both have a crisp texture and sweet, pleasant taste with a slight coconut aftertaste.

Some recommend cooking salsify first to make peeling easier. I find scorzonera quite easy to peel raw and more difficult to peel when cooked because the roots become limp and the skins stick. You may opt for plastic gloves when peeling to avoid a temporary brown stain from the peels.

To avoid discoloration, keep peeled and cut pieces in water with a little lemon juice or vinegar added. Look for crops from California from late September through June.

Select firm, blemish-free roots.

Store loosely wrapped in the refrigerator for up to a week.

SALSIFY WITH CREAM

This is one of the simplest yet most satisfying ways to enjoy salsify.

Preparation time: 10 minutes
Microwave time: 6 minutes
Servings: 4

1 pound salsify
¼ cup water
1 tablespoon fresh lemon juice
2 tablespoons butter
¼ teaspoon salt
⅛ teaspoon freshly ground
  pepper
¼ cup cream

1. Peel salsify roots. Trim away ends. Julienne roots.
2. Put julienned salsify, water, and lemon juice in 1-quart casserole. Cover. MICROWAVE (high) 4 minutes, until still a bit crisp, stirring twice. Drain.
3. Stir in butter. Stir in salt, pepper, and cream. MICROWAVE (high), uncovered, 2 minutes, until cream thickens and salsify is just tender. Serve.

TIP: *Put peeled salsify in a bowl of water with 1 tablespoon lemon juice to keep its fine white color.*

TIP: *Note that the salsify is still undercooked by the end of step 2. It finishes cooking with the cream.*

SALSIFY VINAIGRETTE

Serve these alone or as an unusual addition to a cold salad plate.

Preparation time: 10 minutes
Microwave time: 6 minutes
Servings: 4

1 pound salsify, peeled, trimmed and julienned
¼ cup water
1 tablespoon fresh lemon juice
1 teaspoon minced garlic
6 tablespoons vegetable oil
2 tablespoons fresh lemon juice
¼ teaspoon salt
⅛ teaspoon freshly ground pepper

1. Put salsify, water, and lemon juice in 1-quart casserole. Cover. MICROWAVE (high) 4–5 minutes, until just tender, stirring once. Let stand, covered, 2 minutes. Drain.
2. In 4-cup measure, whisk remaining ingredients. MICROWAVE (high) 1 minute to soften garlic and blend flavors. Whisk again. Pour dressing over salsify while still warm. Toss. Serve slightly warm or refrigerate, covered, and serve chilled.

SALSIFY PUREE

Salsify and a little Swiss cheese make a fine puree. The salsify needs to be cooked until quite tender to avoid a grainy puree.

Preparation time: 20 minutes
Microwave time: 9 minutes
Servings: 4

1 pound salsify, peeled and chopped
¼ cup water
1 tablespoon fresh lemon juice
2 tablespoons butter
¼ cup cream
¼ cup grated Swiss cheese
¼ teaspoon salt
⅛ teaspoon freshly ground pepper

1. Put salsify, water, and lemon juice in 1-quart casserole. Cover. MICROWAVE (high) 7–9 minutes, until quite tender. Let stand, covered, 2 minutes. Drain.
2. Puree salsify in blender or processor. Stir in butter, then cream. Stir in cheese, salt, and pepper. If the salsify is still warm, the cheese will melt. To reheat puree, MICROWAVE (high) 2 minutes.

SALSIFY AND OYSTER FLORENTINE

I devised this unusual and attractive dish of salsify and oysters cooked in nutmeg-enhanced cream and served on a bed of spinach to test the theory that salsify tastes like oysters. (I don't think it does, but invite some friends over for your own taste testing.)

Preparation time: 25 minutes
Microwave time: 20 minutes
Servings: 4

2 pounds fresh spinach *or* 2 10-ounce boxes frozen
¼ cup minced onion
4 tablespoons butter
1 pound salsify, peeled, trimmed and cut into 2-inch julienne strips
2 tablespoons flour
¼ teaspoon ground nutmeg
¼ teaspoon salt
⅛ teaspoon freshly ground white pepper
½ cup cream
1 pint oysters, drained, liquid reserved
2 tablespoons minced fresh parsley

1. Wash fresh spinach well. Trim stems. Put spinach in 3-quart casserole. (The water that clings to leaves after cleaning is enough to cook the spinach.) Cover. MICROWAVE (high) 7–8 minutes, until tender, stirring after 3 minutes. Drain. Chop. Reserve.
2. Put onion and butter in 2-quart casserole. MICROWAVE (high) 2 minutes, until tender, stirring once. Stir in salsify and coat well with butter. Cover. MICROWAVE (high) 4–5 minutes, until just tender.
3. Blend in flour, nutmeg, salt, and pepper. Stir in cream, oysters, and 1 tablespoon of oyster broth. Cover with plastic wrap, turned back at one corner to create a vent. MICROWAVE (high) 3–5 minutes, until oysters curl around the edges, stirring every minute.
4. Arrange spinach on serving platter. Reheat if necessary. Use slotted spoon to lift out salsify and arrange in spokelike fashion on spinach. Lift out oysters and place a few among the salsify and the rest in the middle of spoke design. Drizzle a little sauce over salsify and serve rest of sauce in a gravy bowl. Sprinkle dish with parsley. Serve.

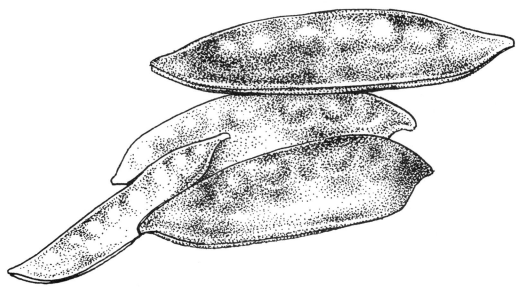

S N O W   P E A S

Snow peas are among the more exciting vegetables to jump from exotic to fairly common status in fresh produce departments.

Many of us discovered the edible pods at Chinese restaurants where drinks came with paper parasols and *moo goo gai pan* starred these flat little peas that you eat pods and all. More recently, nouvelle cuisine and California cooking movements, heavily influenced by Japanese cooking, adopted colorful, crisp snow peas. Growers took the hint to heart—and to stock.

Snow peas may seem expensive per pound. However, you need only a half pound to feed four royally.

Sugar peas, which look like common English peas, are another variety of completely edible pod. These are not yet readily available in American markets but are very easy to grow in your garden. Because they are larger than the flat snow peas, they take just a little longer in the microwave.

It takes a couple of minutes to pull the threads off the tops, and preferably also off the bottoms if you are using sugar peas. The effort is worth it. Start to pull the top thread from the blossom end and the bottom thread from the tip end.

Take care not to overcook snow peas. To preserve their crisp texture, I use no water and microwave them for just 2 minutes. Add them at the end of most recipes.

Select crisp, smooth snow pods with tiny flat seeds and a medium green color. (The pods darken to more familiar dark green when cooked.) Avoid yellowed or limp pods.

Store wrapped in plastic in the refrigerator for up to three days.

TOASTED SESAME SEED SNOW PEAS

A few shakes of sesame oil add wonderful flavor and a pretty sheen to fresh snow peas. Note that to keep pods as crisp as possible no liquid is used to microwave them. Serve as a side dish or gracefully arrange them around a fish or meat entree.

Preparation time: 5 minutes
Microwave time: 5 minutes
Servings: 4

1 tablespoon sesame seeds
8 ounces fresh snow peas
½ teaspoon sesame oil

1. Put seeds in a 1-cup measure. MICROWAVE (high) 3 minutes to toast.
2. Meanwhile, cut off ends of snow peas and remove upper and lower threads as needed. Put pods on dish or pie plate. Cover. MICROWAVE (high) 2 minutes, until warmed through but still crunchy. Toss with oil. Sprinkle with seeds.

TIP: *Use the same microwave technique to toast or revive slightly old nuts in other recipes. Put nuts in a measuring cup and MICROWAVE (high) 3 minutes.*

GRASS SOUP

One of my earliest chores was to pick the "grass" that my older sisters would mysteriously make into soup for lunch. To this day, I don't know where they hid my selected greenery. But I offer these finely sliced snow peas as an ultimately finer choice to enliven a simple bowl of chicken soup.

Preparation time: 15 minutes
Microwave time: 21 minutes
Servings: 4

2 boneless skinned chicken breasts
1 tablespoon fresh lemon juice
4 cups chicken broth or stock
1 cup cooked rice
¼ pound snow peas, ends trimmed, top and bottom threads removed, sliced lengthwise into very thin slivers

1. Put chicken breasts in 2-quart casserole. Sprinkle with lemon juice. Cover. MICROWAVE (high) 6–8 minutes, until meat turns from pink to white, turning over after 3 minutes. Leaving broth in casserole, remove chicken. Dice. (One cup cooked, diced chicken may be substituted for this step.)

2. Add 4 cups chicken broth and rice to casserole. Cover. MICROWAVE (high) 9–11 minutes, until boiling. Add chicken. Cover again and MICROWAVE (high) 2 minutes to return to boiling. Add pea pods. Let stand, covered, 1 minute, to slightly soften pods but keep that fresh "grassy" flavor.

SNOW PEAS AND MUSHROOM SALAD

Quickly cooked snow peas and mushrooms taste fine warm and also make a fine cold salad. They are topped here with a creamy, anchovy-spiked dressing that tastes best after resting at room temperature for a half hour.

Preparation time: 20 minutes
Microwave time: 4 minutes
Servings: 2–4

½ **pound fresh mushrooms, washed and cut into ¼-inch slices**
2 **tablespoons water**
¼ **pound fresh snow peas, ends trimmed, top and bottom threads removed**
½ **teaspoon minced garlic**
2 **anchovy fillets**
1 **green onion, white and first 2 inches of green, sliced**
2 **tablespoons minced fresh parsley**
1 **tablespoon wine vinegar**
¼ **cup sour cream**
½ **cup mayonnaise**

1. Put mushrooms and water in 2-quart casserole. Cover. MICROWAVE (high) 2 minutes, until mushrooms start to let out juices. Stir in snow peas. Cover. MICROWAVE (high) 1½ minutes, stirring once. Drain. Chill, covered, in refrigerator for an hour.

2. To make dressing, mash garlic, anchovies, onion, parsley, and vinegar in small bowl. Blend in sour cream and mayonnaise. Let stand at room temperature for a half hour to develop flavor. Or make ahead, chill covered in the refrigerator, and remove a half hour before serving to reach room temperature.

SNOW PEAS WITH SHRIMP AND CASHEWS

Juicy, succulent shrimp and colorful snow peas make a favorite combination in this Chinese dish, adapted for the microwave.

Preparation time: 10 minutes
Microwave time: 11 minutes
Servings: 4

1 medium onion, sliced
1 teaspoon freshly grated ginger *or* **½ teaspoon dried ground**
3 tablespoons vegetable oil
1 pound large fresh or defrosted frozen shrimp, cleaned, peeled, and patted dry
½ pound fresh snow peas, top and bottom threads removed
1 tablespoon cornstarch
⅓ cup cold water
2 tablespoons soy sauce
1 tablespoon sherry
2½ ounces salted cashews (about ⅔ cup)

1. Mix onion, ginger, and oil in 3-quart casserole. Cover. MICROWAVE (high) 2–3 minutes until onion is just crisp, stirring once.
2. Stir in shrimp. Cover with plastic wrap. Turn back a corner to form vent. MICROWAVE (high) 1–2 minutes, stirring once. Add snow peas. MICROWAVE (high) 1 minute, until shrimp start to turn pink and peas just start to soften. Set aside, loosely covered.
3. Blend cornstarch, water, soy sauce, and sherry in 2-cup measure until dissolved and smooth. MICROWAVE (high) 1–2 minutes, stirring twice, until mixture starts to thicken.
4. Add cornstarch mixture and cashews to shrimp. MICROWAVE (high) 2–3 minutes to thicken slightly. The sauce still will be thin enough to pour over rice or noodles.

TIP: *Shrimp are tricky. In less than a minute they zap from succulent to tough and dry. This recipe works with large shrimp that have been patted dry. If using smaller shrimp, cut back microwave time by at least a minute.*

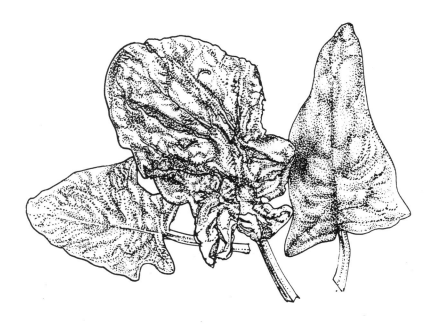

SPINACH

Being far too young, I never had the shock of opening a fresh copy of the December 8, 1928, *New Yorker* magazine to find what is touted to be the most famous cartoon about spinach.

In the cartoon, a well-meaning mother faces her young son and says: "It's broccoli, dear." The disgruntled youngster returns: "I say it's spinach, and I say the hell with it."

I say, what are they talking about?

Fresh, young spinach has a delightful, delicate flavor and cooks to a comforting texture. Plus, it boasts plenty of vitamins A and C, iron, and potassium, all at a mere 23 calories per 3½-ounce serving.

Granted, spinach can deliver a bitter aftertaste. This comes from tannins, chemical compounds that cause astringency. The problem may occur in overmature or poorly stored spinach. The solution is to select fresh, young spinach and eat it soon.

Or use frozen spinach. The taste and texture of frozen spinach is just fine for many cooked dishes. And studies have shown that frozen spinach can be superior nutritionally to fresh spinach that has been stored too long or stored improperly.

Groceries tend to carry crinkly, savoy-type spinach. I prefer this type in salads because its curly shape looks pretty and provides good nooks for salad dressing. The straighter variety, however, is easier to clean and more tender.

Select small-leafed greens with good green color. Avoid wilted leaves. If bagged, make sure spinach is not dry or slimy.

Store loosely wrapped in the refrigerator for two or three days.

SESAME SPINACH

Fast and tasty, this is one of our favorite ways to enjoy fresh spinach.

Preparation time: 10 minutes
Microwave time: 8 minutes
Servings: 4

1½ **pounds fresh spinach,**
  washed, stems trimmed
  4 **tablespoons soy sauce**
  2 **tablespoons sesame seeds**

1. Put spinach in 3-quart casserole. Cover. MICROWAVE (high) 7–8 minutes until tender, stirring after 3 minutes. Drain.
2. Put spinach in serving bowl. Chop if desired (see Tips). Mix in soy sauce and sesame seeds. Serve.

TIP: To wash fresh spinach, swirl in sink of cool water. Lift out spinach. Drain water. Repeat.

TIP: It is faster and easier to chop spinach after it is cooked, right in the bowl. Use two dinner knives, one in each hand, and cut in opposite directions as if rubbing shortening to make pie pastry.

CREAMED SPINACH AND MUSHROOMS

Fresh sour cream and a bit of leftover blue cheese turn staple products like frozen spinach and a can of mushrooms into a delightful side dish. Serve with a handsome ham roast or cornish hens.

Preparation time: 10 minutes
Microwave time: 14 minutes
Servings: 4

  2 **10-ounce packages frozen**
  chopped spinach
  ¾ **cup sour cream**
  2 **tablespoons crumbled blue**
  cheese
  ⅛ **teaspoon freshly ground white**
  pepper
  1 **4-ounce can sliced mushrooms,**
  drained

1. Put unwrapped spinach in 2-quart casserole. Cover. MICROWAVE (high) 8 minutes, breaking up spinach after 4 minutes. Drain well.
2. Put sour cream, blue cheese, and pepper in 2-quart casserole. Stir until smooth. Stir in spinach and mushrooms.
3. Cover. MICROWAVE (high) 2 minutes. Stir. Cover. MICROWAVE (medium-high) 2–4 minutes, stirring once to blend.

WILTED SPINACH SALAD

Classic spinach salad is ready even faster in the microwave because of the ease in cooking bacon.

Preparation time: 20 minutes
Microwave time: 11 minutes
Servings: 4–6

½ **pound (about 10 slices) bacon, cut into 1-inch slices**
5 **tablespoons white wine vinegar**
½ **teaspoon sugar**
1 **tablespoon Dijon mustard**
½ **pound fresh mushrooms, sliced thin**
10 **ounces fresh spinach, cleaned, stems trimmed, torn into bite-sized pieces, patted dry**
1 **cup croutons (see "Chayote" chapter)**

1. Put bacon in 4-cup measure. MICROWAVE (high) 8–10 minutes, uncovered, until crisp. Remove bacon with slotted spoon, leaving fat in measure. Place bacon between paper towels to dry.
2. Whisk vinegar, sugar, and mustard with bacon fat in measure. MICROWAVE (high) 30 seconds to heat. Whisk.
3. In large serving bowl, toss mushrooms, spinach, crumbled bacon bits, and all but 1 tablespoon of dressing.
4. Add croutons to measure with the last tablespoon of dressing. Toss to soften croutons slightly. Add to top of salad. Serve.

QUICK SPINACH WITH GARLIC AND OLIVE OIL

Frozen spinach is a fine product, but it tastes even better with a little help. The garlic tastes nice and light the first night, but grows stronger in leftovers.

Preparation time: 10 minutes
Microwave time: 12 minutes
Servings: 4

2 **10-ounce packages frozen chopped spinach**
2 **tablespoons olive oil**
1 **teaspoon minced garlic**
¼ **teaspoon salt**

1. Put unwrapped spinach in 2-quart casserole. Cover. MICROWAVE (high) 8 minutes, breaking up spinach after 4 minutes. Drain well.
2. Put olive oil and garlic in 2-quart casserole. MICROWAVE (high) 2 minutes, stirring once. Mix in spinach. Cover. MICROWAVE (high) 2 minutes, until heated through. Mix in salt. Serve.

SPINACH LASAGNA

There's no need to precook noodles for this dish. The quick-cooking microwave and preheated sauce do the trick.

Preparation time: 30 minutes
Microwave time: 45 minutes
Servings: 6–8

½ cup chopped onion
1 tablespoon olive oil
4 cups homemade Tomato Sauce (see index)
2 cups (16 ounces) ricotta cheese
½ cup grated Parmesan cheese
1 egg
2 tablespoons fresh oregano *or* 1 teaspoon dried
8 uncooked lasagna noodles
3 10-ounce packages frozen chopped spinach, defrosted and drained
2 cups shredded mozzarella cheese

1. Put onion and olive oil in 1½-quart casserole. MICROWAVE (high) 1–2 minutes, until just tender. Add Tomato Sauce. Cover. MICROWAVE (high) 4–5 minutes, until boiling.
2. In a bowl, blend ricotta cheese, half (¼ cup) of the Parmesan cheese, egg, and oregano.
3. Spread 1 cup sauce on bottom of 11″ × 8″ × 2″ baking dish. Overlap 4 uncooked noodles over sauce. Spread on in order: 1 cup ricotta cheese mixture, all of spinach, 1 cup mozzarella cheese.
4. Spread on in order: 2 cups sauce, 4 overlapping uncooked noodles, remaining ricotta cheese mixture, remaining sauce.
5. Cover. MICROWAVE (high) 10 minutes. Rotate dish a half turn. MICROWAVE (medium) 22–28 minutes, until noodles are tender. Let stand, covered, 10 minutes. Top with remaining mozzarella and Parmesan cheeses. Serve.

TIP: A 15½-ounce jar of prepared spaghetti sauce and one 8-ounce can tomato sauce may be substituted for the 4 cups of homemade Tomato Sauce.

TIP: Note that the final cheese topping is added after the dish has been standing. The large casserole holds so much heat that the cheese melts attractively just in time for dinner.

TIP: Since grating the cheese and layering the lasagna take a bit of time, it is wise to set the spinach from the freezer into the refrigerator to defrost the night before.

CHICKEN BREASTS WITH SPINACH AND RICE

A spinach and sour cream mixture is added atop chicken breasts to give the chicken color and let it absorb flavor. Serve with extra rice, ripe tomato slices, and a salad.

Preparation time: 20 minutes
Microwave time: 23 minutes
Servings: 4–6

1 **pound fresh spinach, washed, stems trimmed**
2 **tablespoons butter**
2–4 **green onions, white portion and first 2 inches of green, sliced**
1 **cup cooked rice**
¾ **cup sour cream**
⅓ **cup pine nuts**
¼ **teaspoon salt**
⅛ **teaspoon freshly ground pepper**
4 **boneless whole chicken breasts (8 halves), skinned**

1. Put spinach in 3-quart casserole. Cover. MICROWAVE (high) 5–8 minutes until tender, stirring after 3 minutes. Drain. Chop.
2. Put butter and green onions in 2-quart casserole. MICROWAVE (high) 2–3 minutes, until tender. Mix in spinach, rice, sour cream, pine nuts, salt, and pepper.
3. Put chicken, smooth side up, in 2-quart rectangular casserole or around edges of pie plate, with thicker portions toward the outside. If necessary, put smallest chicken piece in center and rotate it out later.
4. Top each piece with spinach mixture. Cover with waxed paper. MICROWAVE (high) 12–14 minutes, rotating casserole a half turn after 6 minutes. Let stand, covered, 3 minutes.

TIP: One 10-ounce package frozen chopped spinach may be substituted. Put unwrapped spinach in 2-quart casserole. Cover. MICROWAVE (high) 5 minutes. Drain thoroughly, pressing to remove excess moisture.

TIP: Wild rice, or a wild rice and white rice mixture, may be substituted for the white rice.

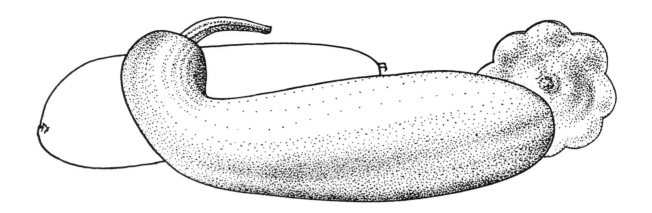

SQUASH, SUMMER

Twenty years ago, restaurants wouldn't dare serve steak accompanied by yellow crookneck or squat pattypan squash. Peas and carrots, or nice green beans, please.

Today, however, squash are in. Tiny yellow squash, one of the most popular mini-vegetables, appear flower and all adorning *au courant* entrees. Little pattypans—as cute as their name—sit nearby. The craze for mini-squashes has sparked a general interest in squash, which can be enjoyed at home with fresh herbs and other summer produce.

Delicate straightneck or crookneck yellow squash and light green or cream-colored pattypans, also called *custard marrow*, are available all year but are more plentiful in summer. Eat them skin, seeds, and all. They have so much natural moisture that little water is needed to cook them in the microwave.

Zucchini is technically a summer squash, but because it is so popular, it gets its own chapter in this book.

Select firm, unblemished squash that are heavy for their size. Smaller ones tend to be sweeter and more tender.

Store loosely wrapped in the refrigerator and use as soon as possible.

YELLOW SQUASH WITH ROSEMARY

Rosemary gives a pleasant, hearty touch to delicate yellow squash. Be sure to crush the herb between your fingers to bring out the flavor.

Preparation time: 5 minutes
Microwave time: 6 minutes
Servings: 4–6

1½ **pounds unpeeled fresh yellow squash, cut into ½-inch slices**
1 **tablespoon butter**
½ **teaspoon dried rosemary, crushed**

Put squash in 2-quart casserole. Cover with waxed paper. MICROWAVE (high) 4–6 minutes, until just tender, stirring after 2 minutes. Drain. Mix in butter and rosemary. Serve warm.

TIP: Soft summer squash has so much water that there's no need to add extra liquid when microwaving. Cook the squash plain to save nutrients. Waxed paper, instead of plastic wrap, leaves the squash crisp.

YELLOW SQUASH WITH CAPERS

Olive oil and capers give a Mediterranean twist to common yellow squash.

Preparation time: 5 minutes
Microwave time: 6 minutes
Servings: 4–6

1½ **pounds unpeeled yellow squash, cut into ½-inch slices**
3 **tablespoons olive oil**
1 **tablespoon fresh lemon juice**
2 **tablespoons drained capers**
3 **tablespoons minced red onion**

1. Put squash in 2-quart casserole. Cover with waxed paper. MICROWAVE (high) 4–6 minutes, until almost tender, stirring after 2 minutes. Drain.
2. In 2-cup measure, whisk olive oil and lemon juice. Stir in capers and red onions. Toss squash with dressing. Serve warm.

MUSHROOM-STUFFED PATTYPANS

Tender, young pattypans are easy to carve and hold up well for stuffing. Filled with mushrooms, they make an unusual appetizer as well as side dish.

Preparation time: 15 minutes
Microwave time: 14 minutes
Servings: 4

4 medium mature pattypan squash
1 cup chopped fresh mushrooms
½ cup chopped onion
2 tablespoons butter
2 tablespoons fine bread crumbs
2 tablespoons grated cheddar cheese

1. Slice off tops of pattypans. Trim away and discard stem and skin from tops. Chop remaining flesh from tops. Scoop out centers, leaving ¼-inch shell. Discard seeds and stringy center. Chop remaining firm flesh from center.
2. Put mushrooms, onion, and butter in 1-quart casserole. MICROWAVE (high), uncovered, 3–4 minutes, until vegetables are tender. Stir in chopped squash. MICROWAVE 3–4 minutes, until tender. Stir in bread crumbs. Fill pattypan shells with mixture.
3. Put filled squash in 2-quart rectangular casserole, at least 1 inch apart. Cover. MICROWAVE (high) 8–10 minutes, until tender, rotating once. Let stand, covered, 5 minutes. Sprinkle with cheese. Serve.

TIP: *Use a melon baller to scoop out the squash.*

SUMMER SQUASH AND AVOCADO SALAD

Looks are deceiving, for this truly lovely salad is very easy to make.

Preparation time: 10 minutes
Microwave time: 6 minutes
Chilling time: 2 hours
Servings: 4–6

1½ **pounds unpeeled fresh crookneck or straight yellow squash, cut into ¼-inch slices**
5 **tablespoons vegetable oil**
2 **tablespoons fresh lemon juice**
1 **tablespoon minced fresh basil** *or* ½ **teaspoon dried**
¼ **teaspoon salt**
⅛ **teaspoon freshly ground pepper**
1 **medium avocado, peeled and cut into ½-inch-thick slices**
3 **⅛-inch-thick slices red onion**

1. Put squash in 2-quart casserole. Cover with waxed paper. MICROWAVE (high) 4–6 minutes, until squash is tender, stirring after 2 minutes. Drain.
2. In 2-cup measure, whisk oil and lemon juice. Stir in basil, salt, and pepper.
3. On serving plate, arrange alternating, overlapping rows of squash and avocado. Separate onion rings and arrange attractively on top. Pour dressing over. Cover with plastic wrap. Refrigerate 2 hours. Serve.

TUNA-STUFFED SUMMER SQUASH

A tuna casserole in an edible container.

Preparation time: 20 minutes
Microwave time: 16 minutes
Servings: 4

**4 straightneck yellow squash,
6–8 inches long**
1 6½-ounce can tuna, drained
½ cup bread crumbs
½ cup cream
**2 green onions, white and first 2
inches of green, sliced**
**¼ teaspoon freshly ground
pepper**
2 tablespoons chopped pimiento
½ cup walnuts

1. Carve out center of each squash, leaving sides high, somewhat like a canoe. Dice inside flesh and reserve, with seeds.
2. Put diced flesh and seeds (about 1½ cups) in 2-quart casserole. Cover. MICROWAVE (high) 5–7 minutes, until soft. Drain.
3. Mix in tuna until well blended. Stir in bread crumbs, cream, green onions, pepper, pimiento, and half (¼ cup) of the walnuts.
4. Fill shells with tuna mixture. Place in rectangular 2-quart casserole, at least 1 inch apart. Cover with waxed paper. MICROWAVE (high) 7–9 minutes, until shells are tender. Top with remaining walnuts. Serve.

TIP: *The amount of cooked centers, bread crumbs, and cream will vary depending on the size squash selected. Just keep this ratio: 3 parts centers to 1 part bread crumbs and 1 part cream (for example, 1½ cups centers, ½ cup bread crumbs, and ½ cup cream).*

TIP: *Skins on summer squash are soft, so they don't need precooking before stuffing.*

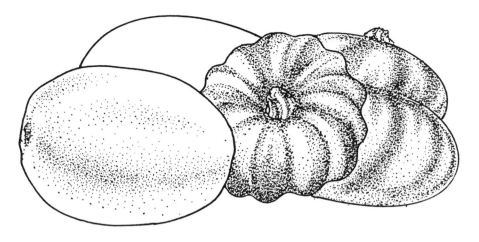

SQUASH, WINTER

I have a theory that the microwave oven was invented by a frustrated cook impatiently drumming her fingers on a hard-shelled acorn squash. "There has to be a better way than 1½ hours in a 375-degree oven," muttered the cook, a former X-ray technician fired from her post for dreaming while the machines were zapping. The rest, as they say, is culinary history.

With a microwave, there are no more excuses for not enjoying acorn, hubbard, spaghetti, turban, butternut, and calabaza squashes as often as you need a jolt of vitamin A from these valuable yellow vegetables. Fifteen minutes is all it takes. (Note that whole squash are pierced before microwaving to allow steam to escape.)

Winter squash is a misnomer, for these hard-shelled varieties are available all year, although the peak season is October through December.

Try traditional acorn squash slathered with honey, remarkable spaghetti squash touched with basil for a pasta look-alike, or sausage-squash pie, a handy vehicle for leftover squash and thus the most useful recipe here.

A warning: Cookbooks—including this one—call for scarce, 1-pound squash. The best theory is that these compact squash are grown by a farmer of great precision, dutifully delivered to grocery shelves but snatched at six in the morning by ardent squash lovers. The rest of us are left with large squash and a lot of leftovers. Or so it seems.

Select firm, unblemished squash that are heavy for their size.

Store in a dry, well-ventilated area at a cool room temperature for up to a month. Do not refrigerate whole squash, or they will suffer chilling injury. Wrap cut pieces in plastic and store in the refrigerator up to three days.

HONEY ACORN SQUASH

Baked squash, which takes more than an hour in a conventional oven, needs only 15 minutes in the microwave. Be sure to let it stand for 5 minutes to finish cooking—it will be too hot to handle anyway!

Preparation time: 5 minutes
Microwave time: 15 minutes
Servings: 4

2 acorn squash, 1 pound each
2 tablespoons butter
2 teaspoons honey

1. Use fork to pierce ¼-inch-deep holes on all sides of squash. Place squash on paper towels on bottom of microwave. MICROWAVE (high) 12–15 minutes, until skin starts to soften, rotating one-quarter turn and turning over every 4 minutes. Let stand 5–10 minutes.
2. Cut squash in half. Remove seeds and save for toasting. Drop ½ tablespoon butter in cavity of each squash. Drizzle edges with honey. Serve hot in the half shell.

TIP: See "Pumpkins" chapter for recipe for toasting seeds.

SAUSAGE-SQUASH PIE

Spices and salt from the sausage drain right into the squash, so there's no need for seasoning beyond an attractive sprinkle of oregano.

Preparation time: 10 minutes
Microwave time: 9 minutes
Servings: 4

2 cups mashed cooked squash
⅓ pound mild Italian sausage
⅛ teaspoon dried oregano

1. Pack the squash on the bottom and up the sides of a 9-inch pie plate. Spread a thin ring of sausage over the squash on the bottom. (Don't put sausage in the very center. This eliminates uneven cooking problems.) Cover with waxed paper.
2. MICROWAVE (high) 7–9 minutes or until the sausage is no longer pink on the inside, rotating the plate every 2 minutes. Sprinkle with oregano. Serve.

PECAN AND ORANGE-BUTTER SQUASH

This southern touch nicely sweetens hubbard squash.

Preparation time: 10 minutes
Microwave time: 17 minutes
Servings: 4–6

**1 1-pound hubbard or other
winter squash**
3 tablespoons butter
2 tablespoons orange juice
¼ cup chopped pecans

1. Cut squash in half lengthwise. Remove seeds. Cut into ½-inch slices.
2. Put squash in 2-quart casserole. Cover. MICROWAVE (high) 10–15 minutes, until just tender, stirring every 3 minutes. Let stand, covered, 5 minutes.
3. Put butter, orange juice, and pecans in 2-cup measure. MICROWAVE (high) 1–2 minutes to slightly soften nuts.
4. Arrange squash on serving platter. Pour pecans and orange-butter over. Serve.

TIP: Cook larger squash longer in the microwave. Keep checking at 2- and then 1-minute intervals until skin softens. Let stand 5–10 minutes.

TIP: Use the microwave to help cut hard winter squash. MICROWAVE (high) the whole squash 4–5 minutes, until the shell softens a bit for easier cutting. Slice and continue with recipe.

SPAGHETTI SQUASH WITH BASIL

A remarkable vegetable, it really does look like golden strands of spaghetti. Serve this warm or cold with crusty French bread.

Preparation time: 15 minutes
Microwave time: 18 minutes
Servings: 4–6

1 spaghetti squash, about 1 pound
¼ cup diced green pepper
¼ cup diced sweet red pepper
3 tablespoons olive oil
1 tablespoon wine vinegar
1 teaspoon minced garlic
¼ cup chopped onion
¼ cup chopped fresh basil

1. Use fork to pierce ¼-inch-deep holes on all sides of squash. Put squash on plate (for easier handling). MICROWAVE (high) 8–12 minutes, until skin is soft to touch, turning over and rotating one-quarter turn every 2 minutes. Let stand 5 minutes.
2. Mix green pepper, red pepper, oil, vinegar, garlic, and onion in 2½-quart rectangular casserole (large enough to hold squash later). MICROWAVE (high), uncovered, 2–3 minutes, until vegetables are tender, stirring twice.
3. Cut open squash. Remove seeds. Use fork to separate flesh into strands.
4. Add squash to casserole. Toss with other vegetables. Cover with waxed paper. MICROWAVE (high) 2–3 minutes until heated through. Add basil and toss again.

TIP: *The whole squash will squirt ferociously when almost done in the microwave. Be sure to use paper towels or a plate underneath.*

APPLE-CHUTNEY-STUFFED SQUASH

Sweet and pungent prepared chutney (Major Grey's is a good brand) and crisp Granny Smith apples team beautifully with naturally sweet squash. Try this with golden acorn squash, which tastes the same as other acorn squash but has a lovely deep yellow shell.

Preparation time: 10 minutes
Microwave time: 22 minutes
Servings: 4

2 1-pound acorn squash
1 tablespoon butter
2 medium Granny Smith apples, peeled, cored, and cubed
3 heaping tablespoons prepared chutney
¼ cup chopped walnuts

1. Use fork to pierce ¼-inch-deep holes on all sides of squash. Place squash on paper towels on bottom of microwave. MICROWAVE (high) 12–15 minutes, until skin starts to soften, rotating one-quarter turn and turning over every 4 minutes. Let stand 5–10 minutes.
2. Put butter and apples in 1-quart casserole. Cover. MICROWAVE (high) 3–4 minutes, until apples are just tender. Stir in chutney and walnuts.
3. Cut squash in half. Remove seeds and save for toasting. Spoon apple mixture into squash cavities. Cover with waxed paper. MICROWAVE (high) 1–3 minutes to warm through. Serve.

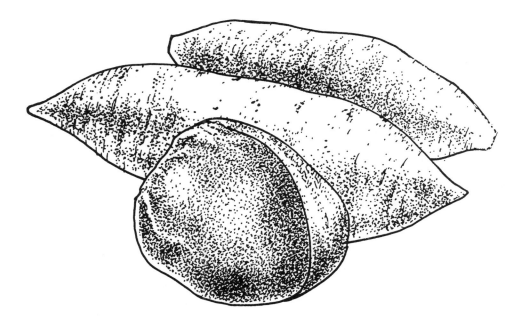

S W E E T   P O T A T O E S

Sweet potato or yam, as it is incorrectly called, is not closely related to the Irish potato but is a member of the morning glory family. In this country sweet potatoes may be either yellow and potatolike in texture or orange, sweet and dense in texture. This latter version, typically grown in the South, is called a yam, but it is not the starchy tuber the rest of the world calls a yam.

Regardless of its billing, a sweet potato's fine yellow or orange color broadcasts an excellent source of vitamin A. A medium sweet potato has about 160 calories. Look for the best supplies, and prices, in August, September, and October.

Microwave ovens are a major asset for those who love sweet potatoes. Four sweet potatoes, which would require 45 minutes in a conventional oven, are baked after less than 15 minutes in the microwave.

A sweet potato is one of the few vegetables that I prefer cooked to well done. When cooked, the sides of a whole sweet potato should feel as soft as the flesh between your thumb and forefinger. If still in doubt, pierce the sweet potato with a knife; if the knife doesn't glide through easily, continue cooking and check every minute.

Select firm, dry sweet potatoes of equal size for even cooking. Avoid those with wet spots or mold.

Store in a cool, dry, well-ventilated spot for up to three weeks. Do not refrigerate.

BAKED SWEET POTATOES WITH CINNAMON AND SUGAR

Here is a good, basic method for baking sweet potatoes in the microwave. The toppings are traditional: butter, cinnamon, and sugar.

Preparation time: 3 minutes
Microwave time: 14 minutes
Servings: 4

4 medium sweet potatoes, washed
4 tablespoons butter
1½ teaspoons sugar
¼ teaspoon ground cinnamon

1. Use fork to pierce sweet potatoes several times. Place in spokelike fashion on four corners of paper towel in microwave. MICROWAVE (high) 12–14 minutes, until sweet potatoes are soft when you give them a good squeeze, rotating paper towel one-quarter turn every 3 minutes. Let stand 5 minutes.
2. Slit open sweet potatoes. Put 1 tablespoon of butter in each to melt. Mix sugar and cinnamon in cup; sprinkle into potatoes.

TIP: The paper towel is a handy microwave device with baked white or sweet potatoes. You can grab the corners and turn all four potatoes at once. It also collects moisture from the potatoes.

TIP: One sweet potato needs about 5 minutes in the microwave; two sweet potatoes need 6 to 10. Standing time for both is 5 minutes. Four large sweet potatoes need up to 20 minutes in the microwave, plus the 5-minute standing time.

TIP: If cooking potatoes with differing sizes, start the larger potato cooking first.

TIP: If sweet potatoes are undercooked, return to microwave and check for tenderness every minute.

SWEET POTATOES AND APPLES

Tart Granny Smith apples pair well with sweet potatoes. Cook the sweet potatoes ahead of time for fast preparation.

Preparation time: 20 minutes
Microwave time: 12 minutes
Servings: 6–8

4 medium-sized sweet potatoes, cooked (see recipe for Baked Sweet Potatoes with Cinnamon and Sugar)
2 medium-sized, tart apples (Granny Smith are good), peeled, cored, and cut into ¼-inch rings
½ cup brown sugar
½ teaspoon ground cinnamon
¼ teaspoon ground nutmeg
½ cup chopped walnuts
4 tablespoons butter, melted

1. Peel potatoes. Cut into ½-inch slices. Arrange alternating and overlapping slices of sweet potatoes and apples in 2-quart rectangular casserole.
2. Combine sugar, cinnamon, nutmeg, and walnuts in small bowl. Sprinkle over sweet potatoes and apples. Drizzle with butter.
3. Cover with waxed paper. MICROWAVE (high) 10–12 minutes, rotating dish one-quarter turn after 5 minutes. Let stand, covered, 2 minutes.

QUICK SWEET POTATOES MARMALADE

A can of sweet potatoes, a jar of marmalade, and a fresh lemon can get you out of a dinner jam in a hurry. Lemon helps cut the sweetness.

Preparation time: 5 minutes
Microwave time: 7 minutes
Servings: 4

1 16-ounce can sweet potatoes, drained
2 tablespoons fresh lemon juice
¼ cup orange marmalade
Zest (grated yellow peel) from 1 1emon

1. Put sweet potatoes in 2-quart rectangular casserole. Drizzle with lemon juice. Spoon marmalade over sweet potatoes. Sprinkle with lemon zest.
2. Cover with waxed paper. MICROWAVE (high) 5–7 minutes, until warmed through.

SWEET POTATO AND TURKEY CURRY SALAD

This dish tastes best with freshly cooked sweet potatoes, but you can use leftover or canned sweet potatoes. Chicken can replace turkey.

Preparation time: 20 minutes
Microwave time: 14 minutes
Servings: 8

4 medium-sized sweet potatoes
¾ cup sour cream
¾ cup mayonnaise
1 tablespoon curry powder
2 green onions, green and first 2 inches of white, sliced
½ cup peanuts
2 cups cubed cooked turkey meat
Chopped fresh coriander (cilantro), for garnish

1. Use fork to pierce sweet potatoes several times. Place in spokelike fashion on four corners of paper towel in microwave. MICROWAVE (high) 12–14 minutes, until sweet potatoes are soft when you give them a good squeeze, rotating paper towel one-quarter turn every 3 minutes. Let stand 5 minutes to finish cooking and to cool enough to handle. Peel. Cube.

2. In 3-quart casserole, mix sour cream, mayonnaise, and curry powder. Stir in sweet potatoes, green onions, peanuts, and turkey. Refrigerate, covered, at least 2 hours. Garnish with coriander.

SWEET POTATO PUDDING GRAND MARNIER

This sweet, soft dessert pudding goes grown-up with a little orange-flavored liqueur.

Preparation time: 10 minutes
Microwave time: 8 minutes
Servings: 6–8

  3 eggs
1½ cups pureed cooked sweet
    potatoes
  2 tablespoons butter
1¼ cups half-and-half
  1 tablespoon Grand Marnier
  ¼ cup flour
  2 tablespoons sugar

1. Beat eggs in 3-quart bowl. Beat in sweet potatoes, then butter, half-and-half, and Grand Marnier. Whisk in flour and sugar.
2. Pour into 2-quart round casserole. Do not cover. MICROWAVE (medium-high) 6–8 minutes, until edges are set and center is a little soft but not sticky, rotating casserole every 2 minutes. Let stand 10 minutes to finish cooking.

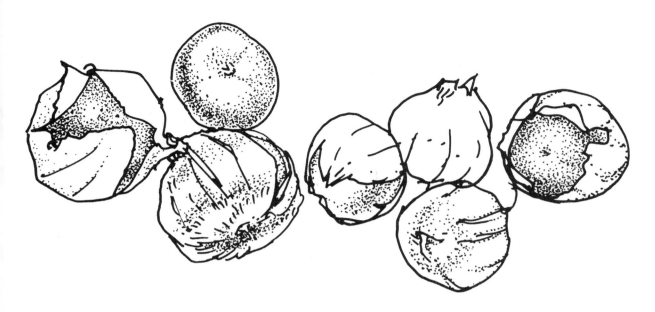

T O M A T I L L O S

Thanks to the still thriving interest in Mexican food, unusual little tomatillos (toe-mah-TEE-yos)—common in Spanish markets—are popping up in major urban groceries.

Though they resemble tomatoes, these small green spheres are not immature versions of everyday tomatoes but full-blown relatives of the Cape gooseberry and ground cherry family. As with ordinary tomatoes, tomatillos technically are fruit but are used in meals as vegetables.

Tomatillos, also called *husk tomatoes*, turn yellow when ripe, but most are sold and eaten green. Their firm texture and slightly tart flavor are the basis of excellent salsas. Or they can be cooked whole, like cherry tomatoes.

The paperlike husks are fun to remove, a pleasant hands-on chore that comes with preparing fresh vegetables.

Select firm, unblemished, shiny green tomatillos with crisp, dry husks.

Store loosely wrapped in the refrigerator for several weeks.

TOMATILLOS IN BUTTER

A little sugar tempers naturally tart tomatillos. Take care not to overcook tomatillos, as they are best with a still slightly firm texture.

Preparation time: 5 minutes
Microwave time: 3 minutes
Servings: 4

1 tablespoon butter 12 tomatillos, papery husks removed ½ teaspoon sugar	Put butter in 2-quart rectangular casserole. MICROWAVE (high) 1 minute to melt. Stir in tomatillos to coat. Do not cover. MICROWAVE (high) 2 minutes, until just tender. Stir in sugar. Let stand 1 minute. Serve.

TOMATILLO SALSA

Firm, tart tomatillos make a terrific-tasting green salsa. Take care not to overcook, or you will lose both texture and tartness. Serve as an appetizer with tortilla chips.

Preparation time: 15 minutes
Microwave time: 5 minutes
Servings: 2 cups

½ cup chopped onion 1 teaspoon minced garlic 1 tablespoon seeded, minced chili pepper 2 tablespoons vegetable oil 10–12 tomatillos, chopped fine 2 tablespoons chopped fresh coriander (cilantro), (optional)	1. Put onion, garlic, pepper, and oil in 2-quart casserole. MICROWAVE (high) 2 minutes to soften, stirring once. 2. Stir in tomatillos. Do not cover. MICROWAVE (high) 3 minutes, until tomatillos just start to release juice. Stir in coriander. Serve warm or at room temperature.

BACON-TOPPED TOMATILLOS

Tomatillos are cooked in bacon grease for extra flavor, then topped with the crumbled bacon. These are wonderful hot from the microwave, but because the fat clings, they don't fare as well for leftovers.

Preparation time: 5 minutes
Microwave time: 7 minutes
Servings: 4

3 strips bacon
8–12 tomatillos, husked and halved
Salt and pepper to taste

1. Put bacon in 2-quart rectangular casserole. Cover with waxed paper to prevent splattering. MICROWAVE (high) 4–5 minutes, until crisp. Remove bacon; leave fat in casserole.
2. Stir in tomatillos while bacon fat is still hot. (If necessary, first reheat fat on high.) Do not cover. MICROWAVE (high) 2 minutes, stirring every 30 seconds, until tomatillos are just tender.
3. Drain well. Add salt and pepper to taste. Top with crumbled bacon.

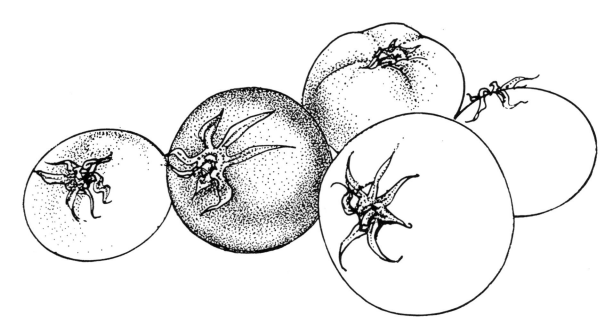

TOMATOES

Tomatoes are at the heart of so much of our cooking that it is difficult to imagine that they were once considered poisonous.

Technically a fruit, tomatoes run in the same family as belladonna or deadly nightshade, a well-respected poison. When explorers brought the native South American plant back to Europe in the 15th century, the populace was less than eager to devour the brilliant red tomato.

Now, of course, fresh tomatoes are a widely sought produce and a favorite garden crop. To satisfy our needs, new seeds seem to arrive each year for larger, earlier, pulpier, or juicier tomatoes. They come in three main types: round slicing tomatoes; pulpy plum tomatoes, excellent for making sauces; and little cherry tomatoes, ideal for salads. And tomatoes don't have to be red; varieties range from pink to deep red and even yellow.

Unfortunately, selections at the grocery are more limited. Most are picked while still green, so quality is impaired, even in summer.

If you don't grow your own, take the time to find a farmer's market in summer. In winter, plum tomatoes or even good-quality canned tomatoes are better than pale, mealy "fresh" ones.

When cooking tomatoes in a microwave, waxed paper often is used instead of plastic wrap so tomatoes cook evenly but don't get soggy.

Select firm, plump, red tomatoes. Avoid soft or bruised ones.

Store at room temperature until fully ripened, then refrigerate for up to three days.

TOMATOES WITH MOZZARELLA AND BASIL

This simple recipe is designed to showcase the best and freshest ingredients: garden-ripe tomatoes, fresh basil, extra-virgin olive oil, freshly ground pepper, and shredded high-quality mozzarella cheese. The dish tastes best when only moderately warm, so plan to let it stand a little before eating it.

Preparation time: 10 minutes
Microwave time: 4 minutes
Servings: 4

4 **tomatoes, cut into ½-inch slices**
3 **tablespoons roughly chopped fresh basil**
1 **tablespoon olive oil**
4 **grinds of fresh pepper**
⅓ **cup shredded mozzarella cheese**

Arrange overlapping tomato slices in 2-quart rectangular casserole. Sprinkle with basil, olive oil, and pepper. Cover with waxed paper. MICROWAVE (high) 3–4 minutes until tender, rotating dish once. Sprinkle with cheese. Let stand 2 minutes.

TIP: *Waxed paper is used with tomatoes instead of plastic wrap so that the tomatoes cook evenly but don't get soggy.*

CURRIED TOMATO HALVES

When summer tomatoes are at their prime, these jazzed-up halves disappear fast. Serve them warm with lamb chops and rice or cold in a vegetable platter.

Preparation time: 10 minutes
Microwave time: 6 minutes
Servings: 3–6

3 **tablespoons butter**
½ **cup minced onion**
1 **teaspoon curry powder**
1 **teaspoon sugar**
2 **tablespoons minced fresh parsley**
¼ **teaspoon salt**
3 **tomatoes, halved horizontally**

1. Put butter, onion, curry powder, sugar, parsley, and salt in 2-cup measure. MICROWAVE (high) 2 minutes, stirring once.
2. Place tomatoes along edge of 9-inch pie plate. Top evenly with curry mixture. Cover with waxed paper. MICROWAVE (high) 4 minutes, rotating once. Let stand 2 minutes. Serve.

TOMATO SAUCE

This basic tomato sauce works well over broiled fish or steamed green beans. For an Italian touch, add ½ teaspoon oregano.

Preparation time: 20 minutes
Microwave time: 16 minutes
Servings: 2 cups

2 pounds fresh, ripe plum tomatoes, peeled, seeded, and sliced, *or* 2 cups canned tomatoes with juice
½ cup chopped onion
1 teaspoon minced garlic
¼ cup olive oil
2 tablespoons chopped fresh basil *or* 1 teaspoon dried
½ teaspoon salt
⅛ teaspoon freshly ground pepper

Put all ingredients in 2-quart casserole. MICROWAVE (high), uncovered, 14–16 minutes, until sauce thickens, stirring twice.

TIP: *Very ripe, fresh summer tomatoes make the best sauce. If the only choice is pale winter tomatoes, opt instead for good-quality canned ones.*

TIP: *Resort to conventional methods to peel tomatoes: plunge a tomato into boiling water for 30 seconds, then into cold water, and peel. It takes too long to boil water for this purpose in the microwave.*

TOMATO-PORT SOUP

America's favorite cream of tomato soup goes upscale with a bit of sweet port or sherry. Note that there is no need to peel tomatoes for this recipe. Once the tomatoes are cooked until tender in the microwave, they make quite a smooth puree in the blender or food processor.

Preparation time: 20 minutes
Microwave time: 25 minutes
Servings: 3–4

4 ripe, medium tomatoes, seeded and chopped coarse
¼ cup chopped onion
1 bay leaf, broken in half
2 tablespoons butter
2 tablespoons flour
1 teaspoon salt
⅛ teaspoon freshly ground pepper
¼ teaspoon sugar
½ teaspoon dried thyme
1 cup milk
¼ cup port or sherry

1. Put tomatoes, onion, and bay leaf in 2-quart casserole. Cover. MICROWAVE (high) 14–16 minutes, until vegetables are very tender, stirring twice. Remove bay leaf. Puree in blender or food processor.

2. Put butter in 2-quart casserole. MICROWAVE (high) 45 seconds to 1 minute to melt. Blend in flour, salt, pepper, sugar, and thyme. Blend in milk. MICROWAVE (high) 4–5 minutes, until thickened, stirring every minute.

3. Slowly stir in tomato mixture. Stir in port or sherry. MICROWAVE (high), uncovered, 2–3 minutes to heat through. Serve with fresh croutons. (See "Chayote" chapter for croutons tip.)

TOMATOES STUFFED WITH CHEVRE

Chevre, or goat cheese, adds a distinctive touch to stuffed tomatoes. Basil is a natural companion, but you may substitute fresh parsley or cilantro.

Preparation time: 20 minutes
Microwave time: 5 minutes
Servings: 4

4 medium to large tomatoes
2 green onions, white portion and first 2 inches of green, sliced
2 tablespoons olive oil
2–3 cups fresh bread cubes
½ teaspoon salt
¼ teaspoon freshly ground pepper
4 tablespoons chopped fresh basil
3 ounces soft, mild chevre (Montrachet is a fine choice)

1. Slice ½ inch off the top of tomatoes. Remove core of flesh and seeds, leaving thick, meaty shell. Discard seeds; chop inner flesh and reserve. Set tomato shells upside down to drain.
2. Put onions and olive oil in 2-quart casserole. MICROWAVE (high) 1 minute to develop flavor. Lightly mix in ¼ cup of reserved, chopped tomato flesh, bread cubes, salt, pepper, basil, and chevre. Smell and taste mixture; adjust seasoning to taste.
3. Fill tomato shells with chevre mixture. Place in a circle on a plate or pie dish. Cover with waxed paper. MICROWAVE (medium) 3–4 minutes, until heated through, rotating plate once.

TIP: *The stuffed tomatoes are microwaved on medium to allow the filling to heat through before the shells get too soft.*

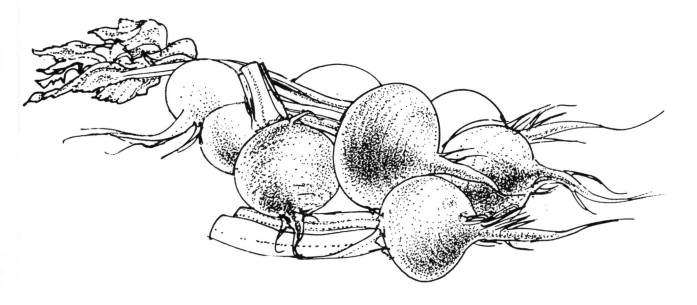

T U R N I P S

Old-fashioned turnips fit squarely into the eighties push for high-carbohydrate, low-fat food. Yet turnips are anything but dull.

Its pleasantly sharp, cabbagelike tang distinguishes this root vegetable and answers yet another modern call for highly flavored, even spicy foods.

Quietly mash turnips and potatoes together and smile as guests try to place the mystery taste. Microwave a turkey breast atop a pile of julienned turnips and watch the tasty strips get stolen before the plate hits the dinner table. The nippy taste of turnips can be addictive.

The most popular turnip has white flesh and purple tops. These peppery tops come as a bonus with a bunch of fresh turnips. And just to encourage you to use them, I start this chapter with a recipe for the tops.

Select small to medium turnips, 2 to 3 inches in diameter, that are hard, smooth, and heavy for their size. Avoid those with yellowed or wilted tops.

Store topped turnips as you would carrots, loosely wrapped in the refrigerator. Remove tops and store separately in the refrigerator, unwashed and loosely wrapped, up to a week.

TURNIP TOPS

Whenever you can, select fresh turnips with leaves still attached. The bonus batch of greens is high in iron and vitamins A and C and adds good color to other turnip dishes. Wash greens just before using by dunking and swirling in a water-filled sink. Lift up the greens, then let the water drain out so the soil won't slip back into the leaves.

Preparation time: 15 minutes
Microwave time: 14 minutes
Servings: 2

**Leafy tops from 3 pounds
   turnips**
1 tablespoon oil
½ teaspoon chopped garlic
2 tablespoons chopped onion
2 tablespoons vinegar
2 dashes Tabasco

1. Cut off and discard stems, tough ribs, and any yellowed leaves of turnip tops. Wash remaining leaves well. The water that clings will be enough to cook the leaves. Mat down on cutting board and cut into ½-inch strips.
2. Put oil, garlic, and onion in 3-quart casserole. MICROWAVE (high) 1–2 minutes, until tender.
3. Add greens. Cover. MICROWAVE (high) 10–12 minutes, until tender, stirring once. Drain. Mix in vinegar and Tabasco. Serve.

TIP: For more recipes for turnip tops, see "Greens" chapter.

TURNIPS IN BROTH

The pure taste of turnips is highlighted by a little chicken broth and a touch of lemon juice.

Preparation time: 10 minutes
Microwave time: 12 minutes
Servings: 4

1 tablespoon butter
1 tablespoon chopped onion
1½ pounds turnips, peeled, trimmed, and cut into ½-inch cubes
¼ cup chicken broth
1½ tablespoons fresh lemon juice
¼ teaspoon salt
⅛ teaspoon freshly ground pepper
1 tablespoon minced fresh parsley

1. Put butter and onion in 1-quart casserole. MICROWAVE (high) 1–2 minutes, until tender. Add turnips and broth. Cover. MICROWAVE (high) 8–10 minutes, until almost tender, stirring once. Let stand 2 minutes. Drain.

2. Stir in lemon juice, salt, and pepper. Sprinkle with parsley. Serve.

TURNIP SLICES WITH APPLES AND PECANS

Fall harvest apples, particularly tart Granny Smiths, team well with crisp turnips. Serve as a side dish with pork or duck.

Preparation time: 15 minutes
Microwave time: 14 minutes
Servings: 4

1 **pound turnips, trimmed, peeled, and sliced into ¼-inch circles**
¼ **cup water**
2 **medium Granny Smith apples, cored, peeled, and cut into ¼-inch slices**
¼ **teaspoon ground cinnamon**
½ **teaspoon sugar**
2 **tablespoons butter**
¼ **cup chopped pecans**

1. Put turnips and water in 2-quart casserole. Cover. MICROWAVE (high) 8–10 minutes, until almost tender, stirring every 3 minutes. Let stand 2 minutes. Drain.
2. Arrange half of apples (1 apple) on top of turnips. Sprinkle with half the cinnamon (⅛ teaspoon) and half the sugar (¼ teaspoon). Dot with half the butter (1 tablespoon). Repeat.
3. Cover with waxed paper. MICROWAVE (high) 3–4 minutes, until apples are tender, gently stirring once. Stir juices from bottom over top. Sprinkle with pecans. Serve.

TIP: If transferring to a serving plate, pour juices over top.

TURNIP AND POTATO PUREE

This smoothy disappears fast, often before guests inquire about the unusual flavor in the mashed potatoes. The proportion of turnips to potatoes is not critical. You can even add a third root vegetable such as parsnips or rutabagas.

Preparation time: 15 minutes
Microwave time: 12 minutes
Servings: 4

1 pound turnips, trimmed, peeled, and diced
1 pound white potatoes, peeled and diced
½ cup water
2 tablespoons butter
½ teaspoon dried thyme
¼ teaspoon salt
½ cup sour cream

1. Put turnips, potatoes, and water in 2-quart casserole. Cover. MICROWAVE (high) 10–12 minutes, until tender, stirring every 3 minutes. Let stand, covered, 2 minutes. Drain. Puree in blender or processor until smooth, taking care not to overprocess.
2. Stir in butter, thyme, salt, and sour cream.

TIP: To reheat, MICROWAVE (high), covered, 2–3 minutes, stirring every minute.

TIP: Pureed turnips and potatoes taste wonderful, even without the butter, sour cream, and herbs. Taste before you add the last four ingredients. You could skip them—and add the calories back at dessert.

APRICOT TURKEY BREAST ON A BED OF TURNIPS

When vegetables start stealing thunder from a roast, you have a winner. Turnips here absorb flavor from both the turkey juices and the apricot basting sauce, creating a rich accompaniment to the fowl. Best of all, the dish is ready in an hour.

Preparation time: 15 minutes
Microwave time: 1 hour
Servings: 6

½ **boneless turkey breast (3–4 pounds), skin on**
⅔ **cup apricot preserve**
¼ **cup apple juice**
1 **pound turnips, trimmed, peeled, and julienned**
1 **medium onion, sliced thin**

1. Put turkey breast skin side down in 2-quart casserole. Coat with half (⅓ cup) the apricot preserve. MICROWAVE (high), uncovered, 25 minutes, rotating casserole once.
2. Lift turkey onto a plate. Mix apple juice, turnips, and onion with juices in bottom of casserole. Return turkey to casserole, placing skin side up on top of turnips. Coat with remaining preserve.
3. MICROWAVE (high), uncovered, 5 minutes. Stir turnips. MICROWAVE (medium) 25–30 minutes or until temperature is 170°F and juices run clear, not pink. Let stand, covered with waxed paper, 10 minutes.

TIP: For a pretty presentation, arrange a can of drained apricot halves around the roast the last 5 minutes of cooking. Let stand as directed above.

W A T E R C R E S S

With its delicate, deep green leaves, watercress is among the most graceful of vegetables to present on dinner plates. And one of the easiest.

It is easy because, frankly, this pretty aquatic plant that thrives along edges of ponds and streams usually is eaten raw. Just rinse a bouquet of dark green watercress under the faucet, dry and crisp it in the refrigerator, then use it to garnish plates, enhance lettuce salads, or star—between slices of buttered, crustless bread—as a classic watercress sandwich.

Then, when you've eaten your fill (or what you can afford of this relatively expensive green), or just before highly perishable watercress starts to wilt and hint about calling it a day, cook up a batch.

Watercress retains its pleasant, peppery flavor when cooked and is a real treat with butter-soaked macadamia nuts. Team it with shallots, sherry, and cream in a cool summer soup or mix it with thyme, sour cream, and cognac to stuff chicken breasts.

Besides tasting good, watercress is high in vitamins A and C.

Select bright, fresh-looking leaves. Watercress usually is sold in small bunches. Avoid yellowed or wilted leaves.

Store loosely wrapped in the refrigerator, with the tie removed from the bundle. Since it is quite perishable, use as soon as possible.

WATERCRESS WITH MACADAMIA NUTS

Watercress is hardly cooked, just wilted slightly, and then drizzled with butter-soaked macadamia nuts.

Preparation time: 5 minutes
Microwave time: 4 minutes
Servings: 4

2 bunches (½ pound) watercress, washed, stems trimmed, leaves left whole

3 tablespoons butter

¼ cup chopped macadamia nuts

1. Put watercress in 2-quart casserole. Cover. MICROWAVE (high) 1–2 minutes, until just wilted. Drain. Arrange neatly on serving dish.
2. Put butter and nuts in 2-cup measure. MICROWAVE (high) 2 minutes, until softened, stirring once. Pour over watercress.

TIP: Wash watercress just before using and do not dry. The water that clings to the leaves will be enough to cook it in the microwave.

CREAM OF WATERCRESS SOUP

The peppery flavor of watercress is tempered with cream and a touch of lemon juice in this green-flecked soup. It tastes best after being chilled in the refrigerator.

Preparation time: 15 minutes
Microwave time: 17 minutes
Chilling time: 2 hours
Servings: 4

2 bunches (½ pound) watercress, washed, stems trimmed
1 tablespoon butter
2 tablespoons chopped shallots
2 tablespoons cream sherry
2 cups chicken broth
1 cup half-and-half
1 tablespoon fresh lemon juice
¼ teaspoon salt
⅛ teaspoon freshly ground pepper

1. Put watercress in 2-quart casserole. Cover. MICROWAVE (high) 3–4 minutes, until leaves are quite tender. Drain. Set aside.
2. Put butter and shallots in 2-quart casserole. MICROWAVE (high) 2 minutes, until tender. Stir in sherry. MICROWAVE (high) 1 minute, until mixture is thick. Stir in chicken broth. MICROWAVE (high) 6–7 minutes, until boiling.
3. Stir in reserved watercress. Puree in blender or food processor.
4. Stir in half-and-half, lemon juice, salt, and pepper. MICROWAVE (high) 2–3 minutes, until soup boils again. Taste and adjust seasoning, adding more lemon juice if soup seems bitter. Serve immediately or refrigerate, covered, for 2 hours and serve cold.

CHICKEN BREASTS STUFFED WITH WATERCRESS

The directions are long, but these elegant stuffed chicken breasts are not difficult to make. Serve with brown rice, Yellow Squash with Rosemary (see index), and fresh tomato slices.

Preparation time: 30 minutes
Microwave time: 13 minutes
Servings: 4

4 boneless, skinned chicken breast halves
2 large bunches watercress, stems discarded, leaves chopped (about 4 cups)
3 green onions, white and first 2 inches of green, sliced
1 tablespoon butter
1 tablespoon chopped fresh thyme plus 1 teaspoon for sauce, *or* ½ teaspoon dried thyme plus ¼ teaspoon for sauce
½ teaspoon salt
⅛ teaspoon freshly ground pepper
2 teaspoons cognac
¼ cup sour cream

1. Remove all fat from chicken breasts and cut away any pieces of membrane. Rinse and pat dry. Place between two pieces of waxed paper and use a veal pounder or side of a cleaver to pound each breast gently to flatten.
2. Put watercress, onions, and butter in 2-quart casserole. Cover. MICROWAVE (high) 4 minutes, until vegetables are tender, stirring after 1 minute. Stir in 1 tablespoon fresh or ½ teaspoon dried thyme, salt, and pepper. Taste and adjust seasonings, if desired.
3. Tilt casserole, squeeze watercress mixture, and let cooking juices collect at the bottom. Save the juices. Divide watercress mixture into four equal portions. Spread over four chicken breasts; roll chicken jelly roll fashion.
4. Arrange stuffed chicken breasts in spoke fashion on dish or pie plate. Cover with waxed paper. MICROWAVE (high) 5–7 minutes, until chicken turns from pink to white and is just firm to the touch, turning pieces after 3 minutes. Let stand 2 minutes; save juices. Cut each stuffed chicken breast into 1-inch slices and arrange attractively on serving dishes.
5. Pour cooking juices from chicken plus any wayward bits of watercress into 2-quart casserole that has cooking juices from the watercress. Stir in cognac. MICROWAVE (high) 1 minute. Stir in sour cream and 1 teaspoon fresh or ¼ teaspoon dried thyme. MICROWAVE (high) 30 seconds to heat, taking care not to boil sauce. Taste and adjust

seasoning if desired. Pour sauce over top of chicken breasts; avoid covering the pretty scroll-like watercress design.

TIP: Adding the wayward watercress to the sauce in the last step not only is economical but creates a pretty green-flecked sauce needed on the pale, microwaved chicken.

TIP: If a small strip of chicken comes loose from the main chicken breast, overlap and pound together.

TIP: A 10-ounce package frozen chopped spinach may be substituted for watercress.

SHRIMP ON BED OF WATERCRESS

Watercress holds its color well and serves as a pretty, leafy backdrop to ginger-sparked shrimp. Serve with rice.

Preparation time: 10 minutes
Microwave time: 12 minutes
Servings: 4

2 **bunches (½ pound) watercress, washed, stems trimmed, leaves left whole**
1 **medium onion, sliced into thin rings, separated**
1 **tablespoon vegetable oil**
2 **teaspoons freshly grated ginger**
1 **pound medium-sized fresh or defrosted frozen shrimp, cleaned**
1 **8-ounce can bamboo shoots, drained**

1. Put watercress in 2-quart casserole. Cover. MICROWAVE (high) 1–2 minutes, until just wilted. Drain.
2. Mix onion, vegetable oil, and ginger in 2-quart rectangular casserole. MICROWAVE (high) 2–3 minutes to soften, stirring once.
3. Stir in shrimp. Cover with plastic wrap. Turn back a corner to form vent. MICROWAVE (high) 2–4 minutes, until shrimp start to turn pink, stirring once. Stir in bamboo shoots. Let stand, covered, 2 minutes.
4. Arrange watercress on serving platter. Top with shrimp mixture. To reheat, cover with plastic wrap and turn back a corner to form a vent. MICROWAVE (medium) 2–3 minutes or until heated through.

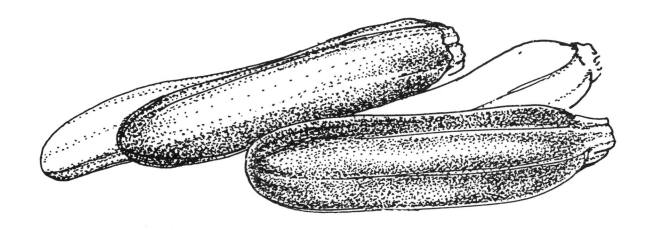

ZUCCHINI

As many jokes as recipes have been written about zucchini, the wonder squash that has conquered American gardens and groceries.

Twenty years ago, attractive green zucchini, or "little squash," was available only in Italian supermarkets. But the zucchini phenomenon has grown, well, like the little squash itself when left alone for a hot week in August. We are knee-deep in the zucchini era—and loving every slice of it.

Although zucchini is identified with Italy, the squash is indigenous to the Americas. Indians introduced the squash to the Pilgrims, who sent it back to Europe. The English adopted its French name, *courgette*, but it is the Italians who made widest use of the squash.

Indeed, it is an Italian—noted cooking authority Giuliano Bugialli—who showed me how to avoid occasional bitterness in zucchini. Select small zucchini, Bugialli advises, but bypass the dark green ones in favor of pale green zucchini. These lighter squashes have a sweeter taste.

Zucchini ranges from greyish to yellow, but the most common variety sold here is green. Despite the healthy-looking green color, zucchini has limited food value. The vegetable is 95 percent water and provides a modest amount of potassium and vitamin C. On the other hand, it has almost no fat or sodium.

Zucchini may be used in any recipes for summer squash; because of its popularity, however, this summer squash gets a chapter of its own.

Select small, firm, blemish-free zucchini that are heavy for their size. Avoid large zucchini (longer than 8 inches), which tend to be bitter.

Store loosely wrapped in the refrigerator for two or three days.

ALMOND ZUCCHINI

Zucchini has so much natural moisture that no more is needed in cooking; butter is added later just for flavor. Parsley is not just for garnish; the combination makes zucchini taste even fresher.

Preparation time: 10 minutes
Microwave time: 7 minutes
Servings: 4

1 pound zucchini (4–5 small), cut into ¼-inch slices
2 tablespoons butter
2 tablespoons sliced almonds
2 tablespoons minced fresh parsley

1. Put zucchini in 2-quart casserole. Cover. MICROWAVE (high) 4–6 minutes, until just fork-tender, stirring twice. Drain.
2. Put butter and almonds in 2-cup measure. MICROWAVE (high) 45 seconds to 1 minute, until butter melts and nuts soften a little. Pour over zucchini. Sprinkle with parsley.

CREAMY ZUCCHINI

Grated zucchini are cooked briefly in a white sauce that is enhanced by marjoram and thickened with sour cream.

Preparation time: 15 minutes
Microwave time: 10 minutes
Servings: 4

2 tablespoons minced onion
1 teaspoon minced garlic
2 tablespoons butter
2 tablespoons flour
¼ teaspoon salt
⅛ teaspoon freshly ground pepper
1 cup milk
1 pound shredded zucchini (3 cups)
2 tablespoons chopped fresh marjoram *or* 1 teaspoon dried
¼ cup sour cream, room temperature

1. Put onion, garlic, and butter in 2-quart round casserole. MICROWAVE (high) 45 seconds to 1 minute to melt butter and soften vegetables. Blend in flour, salt, and pepper. Whisk in milk until smooth. MICROWAVE (high) 5–6 minutes, until sauce thickens, stirring after 1½ minutes, then every minute.
2. Stir in zucchini and marjoram. MICROWAVE (high) 3 minutes, until zucchini is just tender. Stir in sour cream.

ZUCCHINI AND TOMATO KABOBS

Presentation is everything here. No sauces, salt, or fats are needed—just fresh vegetables.

Preparation time: 15 minutes
Microwave time: 5 minutes
Servings: 4

1 medium tomato
2 medium zucchini, cut into ½-inch slices
1 small onion, peeled, quartered, and separated into pieces
4 mushroom caps

1. Cut tomatoes into 6 wedges, then cut each in half to make 12 pieces. Arrange vegetables on four wooden skewers: tomatoes, which cook fastest, should be in the middle; zucchini on either side of tomatoes; onion pieces at the ends; and a mushroom at the tip.
2. Place skewers in a row on a 9-inch plate. Do not cover. MICROWAVE (high) 2 minutes. Rearrange skewers, moving the inner two to the outside. MICROWAVE (high) 3 minutes, until zucchini are tender but tomatoes are still firm enough to stay on skewer. Serve skewers intact and let diners slide vegetables onto their plate.

TIP: Because microwaves pass through wood, skewers remain cool while vegetables cook.

TIP: To make mushrooms easier to skewer, first MICROWAVE (high) 1 minute.

TIP: Vegetables (except tomatoes) can be marinated in a vinaigrette for 20 minutes before cooking. Drizzle with remaining vinaigrette after cooking.

TIP: Try other vegetables, arranging the fastest-cooking ones in the middle and the slowest ones at the ends: cucumber (middle), green peppers (ends), yellow squash (middle).

QUICK ZUCCHINI AND TOMATOES

Fresh zucchini is cooked with stewed tomatoes, then topped with chopped basil. For this dish I prefer to cook zucchini until quite tender. To get all the vitamins, serve in small bowls and consume the broth as well as vegetables.

Preparation time: 10 minutes
Microwave time: 9 minutes
Servings: 4

½ **pound zucchini (2–3 small), cut into ¼-inch slices**
1 **16-ounce can stewed tomatoes**
2 **tablespoons chopped fresh basil *or* 1 teaspoon dried**

Put zucchini and tomatoes in 2-quart casserole. Cover. MICROWAVE (high) 7–9 minutes, until zucchini is tender. Let stand, covered, 2 minutes. Sprinkle with basil.

ZUCCHINI AND POTATO STROGANOFF

Beef, mushrooms, and sour cream—major components of a stroganoff—are topped with sliced potatoes and zucchini for a hearty one-dish meal.

Preparation time: 20 minutes
Microwave time: 21 minutes
Servings: 4–6

1 **pound ground chuck**
½ **pound fresh mushrooms, sliced**
½ **cup chopped onion**
1 **teaspoon minced garlic**
1 **cup sour cream**
½ **teaspoon salt**
¼ **teaspoon freshly ground pepper**
1 **medium potato, cut into ¼-inch slices**
2 **tablespoons chopped fresh basil *or* 1 teaspoon dried**
1 **pound zucchini, cut into ¼-inch slices**
1½ **cups shredded mozzarella cheese**

1. Put ground chuck, mushrooms, onion, and garlic in 2-quart rectangular casserole. MICROWAVE (high) 5–7 minutes, until meat no longer is pink, breaking up meat with spoon every 2 minutes. Drain. Stir in sour cream and half the salt (¼ teaspoon) and pepper (⅛ teaspoon).
2. Layer potatoes on top. Cover. MICROWAVE (high) 5–7 minutes, until potatoes are just tender, gently rearranging once. Sprinkle with remaining salt and pepper and the basil.
3. Layer zucchini on top. Cover. MICROWAVE (high) 5–7 minutes, until zucchini is just tender. Sprinkle with cheese. Let stand 3 minutes.

ZUCCHINI BREAD

This zucchini bread, loaded with nuts and currants, is great by itself. But for a treat, serve it topped with whipped cream cheese.

Preparation time: 30 minutes
Microwave time: 15–20 minutes
Servings: 1 bread ring

2 tablespoons shortening **¼ cup graham crackers, crushed** **1½ cups flour** **1½ cups light brown sugar** **1 teaspoon salt** **1 teaspoon baking soda** **¼ teaspoon baking powder** **1 teaspoon ground cinnamon** **¼ teaspoon ground cloves** **½ cup vegetable oil or** **shortening** **⅓ cup water** **2 eggs, slightly beaten** **1 teaspoon vanilla** **1 10½-ounce package sliced** **almonds, chopped** **⅓ cup dried currants** **1½ cups grated zucchini, tightly** **packed (1 medium, about ¼** **pound)**	1. Grease 10-cup bundt pan thoroughly with 2 tablespoons shortening. Coat with graham cracker crumbs. 2. In mixing bowl, combine flour, sugar, salt, baking soda, baking powder, cinnamon, and cloves. Add oil, water, eggs, and vanilla. Mix with electric mixer at low speed, scraping sides, until blended. Fold in almonds, currants, and zucchini. Mixture will be thick. 3. Pour into prepared baking pan. Put pan on inverted pie plate. Cover with waxed paper. 4. MICROWAVE (medium-high) 15–20 minutes, rotating one-quarter turn every 5 minutes. Bread is done when top feels dry and springs back when lightly touched. 5. Let stand, uncovered, 10 minutes on heatproof counter or surface. Invert onto plate and allow to cool completely before cutting. Wrap leftovers in foil and store in refrigerator for up to a week.

TIP: Take time to grease pan well, especially the ridges. This helps the finished bread slip out easily. Graham crackers help give the bread color.

TIP: Note that the bread is placed on a surface, not a rack, to cool. This retains heat and lets the bread finish cooking.

ZUCCHINI-CHICKEN NACHOS

This is a wonderfully messy dish to eat with fingers: tortilla chips covered with slightly spicy tomatoes, zucchini, and chicken, all covered with cheese.

Preparation time: 20 minutes
Microwave time: 16 minutes
Servings: 4–6

4 chicken breast halves, skinned and boned
1 tablespoon fresh lemon juice
¼ cup chopped onion
1 teaspoon minced garlic
1 tablespoon olive oil
1 pound zucchini, cut into ⅜-inch slices
1 16-ounce can tomatoes, drained and chopped
1 teaspoon minced fresh chili or 6 good shakes hot pepper sauce
¼ teaspoon ground cumin
¼ teaspoon dried oregano
⅛ teaspoon freshly ground pepper
Tortilla chips
1 cup grated cheddar cheese

1. Put chicken in 2-quart rectangular casserole. Sprinkle with lemon juice. Cover with waxed paper. MICROWAVE (high) 5–7 minutes, until juices no longer run pink, turning over after 3 minutes. Drain. Set aside.
2. Put onion, garlic, and olive oil in same 2-quart rectangular casserole. MICROWAVE (high) 1 minute. Stir in zucchini, tomatoes, chili, cumin, oregano, and pepper. Cover. MICROWAVE (high) 4–6 minutes, until zucchini is just tender, stirring twice.
3. Dice chicken. Add to zucchini mixture. Do not cover. MICROWAVE (high) 2 minutes to warm through. Spread over tortilla chips. While still warm, top with cheese.

BABY VEGETABLES

Tiny zucchini, precious little pattypans, delicate strands of green beans, and baby corn, still wet behind the ear. These are the darlings of the vegetable craze.

Baby or mini vegetables are not immature versions of regular-sized vegetables, but new—and pricey—varieties grown largely in California and Florida. Hot, trendy restaurants were the first to adopt the babies, but upscale groceries in urban areas now carry seasonal samplings.

Don't destroy the charm of these little gems by cutting them up or covering them with heavy sauces. Keep the preparation simple so that diners can identify them. If you stuff some pattypans (they are just large enough to hold one snail or bits of chopped mushrooms), leave a few pattypans whole.

If you have time, make a plate with several varieties of vegetables and treatments. Or, quick-cook several varieties and give them all the same lime-butter sauce—the various vegetables themselves will be enough to hold interest.

Select the small varieties just as you would the larger. In general, look for firm vegetables with no signs of wilting.

Store as you would regular summer vegetable varieties, generally loosely wrapped in the refrigerator.

MINI-ZUCCHINI WITH LIME BUTTER

No one has problems identifying mini-zucchini—they just want to know if they are real. Leave them whole, cook them briefly, and serve with a simple lime butter.

Preparation time: 3 minutes
Microwave time: 3 minutes
Servings: 4 small

16 mini zucchini
2 tablespoons water
2 tablespoons butter
2 tablespoons fresh lime juice

1. Put zucchini and water in 1-quart casserole. Cover. MICROWAVE (high) 2–3 minutes, until just crisp, stirring after 1 minute. Drain.
2. Put butter in 2-cup measure. MICROWAVE (high) 30–45 seconds, until melted. Stir in lime juice. Pour over zucchini and toss lightly.

ROSEMARY GREEN BEANS

Firm little green beans need only a brief cooking and a touch of rosemary for extra interest.

Preparation time: 5 minutes
Microwave time: 3 minutes
Servings: 4

6 ounces mini green beans
¼ cup water
2 tablespoons butter
½ teaspoon dried rosemary, crushed

1. Put green beans and water in 1-quart casserole. Cover. MICROWAVE (high) 2–3 minutes, until just tender. Drain.
2. Put butter in 2-cup measure. MICROWAVE (high) 30–40 seconds to melt. Stir in rosemary. Pour over green beans and toss gently.

PRINCESS PATTYPANS

Scooped out, filled with cream cheese, and topped with jewellike red caviar, little pattypan squash look like mini crowns.

Preparation time: 10 minutes
Microwave time: 2 minutes
Servings: 4 small

16 mini pattypan squash
 2 tablespoons cream cheese
Red caviar (lumpfish roe)

1. Use small knife to cut thin slice off bottom (blossom end) of each pattypan so that they will sit flat. Slice off stem end, being careful not to cut too low, or you will lose the pretty shape of the little squash. Use spoon (a grapefruit spoon works well) to scoop out center, leaving ¼-inch-thick shell.
2. Fill each pattypan with an equal amount of cheese. Place pattypans around edges of serving dish or pie pan. Do not cover. MICROWAVE (high) 1–2 minutes, until vegetables start to feel soft to the touch but still hold their shape well. Top with caviar "jewels." Serve.

TIP: Caviar (lumpfish roe) may be replaced by very thin strips of smoked salmon. Or, try blue cheese or cheddar cheese, topped with minced green onions.

TIP: Note that stuffed mini squash are not covered when cooked. This helps retain their shape.

TIP: To cook whole pattypans, trim stem and blossom ends if desired. Arrange around edges of plate. Add 2 tablespoons water. Cover. MICROWAVE (high) 2–3 minutes, until vegetables are just tender. Serve with a light butter sauce or vinaigrette.

FIVE-MINUTE VEGETABLES

There are times when sitting down together for a meal is more important than making every dish from scratch. So don't snub your nose at convenience products like frozen or canned vegetables. They will get you out of a jam and down to the dinner table—fast.

You probably will sacrifice some texture in the convenience products, but unless your produce in the refrigerator is pristinely fresh, the frozen and canned products may be just as good or even superior in nutrition.

One of the tricks to fast and delicious vegetables is to have your larder stocked with tasty additions such as canned olives, canned tomatoes, sesame oil, jalapeño peppers, pine nuts, cheese, and herbs. When it is time to use them up, you'll create even more wonderful combinations.

Because these Five-Minute Vegetables are ready so fast, you can make two or three and keep them warm, covered, in a low conventional oven.

For even more ideas, thumb through the main text of this book, looking at the first recipe in each chapter. The first dish for each vegetable is designed to be fairly simple, one you can enjoy frequently.

ARTICHOKES AND PEAS

I threw this dish together one night after I remembered that I was supposed to bring a vegetable dish to a party. The freezer and larder came to the rescue.

Serves: 4

1 10-ounce package frozen tiny peas
1 tablespoon butter
1 can (6–8 count) artichoke bottoms, rinsed, drained, and quartered
½ cup pine nuts
2 green onions, white and first 2 inches of green, sliced
1 tablespoon fresh chervil *or* ½ teaspoon dried

Put peas in 2-quart casserole. Cover. MICROWAVE (high) 3 minutes, stirring once. Drain. Stir in butter, artichokes, and pine nuts. Cover. MICROWAVE (high) 2 minutes. Stir in onions and chervil.

ORIENTAL BROCCOLI

Frozen packages of broccoli call for about 8 minutes in the microwave, but you can reduce this time by quickly rinsing off the ice crystals under running water.

Servings: 3–4

1 10-ounce package frozen chopped broccoli
½ teaspoon soy sauce
¼ teaspoon sesame oil
1 tablespoon sesame seeds

Rinse broccoli under faucet to melt ice crystals. Put in 1-quart casserole. Cover. MICROWAVE (high) 5 minutes, stirring once to break up broccoli. Drain if necessary. Stir in remaining ingredients.

CURRIED CARROTS

Fresh carrots can be cooked in 5 minutes; frozen need 1 more minute. Curry powders vary in strength, so use the amount here only as a guide.

Servings: 3–4

1 **pound fresh carrots, julienned, or 1 10-ounce package frozen**
2 **tablespoons water (if using fresh carrots)**
1 **tablespoon butter**
½ **teaspoon curry powder**
2 **tablespoons pine nuts**

If using fresh carrots, put in 1-quart casserole with water. For frozen, first rinse under faucet to remove ice, then put in casserole without extra water. Cover. MICROWAVE (high) 5 minutes (6 for frozen), stirring after 3 minutes. Drain. Stir in butter, then curry powder and pine nuts.

CAULIFLOWER WITH CHEESE

If you take 5 minutes in the morning to cut the cauliflower into flowerets, it takes only another 5 minutes to cook them for dinner. Take care to sprinkle the cheese evenly for a more attractive dish.

Serves: 4

2 **cups cauliflower flowerets**
¼ **cup water**
¼ **cup grated cheddar cheese**

Put cauliflower and water in 1½-quart casserole. Cover. MICROWAVE (high) 5 minutes until tender, stirring once. Let stand, covered, 2 minutes. Drain. Sprinkle with cheese.

CORN 'N' CROUTONS

Seasoned croutons are added to absorb moisture from cooked corn, tomatoes, and black olives. When they do their job well, the croutons turn tasty but soggy; if you prefer them crisp, stir them in at the end, just before serving.

Serves: 4–6

1 **10-ounce package frozen corn**	Put corn in 2-quart casserole. Cover. MICROWAVE (high) 3 minutes, stirring once. Drain. Stir in remaining ingredients. Do not cover. MICROWAVE (high) 2 minutes. Stir and serve.
2 **tablespoons butter**	
1 **cup pitted black olives, drained well**	
1 **14½-ounce can tomatoes, drained and chopped coarse**	
1 **cup seasoned croutons**	
¼ **teaspoon salt**	
⅛ **teaspoon freshly ground pepper**	

MUSHROOMS IN WINE

The quality of wine makes a difference, so use 2 tablespoons of the wine you are serving for dinner.

Servings: 4

½ **pound fresh mushrooms, wiped clean and sliced**	Put all ingredients in 1-quart casserole. MICROWAVE (high) 5 minutes, stirring after 2 minutes. Let stand, covered, 2 minutes. Use cooking broth over entree if suitable or save for soups or gravies.
1 **tablespoon butter**	
2 **tablespoons red wine**	

SWEET ONION–TOMATOES

Fresh onion rings are sweetened with brown sugar, then generously served on slices of fresh tomatoes. The tomatoes, too, can be heated in the microwave if you desire; put on a plate, cover with waxed paper, and cook on high for 2 minutes.

Serves: 4

1 medium onion, peeled, cut into ¼-inch slices, and separated into rings
2 tablespoons water
1 tablespoon butter
1 tablespoon brown sugar
4 1-inch-thick tomato slices

Put onion rings and water in 1-quart casserole. Cover. MICROWAVE (high) 3 minutes. Drain. Stir in butter and brown sugar. Do not cover. MICROWAVE (high) 2 minutes. Stir. Top tomatoes with onions.

PEAS AND LETTUCE

Wilted lettuce makes a pretty addition to peas. Give the peas a two-minute head start (just enough time to shred the lettuce), then stir in the lettuce. You'll need the 2-quart casserole to contain the lettuce until it cooks down.

Servings: 3–4

1 10-ounce package frozen peas
1 tablespoon butter
2 cups shredded lettuce
¼ teaspoon salt
1 tablespoon chopped fresh dill
    or ½ teaspoon dried

Put peas and butter in 2-quart casserole. Cover. MICROWAVE (high) 2 minutes. Stir in lettuce. Cover. MICROWAVE (high) 3 minutes. Mix in salt and dill.

SPICY GREEN PEPPERS

Sweet bell peppers are cooked with olive oil for flavor, jalapeño pepper for spicy interest, and tomatoes for color. If you take 2 minutes to chop the green peppers, they need only 5 minutes in the microwave. Tomato is added toward the end, and cooking continues uncovered so that tomatoes don't add too much moisture to the dish.

Servings: 4

2 green peppers (sweet bell peppers), cored and chopped
2 tablespoons olive oil
1 teaspoon minced jalapeño pepper
¼ cup diced tomato (about 2 slices)

Put green peppers, olive oil, and jalapeños in 1-quart casserole. Cover. MICROWAVE (high) 2 minutes. Stir in tomatoes. Do not cover. MICROWAVE (high) 3 minutes.

CREAMY SPINACH

We stretched the 5-minute rule here because frozen spinach needs a full 6 minutes in the microwave—still not bad for a quick vegetable.

Servings: 2–3

1 10-ounce package frozen chopped spinach
⅛ teaspoon garlic powder
2 tablespoons sour cream

Rinse spinach under faucet to remove ice. Put in 1-quart casserole. Cover. MICROWAVE (high) 6 minutes, breaking up with fork after 4 minutes. Drain well. Stir in garlic powder and sour cream.

NUTTY SWEET POTATOES

Use the soft texture of canned sweet potatoes to an advantage: mash them lightly, then top with peanuts.

Servings: 4

1 **16-ounce can sweet potatoes, drained**	Put sweet potatoes in 1-quart casserole. Cover. MICROWAVE (high) 4 minutes to heat through.
2 **tablespoons butter**	Use fork to lightly mash in butter. Sprinkle with
2 **tablespoons chopped peanuts**	peanuts.

ROSEMARY ZUCCHINI

Rosemary is a good, assertive herb to wake up a favorite vegetable. Be sure to crush first to release flavor.

Servings: 4

1 **pound zucchini, cut into ¼-inch slices**	Put zucchini in 2-quart casserole. Cover. MICROWAVE (high) 5 minutes. Drain. Stir in dressing and rosemary.
2 **tablespoons prepared Italian dressing**	
½ **teaspoon dried rosemary**	

BIBLIOGRAPHY

Among the many books and publications used to research this book, these were particularly useful:

Brennan, Georgeanne, Isaac Cronin, and Charlotte Glenn. *The New American Vegetable Cookbook*. Berkeley, California: Aris Books, 1985.

"Commercial Storage of Fruits, Vegetables, and Florist and Nursery Stocks." Washington, D.C.: USDA Handbook No. 66, rev. 1986.

"Composition of Foods: Vegetables and Vegetable Products." Washington, D.C.: USDA Handbook No. 8–11, rev. August 1984.

Grigson, Jane. *Jane Grigson's Vegetable Book*. Harmondsworth and New York: Penguin Books, 1981.

Hawkes, Alex D. *A World of Vegetable Cookery*. New York: Simon and Schuster, 1985.

Morash, Marian. *The Victory Garden Cookbook*. New York: Knopf, 1982.

Murdich, Jack. *Buying Produce*. New York: Hearst Books, 1986.

The Packer 1986 Produce Availability & Merchandising Guide. Shawnee Mission, Kansas: The Packer, 1986.

Schneider, Elizabeth. *Uncommon Fruits & Vegetables, a Commonsense Guide*. New York: Harper & Row, 1986.

"Unusual Vegetables, Something New for This Year's Garden." *Organic Gardening and Farming*. Anne Moyer Halpin, editor. Emmaus, Pennsylvania: Rodale Press, 1978.

RECIPES LIST

Appetizers
Artichoke Kabobs in Mustard-
  Cheese Sauce
Artichokes in Lemon Sauce
Blue Cheese–Stuffed Mushrooms
Carrot Won Tons
Fiddlehead Ferns and Cheese
Garlic-Studded Whole Artichokes
Goat Cheese on Belgian Endive
  Spears
Green Beans in Prosciutto
Jicama and Shrimp Rumaki
Marinated Mushrooms
Sausage-Stuffed Artichokes
Toasted Pumpkin Seeds
Tomatillo Salsa
Zucchini-Chicken Nachos

Salads
Asparagus and Artichoke Salad
Beets and Capers Salad
Belgian Endive Hearts with
  Roquefort Dressing
Belgian Endive with Warm
  Anchovy Sauce
Carrot-Dill Salad
Celeriac and Pineapple Salad
Chicken-Chayote Salad
Goat Cheese on Belgian Endive
  Spears
Hawaiian Breadfruit Salad
Hot German Potato Salad
Hot Jicama Slaw
Hot Waldorf Salad
Leeks Vinaigrette
Marinated Fiddlehead Ferns
Marinated Mushrooms
Niçoise Salad
Radicchio with Caper-Hollandaise
  Sauce
Radicchio with Warm Anchovy
  Dressing
Salsify Vinaigrette
Skid-Free Okra Salad
Snow Peas and Mushroom Salad
Summer Squash with Rosemary
Tomatoes with Mozzarella and
  Basil
Warm Bok Choy Salad with
  Peanuts
Wilted Spinach Salad

Soups
Artichoke and Oyster Soup
Beet and Cabbage Soup
Cabbage Potage
Carrot Soup
Carrot Won Tons
Cauliflower Soup
Chicken Gumbo
Chilled Red Pepper Soup
Classic Onion
Cold Green Soup
Garlic Soup
Gila's Extra-Creamy Vichyssoise
Grass Soup
Japanese Noodle Soup
Jicama and Shrimp Soup
Kohlrabi Soup
Micro Shabu Shabu
Mushroom Soup
Mushroom-Beef Stew
Mustard Greens Soup
Oyster-Celery Stew
Pea Soup
Pumpkin-Chestnut Soup-in-the-
  Shell
Rutabaga Ragout
Spicy Cucumber Soup
Tomato Soup

Side Dishes
Almond Zucchini
Apple-Chutney-Stuffed Squash
Aromatic Asparagus in Parchment
Artichoke Kabobs in Mustard-
  Cheese Sauce
Artichokes and Peas
Artichokes in Lemon Sauce
Asparagus with Hollandaise Sauce
Bacon-Topped Tomatillos
Baked Apples with Leeks and
  Sausage
Baked Breadfruit
Baked Jerusalem Artichokes
Baked Whole Radishes
Beets and Mandarin Oranges
Beets with Tops
Belgian Endive Braised in Wine
Blackened Eggplant
Blue Cheese–Stuffed Mushrooms
Braised Chards
Brandied Parsnips with
  Macadamia Nuts

Broccoli with Hot Peppers and
  Garlic
Broccoli with Lemon Juice
Broccoli with Macadamia Nuts
Broccoli with Oyster Sauce
Brussels Sprouts with Apples and
  Onions
Cabbage Wedges Vinaigrette
Cauliflower Custard Ring
Cauliflower with Cheese
Cauliflower with Lemon-Crumb
  Topping
Celeriac and Potato Puree
Celery au Gratin
Celery with Cheddar Cheese
  Sauce
Celery with Olives and Pine Nuts
Chard with Anchovy-Roquefort
  Dressing
Chard with Tiny Onions
Chayote in Hot Tomato Sauce
Chayote Slices with Bread
  Crumbs
Chayote with Butter and Pepper
Cheddar Beans
Chopped Beans with Shrimp
Chopped Green Peppers
Cooked-Up Greens
Corn Maque Choux
Corn 'n' Croutons
Corn on the Cob
Creamed Onions
Creamed Parsnips with Fine
  Herbs
Creamed Spinach and Mushrooms
Creamy Cabbage with Caraway
  Seeds
Creamy Spinach
Creamy Zucchini
Cucumber-Chicken Salad
Cucumbers with Dill
Curried Carrots
Curried Onion Rings
Curried Parsnips
Curried Tomato Halves
Dirty Potatoes
Double Cheese Corn Eggs
Duxelles
Eggplant and Apples with Malt
  Vinegar
Eggplant and Basil Bake
Eggplant Under Blue Cheese Sauce

INDEX